Both English and Latin

Bilingualism and Biculturalism in Milton's Neo-Latin Writings

CONTENTS

Acknowledgments
Abbreviations
Introduction 1

Chapter 1	The Development of the Bilingual: St Paul's School	9
	1.1 "Clad in a Double Garment": Bilinguality and Translation	9
	1.2 *Mataphrasis*: Milton's Rendering of Horace, *Odes* 1.5	15
	1.3 *Paraphrasis*: "Awake, Arise, or Be For Ever Fall'n"	25
	1.4 "The Turning of Verses": Milton's *Apologus de Rustico et Hero*	36

Chapter 2	Bilingualism and Biculturalism: Cambridge and Beyond	55
	2.1 Bicultural Self-Fashioning: Both Londoner and Roman	58
	2.2 Tricultural "Cross-Comparison": Milton, Ovid, Young	62
	2.3 "Overleaping" Convention: Lamenting the Dead	65
	2.4 "Both Latin and English"?: *Naturam Non Pati Senium*	75
	2.5 Bipartite and Bilingual Signifiers: *Elegia Sexta*	80
	2.6 "Overleaping" Linguistic Walls	88

Chapter 3	Both Latin and Tuscan: Milton and the Italian Academies	95
	3.1 Both Latin and Tuscan: Milton's Letter to Buonmattei	104
	3.2 *Novae Patriae Linguae Institutiones*: Buonmattei as Quintilian	115

Chapter 4	Italy, Bilingualism, and Biculturalism	119
	4.1 *Ad Salsillum*	119
	4.2 *Mansus*	124
	4.2.1 Balanced Biculturalism in *Mansus*: Milton and Marino	126
	4.2.2 Bicultural Assimilation in *Mansus*: Milton and Tasso	129
	4.3 *Thuscus Tu Quoque*: Bicultural Identities in *Epitaphium Damonis*	132
	4.3.1 A Phoenix Reborn: *Epitaphium Damonis* and "La Questione della Lingua"	135
Chapter 5	"Both English and Latin": The 1645 Volume	141
	5.1 *Gemellus Liber*	141
	5.2 *Geminus Auctor*	146
	5.3 *Geminae Frontes*	150
	5.4 *Geminus Miltonus?*	152
	5.5 *Geminae … Linguae*	158
Chapter 6	After "Word": Surprised by Syntax: The *Vox Bilinguis* of *Paradise Lost*	167
	6.1 Epic Openings: "Of Man's First"/*Arma Vir*	170
	6.2 "Thee I Revisit"/*Sociosque Revisit*	175
	6.3 *Serpens Bilinguis*: "Tongue of Brute"/*Brutus Orator*	180
	6.4 "Words" and the "Sword": Assassinating Eve?	186
	6.5 Epic Endings: *Facies*/Faces/Firebrands	190
Bibliography		199
Index Nominum		213

ACKNOWLEDGMENTS

I wish to thank the Queen's University Research and Scholarships Committee for funding trips to the British Library, London, and the Bodleian Library, Oxford, and the authorities of those institutions for permitting me to consult manuscripts and early printed books relevant to my research. I am particularly indebted to the Library staff of the Biblioteca Nazionale Centrale, Florence, for making accessible to me manuscripts pertaining to the Florentine Academies. Thanks are also due to the Queen's University Library, especially its Special Collections and Inter-Library Loans divisions.

Some portions of this book appeared in an earlier form in *Medievalia et Humanistica*, *Renaissance Studies*, and *Notes and Queries*. Part of Chapter 1 reworks material originally published in *Metaphrastes Or Gained in Translation: Essays and Translations in Honour of Robert H. Jordan* (Belfast Byzantine Texts and Translations 9: Belfast, 2004).

Finally I wish to thank my husband, Tony Sheehan, Humanities Computing Manager at Queen's, for his technical assistance and advice throughout and also, and especially, for his support in so many ways. To him I dedicate this monograph as a small token of a very great love.

EH

ABBREVIATIONS

AJP	*American Journal of Philology*
CJ	*Classical Journal*
CLS	*Comparative Literature Studies*
CM	*The Works of John Milton*, eds. F.A. Patterson *et al.* (New York: Columbia University Press, 1931-1940), 18 vols.
CP	*Classical Philology*
CW	*Classical World*
DBI	*Dizionario Biografico degli Italiani* (Rome: Istituto della Enciclopedia Italiana, 1977)
ELR	*English Literary Renaissance*
EMLS	*Early Modern Literary Studies*
ERA	*English Research Association of Hiroshima*
ES	*English Studies*
ESC	*English Studies Collection*
G&R	*Greece and Rome*
HL	*Humanistica Lovaniensia: Journal of Neo-Latin Studies*
HLQ	*Huntington Library Quarterly*
HSCP	*Harvard Studies in Classical Philology*
JEGP	*Journal of English and Germanic Philology*
JRS	*Journal of Roman Studies*
MH	*Medievalia et Humanistica*
MLN	*Modern Language Notes*
MLQ	*Modern Language Quarterly*
MLR	*Modern Language Review*
MP	*Modern Philology*
MQ	*Milton Quarterly*
MS	*Milton Studies*
N&Q	*Notes and Queries*
OLD	*Oxford Latin Dictionary*
PBA	*Proceedings of the British Academy*
PMLA	*Publications of the Modern Language Association of America*
PQ	*Philological Quarterly*
RES	*Review of English Studies*
RR	*Renaissance and Reformation*
SEL	*Studies in English Literature*
ShQ	*Shakespeare Quarterly*
SP	*Studies in Philology*
TAPhA	*Transactions of the American Philological Association*
TLS	*Times Literary Supplement (London)*

Introduction

> I will point ye out the right path of a vertuous and noble Education; laborious indeed at the first ascent, but else so smooth, so green, so full of goodly prospect, and melodious sounds on every side, that the Harp of Orpheus was not more charming. (Milton, *Of Education*)[1]

According to John Aubrey, John Milton was already a poet when he had his portrait painted at ten years of age.[2] Although such a viewpoint remains uncorroborated, it led the editors of the Columbia Milton to make the justifiable speculation that among "fugitive, lost, and projected works" by Milton might be included "poems composed at the age of ten."[3] Aubrey's statement is teasingly brief. It does not tell us whether these purported poems constituted, for example, pedagogical exercises in verse-composition regularly set at St Paul's School, London,[4] nor does it name the language in which they were written. Were they perhaps cast in Latin in the same quasi-Ovidian vein as the verses on the theme of early rising[5] (a theme regularly prescribed as the basis of school

---

[1] *The Works of John Milton*, eds. F.A. Patterson *et al.* (New York: Columbia University Press, 1931-1940), 18 vols, volume 4, 280. Unless indicated otherwise, all quotations from Milton's prose works are from this edition, hereinafter abbreviated to *CM*.

[2] "Anno Dom.1619, he was ten yeares old, as by his picture: & was then a Poet," John Aubrey, "Minutes of the Life of Mr John Milton," in *The Early Lives of Milton*, ed. Helen Darbishire (London, 1932), 2. On Milton's widow as the source of the comment, which was purported to have been made while she and Aubrey were looking at the portrait, see W.R. Parker, *Milton: A Biography*, ed. Gordon Campbell (Oxford, 1996), II, 708-709. For discussion of the portrait, see Leo Miller, "Milton's Portraits: An Impartial Inquiry Into Their Authentication," *MQ* special issue (1976), 1-43.

[3] *CM*, 18, 536.

[4] See in particular Milton's translation of Horace, *Odes* 1.5, *Carmina Elegiaca*, and *Apologus De Rustico et Hero* discussed in Chapter 1.

[5] The Columbia editors remark in a note to their comment re the speculated lost poems: "Candy alone seems to have thought he had trace of some of them in the 'Milton-Ovid stanzas,' but of this he has satisfied few save himself" (*CM* 18, 536). See H.C.H. Candy, *Some Newly Discovered Stanzas Written by John Milton on Engraved Scenes Illustrating Ovid's Metamorphoses* (London, 1924) first announced

exercises in Latin *imitatio*)[6] discovered by Horwood toward the end of the nineteenth century, and in all likelihood the earliest examples of Milton's Latin poetry to survive?[7] Did they by contrast exemplify the young Milton's independent attempts at English poetry? Or was he perhaps already experimenting poetically in both languages? Here the question of the linguistic medium employed by Milton, the ten-year old "poet," is an issue that remains unresolved.

Further irresolution results from the loss of the records of St Paul's School in the Great Fire of London in 1666.[8] Nonetheless, it is not unreasonable to speculate that Milton's initiation into the rudiments of both English and Latin preceded the inception of his formal schooling (the latter occurring probably at about the usual age of seven).[9] Sir Thomas Elyot had castigated "old authors" for their conviction "that before the age of seven years a child should not be instructed in letters."[10] And the Statutes of St Paul's, as ordained by its founder Dean Colet, could proudly proclaim:

---

in *TLS* 26 Jan. 1922. Here Candy attributed to Milton English verses inscribed on blank verso pages of a text of Ovid, an attribution almost universally dismissed by subsequent Milton scholarship.

[6] For the suggestion that the *Carmina Elegiaca* conform to a specific grammar school exercise, see pages 28-34.

[7] See page 28.

[8] This loss has rightly been described as "considerable and frustrating" by Edward Jones. See "'Ere Half my Days': Milton's Life, 1608-1640," in *The Oxford Handbook of Milton*, eds. Nicholas McDowell and Nigel Smith (Oxford, 2009), 3-25, at 6.

[9] See T.W. Baldwin, *Shakspere's Small Latine and Lesse Greeke*, 2 vols. (Urbana: University of Illinois Press, 1944), I, 441-442. The loss of the records prevents unqualified acceptance of Donald Clark's confident assertion that Milton "entered school in 1615 at the normal age of seven" (D.L. Clark, *John Milton at St Paul's School* [New York, 1948; rpt Hamden, 1964], 32). B.K. Lewalski, *The Life of John Milton* (Blackwell, 2000), 6, considers the possibility that he entered in 1615, but favours 1620. Gordon Campbell and T.N. Corns, *John Milton, Life, Work, and Thought* (Oxford, 2008), 19, believe that Milton "may have entered the school any time between 1615 and 1621."

[10] Sir Thomas Elyot, *The Book Named the Governor* (1531), ed. S.E. Lehmburg (London, 1962), 66.

> If your chylde can rede and wryte latyn and englisshe sufficiently, soo that he be able to rede and wryte his owne lessons, then he shall be admytted into the schole for a scholar.[11]

That the pre-school Milton could do much more than "rede and wryte latyn and englisshe sufficiently" seems highly likely given the fact that in addition to, and quite likely in advance of, his formal schooling, he was "exercis'd to the tongues" from his "first yeeres" by "sundry masters and teachers both at home and at the schools."[12] Indeed it was under the tutelage of Thomas Young[13] that, he says, he "first drank of the streams of the Muses" (*primus ego ... illo praeeunte .../Pieriosque hausi latices* [*Elegia Quarta* 29-31]),[14] a tutelage heralded as surpassing that provided by the illustrious instructors of famous heroes of classical mythology.[15] Milton's comparison of Young to a range of classical educators is insightful,[16] suggesting perhaps that he played a formative role in Milton's classical education,[17] functioning perhaps as his earliest Latin tutor, in addition to his generally accepted role as a private tutor in modern languages.[18] That Milton received this privilege[19] at his father's

---

[11] J.H. Lupton, *Life of Dean Colet* (London, 1887), Appendix B, 285.

[12] Milton, *Reason of Church Government* (*CM* 3, 235). See Lewalski, *Life*, 5-6; Campbell and Corns, *Life, Work, and Thought*, 16-18.

[13] On the Scots Presbyterian Thomas Young (1587?-1655), see *ODNB*. On his relationship with Milton, see H.F. Fletcher, "Milton and Thomas Young," *TLS* 21 Jan. (1926), 44; W.R. Parker, "Milton and Thomas Young, 1620-1628," *MLN* 53 (1938), 399-407.

[14] Unless otherwise indicated, all quotations from Milton's Latin and minor English poetry are from *John Milton: Complete Shorter Poems*, ed. John Carey (London and New York, 1997). I have modernized punctuation.

[15] Milton, *Elegia Quarta*, 23-28. See also pages 62-65.

[16] Insightful also perhaps is Milton's consistent recourse to Latin as linguistic medium for his poetic and epistolary communications with his former tutor.

[17] Lewalski, *Life*, 6, likewise considers the possibility that these lines intimate "that Young was Milton's first teacher in classics, beginning around 1615 when he was seven."

[18] See Clark, *John Milton at St Paul's School*, 18; Campbell and Corns, *Life, Work, and Thought*, 16.

[19] Parker, *Biography*, ed. Campbell, I, 12, speculates: "presumably the tutor visited his pupil at hours set for teaching." Campbell and Corns, *Life, Work, and Thought*, 17, point out, however, that "the comfortable assumption that tuition took place in Bread

expense is evident from expressions of gratitude articulated in *Ad Patrem*[20] and *Defensio Secunda*[21] towards one who is depicted as the ideal Renaissance educator, and who is appropriately addressed as *pater optime* (*Ad. Pat.* 6, 78).[22] After all, Richard Mulcaster had stated that "the parent himselfe ought in reason to be more than halfe a judge of the entrie to schooling, as being best acquainted with the particular circumstances of his owne child."[23] Milton père may have exercized such a judgement, and perhaps much more. If so, he may well have been instrumental in facilitating and enhancing the childhood bilingualism[24] of his son.

Street is destabilized by evidence that links Young to Rotherhithe and further afield (Essex, and Ware, in Hertfordshire)."

[20] Milton, *Ad Patrem* 78-85. Here he states that it was at his father's expense (*tuo ... sumptu* [78]) that he was enabled to learn Latin, Greek, French, Italian and Hebrew.

[21] Milton, *Defensio Secunda*: *pater me puerulum humaniorum literarum studiis destinavit ... et in ludo literario, et sub aliis domi magistris erudiendum quotidie curavit* (*CM* 8, 118-120).

[22] On Milton's presentation of his father as an ideal Renaissance educator, see Estelle Haan, "Milton's Latin poetry and Vida," *HL* 44 (1995), 282-304, at 283-292; Estelle Haan, "Milton's *Ad Patrem* and Grotius's *In Natalem Patris*," *N&Q* 45.4 (1998), 442-447.

[23] Richard Mulcaster, *Positions* (1581), ed. R.H. Quick (London, 1888), 21. Cf. Petrus Paulus Vergerius, *De Ingenuis Moribus*: *neque enim opes ullas firmiores aut certiora praesidia vitae parare filiis genitores possunt quam si eos exhibeant honestis artibus et liberalibus disciplinis instructos*. Text is that of *Humanist Educational Treatises*, ed. and trans. C.W. Kallendorf (I Tatti Renaissance Library, 2002), 4.

[24] Cf. Colin Baker, *A Parents' and Teachers' Guide to Bilingualism* (Clevedon, 1995), 44: "If the home conditions allow it, there is much value in developing children's bilingualism earlier rather than later." I employ the term "childhood bilingualism" in accordance with the definition provided by linguistic theorists. See, for example, Jean Lyon, *Becoming Bilingual: Language Acquisition in a Bilingual Community* (Philadelphia, 1996), 48: "The bilingual acquisition of language, both simultaneous and sequential, and childhood second language learning are all included in the term 'childhood bilingualism.'" For studies of early childhood bilingualism, see, among others, Jules Ronjat, *Le Développement du Lange Observé chez un Enfant Bilingue* (Paris, 1913); Millivoïe Pavlovitch, *Le Lange Enfantin: Acquisition du Serbe et du Français* (Paris, 1920); Eugene García, *Early Childhood Bilingualism* (Albuquerque, 1983); W.F. Leopold, *Speech Development of a Bilingual Child: A Linguist's Record* (New York, 1939-49); Traute Taeschner, *The Sun is Feminine: A Study of Language Acquisition in Bilingual Children* (Berlin, 1983); Brian MacWhinney, "A Unified Model of Language Acquisition," in *Handbook of Bilingualism: Psycholinguistic Approaches*, eds. J.F. Kroll and A.M.B. De Groot (Oxford, 2005), 49-67.

Recent studies of bilinguality indicate that the outcome of a bilingual education[25] "depends upon a number of pre-school factors as well as upon the way the two languages are planned in education."[26] Likewise the age of language acquisition has been seen to play a significant role in the development of the bilingual on a whole series of levels, not least of which are the linguistic and the cognitive.[27] Although an infant who is learning his first language is in effect "learning how to mean,"[28] second-language acquisition has been found to work most efficiently when it follows rapidly thereupon and when it occurs in early childhood—a period viewed by many linguists as the "critical period."[29] In *Of Education* Milton strongly advocates a rapidly condensed timescale in regard to second-language acquisition, whether that language be Latin or Greek:

> First we do amiss to spend seven or eight years meerly in scraping together so much miserable Latine and Greek, as might be learnt otherwise easily and delightfully in one year.[30]

Milton's own experience in terms of his acquisition of 1) a "native language" that "didst move my *first* endeavouring tongue to speak,"[31] and

---

[25] On bilingualism and education, see, for example, E. G. Lewis, *Bilingualism and Bilingual Education* (Perganon Press, 1981); J.F. Hamers and M.H.A. Blanc, *Bilinguality and Bilingualism* (Cambridge, 1989); Colin Baker, *Foundations of Bilingual Education and Bilingualism* (Clevedon, 1996).

[26] Hamers and Blanc, *Bilinguality and Bilingualism*, 196.

[27] See Núria Sebastián-Gallés and Laura Bosch, "Phonology and Bilingualism," in *Handbook of Bilingualism*, 68-87; Robert De-Keyser and Jenifer Larson-Hall, "What does the Critical Period Really Mean?" *Handbook of Bilingualism*, 88-108; Ton Dijkstra, "Bilingual Visual Word Recognition and Lexical Access," *Handbook of Bilingualism*, 179-201.

[28] See M.A.K. Halliday, *Learning How to Mean: Explorations in the Development of Language* (London, 1975). Cf. Lyon, *Becoming Bilingual*, 5: "The early attempt at communication with another person is the beginning of language."

[29] See Hamers and Blanc, *Bilinguality and Bilingualism*, 10, 75. However, De-Keyser and Larson-Hall, "Critical Period," 88, note that "the younger is better argument has been both used and abused."

[30] *CM* 4, 277.

[31] *At a Vacation Exercise*, 1-2. Italics are mine. Cf. in general John Brinsley, *Ludus Literarius or The Grammar School*, ed. E.T. Campagnac (Liverpool and London, 1917), 12: "How the Scholler may be taught to reade English speedily, to fit him the sooner, and better for the Grammar Schoole"; *ibid.*, 15: "First the childe is to be

probably quite soon thereafter (and in all likelihood "easily and delightfully") of 2) the basic rudiments of the Latin language, might meaningfully be read as an early modern instance of consecutive childhood bilinguality.[32] Thus the definition of the latter as one who "acquires a second language early in childhood but after the basic linguistic acquisition of his mother tongue has been achieved"[33] is potentially applicable to the pre-school Milton and certainly applicable to the Milton of St Paul's and Cambridge. John Brinsley had proclaimed: "What they are not able to utter in Latine, remember to cause them first to utter in English."[34] For Charles Hoole it is "by teaching English more Grammatically" that a schoolmaster can best "prepare his Scholars for Latine."[35]

Furthermore studies of consecutive childhood bilinguality attest to its facilitating the transfer of skills to the new language. This in turn results in "a functional representation in which the two languages are interchangeable."[36] Linguistic interchangeability would certainly come to manifest itself some thirty years later in the Milton of *Lycidas* and *Epitaphium Damonis*,[37] two pastoral laments cast in English and Latin, respectively, which engage in imaginatively contrasting ways with shared Theocritean and Virgilian intertexts. Here Milton's language "use," namely, "the capacity to call on either language,"[38] amply demonstrates that "both of a bilingual's languages are always active to some degree."[39]

---

taught, how to call every letter, pronouncing each of them plainly, fully and distinctly." For further discussion of *At a Vacation Exercise*, see pages 88-93.

[32] Hamers and Blanc, *Bilinguality and Bilingualism*, 10.

[33] Hamers and Blanc, *Bilinguality and Bilingualism*, 10.

[34] Brinsley, *Ludus Literarius*, 206.

[35] Charles Hoole, *A New Discovery of the Old Art of Teaching Schoole*, ed. E.T. Campagnac (Liverpool and London, 1913), 7.

[36] Hamers and Blanc, *Bilinguality and Bilingualism*, 75.

[37] See pages 132-139.

[38] Cf. Hamers and Blanc, *Bilinguality and Bilingualism*, 11-12: "The notion of 'use' means that the bilingual individual has the capacity to call on either language, and this implies that he must have a minimal competence in both languages."

[39] E.B. Michael and T.H. Gollan, "Being and Becoming Bilingual: Individual Differences and Consequences for Language Production," in *Handbook of Bilingualism*, 389-407, at 390.

His language selection and use were doubtlessly informed by context,[40] and ultimately perhaps by a poet's "self-fashioning."[41] What remains indisputable is the fact that for the young Milton linguistic experimentation and an associated linguistic interchangeability would have been both nurtured and enhanced by his experiences at St Paul's School, London,[42] and later at Cambridge University, where Latin came to function as his *preferred* linguistic medium for interrogating things English and for challenging established university norms. Similarly in the course of his Italian journey it was Latin that came to constitute his code selection for formal performance in Florentine academies, and for private epistolary communication with Italian academicians. At times he is both English and Latin; at others both Latin and Tuscan. It is highly significant that Milton's first collection of poetry published in 1645 self-consciously proclaims its author as a bilingual poet, entitled, as it is: *Poems of Mr John Milton Both English and Latin*.

This study examines the interplay of Latin and English in a selection of Milton's neo-Latin writings composed at St Paul's, at Cambridge University, and in the course of his Italian journey. It argues that this interplay is indicative of an inherent bilingualism that proceeds hand in hand with a self-fashioning that is bicultural in essence. Interlingual flexibility, it is argued, would ultimately prove central to the poet of *Paradise Lost*, an epic that is uniquely characterized by its Latinate vernacular and its vernacular *Latinitas*.

---

[40] R.F.I. Meuter, "Language Selection in Bilinguals: Mechanisms and Processes," in *Handbook of Bilingualism*, 349-370, at 365, notes that "language selection is determined by a number of factors, including relative proficiency, contextual cues, and monitoring ability."

[41] See Stephen Greenblatt, *Renaissance Self-Fashioning: From More to Shakespeare* (Chicago, 1980).

[42] See A.F. Leach, "Milton as Schoolboy and Schoolmaster," *PBA* 3 (1908), 295-318.

Chapter 1

The Development of the Bilingual: St Paul's School

1.1 "Clad in a Double Garment": Bilinguality and Translation

> It were as wise to cast a violet into a crucible that you might discover the formal principle of its colour and odour, as seek to transfuse from one language into another the creations of a poet. (Shelley, *A Defence of Poetry*)[1]

Thus proclaimed Percy Bysshe Shelley, issuing a famously memorable caveat about the perils of translation. A whole host of literary examples spanning several centuries and as many languages could be cited as a means of determining the truth or otherwise of this statement. But something of its rather blinkered nature, at least in regard to the pedagogical training of the early modern child, emerges once it is acknowledged that translation may enhance not only language acquisition, but bilinguality itself.

Indeed many Renaissance educational theorists and practitioners would have taken issue with such a caveat as that voiced by Shelley, promoting as they did the "wisdom" that was both inherent in and could accrue from translation. According to Roger Ascham translation "is most common, and most commendable of all other exercises for youth."[2] It is a means "whereby your scholer shall be brought not onelie to like eloquence, but also, to all trewe understanding and right iudgement, both of writing and speaking."[3] For John Brinsley it is "a most speedy way to learning."[4] Crucially it possesses an ability to recreate. Viewed in this sense the very act (and art) of "transfusing" an original creation from one

---

[1] Text is that of *Percy Bysshe Shelley: Selected Poetry and Prose*, ed. A.D.F. Macrae (London and New York, 1991), 209.

[2] Ascham, *The Scholemaster* (1570), ed. Edward Arber (London, 1870), 92 (under *Translatio Linguarum*).

[3] Ascham, *The Scholemaster*, 95.

[4] Brinsley, *Ludus Literarius*, 108.

language into another, of transposing a source message written in L_A into a written form in the target language L_B, can serve a purpose that is both educational and liberating. This may even result in the enrichment of the language into which that message has been "transfused." Or as Brinsley puts it:

> I seeme to my selfe, to finde as sensible and continuall a growth amongst all my Schollers, in their English tongue as in the Latine ... how to expresse the meaning of the Latine in proprietie, and puritie of our owne tongue.[5]

Translation formed a crucial part of the educational system of early modern England, functioning, as Moss has argued, as "the 'natural' medium through which pupils learn[ed] to manipulate the phraseology of 'rhetorically' contrived Latin."[6] It was a system that was "aimed quite explicitly at bringing the English language within the scope of the verbal competence inculcated by classroom method."[7] The teaching of Latin through the medium of translation was a key tenet and precept of several Renaissance educators. Ascham, for example, recommended that it "be exercised, speciallie of youth, for the ready and sure obteining of any tung,"[8] and Brinsley proposed the regular "use of translating *both into English, and Latine*," stating that "continuall translating *both wayes* is a most speedy way to learning, as Mr Ascham proveth at large."[9] These precepts are exemplified in practice by Charles Hoole's translation of Comenius's *Orbis Sensualium Pictus* (1659), in which a series of pictures marked with numerical assignments directs the very young pupil's gaze to parallel English and Latin phrases describing the image in question.[10] The bilingual nature of the pedagogical methodology is signaled in the Preface:

---

[5] Brinsley, *Ludus Literarius*, 21.

[6] Ann Moss, *Printed Commonplace-Books and the Structuring of Renaissance Thought* (Oxford, 1996), 216.

[7] Moss, *Printed Commonplace-Books*, 216. For further discussion of links between bilingualism and Renaissance pedagogy, see Estelle Haan, *Andrew Marvell's Latin Poetry: From Text to Context* (Collection Latomus 275: Brussels, 2003), 66-72; Estelle Haan, "From Neo-Latin to Vernacular: Marvell's Bilingualism and Renaissance Pedagogy," in *New Perspectives on Andrew Marvell*, ed. Gilles Sambras (Reims, 2008), 43-64.

[8] Ascham, *The Scholemaster*, 92.

[9] Brinsley, *Ludus Literarius*, 108. Italics are mine.

[10] For example, 'water' is matched by *aqua*; 'dew' by *ros*.

enriching the Latin language itself,[21] and Quintilian announced that in the very act of translating Greek into Latin "we may use the very best words since all that we use are our own."[22] As Donald Clark succinctly puts it, "Milton had to become a little Roman boy of sorts before he could make Latin translations."[23] In this respect the Anglo-Roman Milton of St Paul's (and indeed much later) might be seen to display that "balanced biculturalism [which] often goes hand in hand with a balanced bilinguality."[24] For in the early modern classroom the teaching of Latin syntax and grammar was conducted via pedagogical methodologies that were, in the words of Milton's 1645 volume, "both English and Latin."[25] Brinsley, in discussing the teaching of Latin syntax, states that "it will much helpe them [schoolboys] ... to speake and to parse in Latine: yet still asking the question also in English, and answering *both in English and Latine*, so farre as need is."[26] He urges that schoolchildren "get the propriety of both the tongues, *both* of Latine and English *together*."[27] Hoole requires "that a childe may have his reading perfect, and ready in *both* the *English and Latine* tongue."[28] At the very heart of this pedagogy lay both translation and, as Moss observes, "the method of imitation, imitation be it in English or in Latin, of Latin authors only."[29] That

---

[21] Cicero, *De Oratore* 1.155: *postea mihi placuit, eoque sum usus adulescens, ut summorum oratorum Graecas orationes explicarem, quibus lectis hoc adsequebar, ut, cum ea, quae legeram Graece, Latine redderem, non solum optimis verbis uterer et tamen usitatis, sed etiam exprimerem quaedam verba imitando, quae nova nostris essent, dum modo essent idonea.* Text is that of *Cicero: De Oratore*, ed. A.S. Wilkins (Oxford, 1879), I, 130.

[22] Quintilian, *De Institutione Oratoria*, 10.5.2: *vertere Graeca in Latinum veteres nostri oratores optimum iudicabant ... nam et rerum copia Graeci auctores abundant et plurimum artis in eloquentiam intulerunt et hos transferentibus verbis uti optimis licet: omnibus enim utimur nostris.* Text is that of *Institutionis Oratoriae Libri Duodecim*, ed. Michael Winterbottom (Oxford, 1970), 607.

[23] Clark, *John Milton at St Paul's School*, 172.

[24] Hamers and Blanc, *Bilinguality and Bilingualism*, 11.

[25] *Poems of Mr John Milton: Both English and Latin* (London, 1645).

[26] Brinsley, *Ludus Literarius*, 80. Italics are mine.

[27] Brinsley, *Ludus Literarius*, 109. Italics are mine.

[28] Hoole, *A New Discovery*, 14. Italics are mine.

[29] Moss, *Printed Commonplace-Books*, 216.

Milton excelled in such exercises is beyond question; that he derived great pleasure from the experience is attested by his later recollection of

> the smooth Elegiack Poets, whereof the Schooles are not scarce. Whom both for the pleasing sound of their numerous writing, which in imitation I found most easie; and most agreeable to natures part in me, and for their matter which what it is, there be few who know not, I was so allur'd to read, that no recreation came to me better welcome. (*Apology for Smectymnuus*)[30]

Milton's emphasis upon his enjoyment of the sound of the Latin language, upon his innate capacity to imitate, upon the magnetism of the subject matter of Latin elegiac verse, and his view of the whole experience as a form of "recreation" interestingly accord with what Baker has described as "the most important factor in the language development of a bilingual child," namely, "making language enjoyable, fun and a thoroughly happy experience for children."[31]

In short, early modern pedagogy was crucially informed (and formed) by a firm conviction that there was much to be gained in translation in linguistic as well as in methodological terms. In his Preface to Ovid's *Epistles*, published in 1680, John Dryden discusses three different types of translation: "metaphrase," "paraphrase," and "imitation."[32] Milton's surviving examples of what in all probability either constitute or approximate such school exercises, demonstrate, as will be argued,[33] a bilingual's "innate skill" in translating from one language into another while retaining the meaning of the original message.[34]

---

[30] *CM* 3, 302.

[31] Baker, *A Parents' and Teachers' Guide to Bilingualism*, 35. On the role of parenting in the development of the bilingual child, see in general Edith Harding and Philip Riley, *The Bilingual Family: A Handbook for Parents* (Cambridge, 1986); Lenore Arnberg, *Raising Children Bilingually: The Pre-School Years* (Clevedon, 1987); George Saunders, *Bilingual Children: From Birth to Teens* (Clevedon, 1988).

[32] See page 16.

[33] See pages 15-25, 25-36, and 36-53.

[34] See Brian Harris and Bianca Sherwood, "Translating as an Innate Skill," in *Language, Interpretation and Communication*, eds. David Gerver and H.W. Sinaiko (New York and London, 1978), 155-170.

1.2 *Metaphrasis*: Milton's Rendering of Horace, *Odes* 1.5

> Translation is so far removed from being the sterile equation of two dead languages that of all literary forms it is the one charged with the special mission of watching over the maturing process of the original language and the birth pangs of its own.
> (Walter Benjamin)[35]

The date of Milton's "translation" of Horace, *Odes* 1.5 is unknown, with suggestions ranging from 1624 to as late as 1655. Fletcher,[36] Hughes[37] and Carey[38] regard it as either a school or university exercise, whereas Clark leaves the question open.[39] By contrast Shawcross and others have argued at length for a later date.[40] Campbell on the other hand has cautiously described the piece as "wholly undatable,"[41] and Revard simply states: "date of composition unknown."[42] True as this may be, there are, however, several factors that might support the argument that

---

[35] Walter Benjamin, "The Task of the Translator," in *Illuminations*, trans. Harry Zohn, ed. Hannah Arendt (London, 1970), 69-82, at 73. For further discussion see Charles Martindale, *Redeeming The Text: Latin Poetry and the Hermeneutics of Reception* (Cambridge, 1993), 75-77.

[36] H.F. Fletcher, *The Intellectual Development of John Milton* (Illinois, 1956), I, 238.

[37] *Milton: The Minor Poems*, ed. M.Y. Hughes (New York, 1947), li.

[38] John Carey, *Milton: Complete Shorter Poems*, 99, suggests late 1629.

[39] Clark, *John Milton at St Paul's School*, 178.

[40] J.T. Shawcross, "Of Chronology and the Dates of Milton's Translation from Horace and the New Forcers of Conscience," *SEL* 3 (1963), 77-84, argues for a late date, noting (80) that the Latin text supplied in the 1673 volume of Milton's poetry seems not to have been published before 1636. Cf. D.P. Harding, *The Club of Hercules: Studies in the Classical Background of Paradise Lost* (Illinois, 1962), 128-134, who detects the development of Milton's mature style, whereas Roy Flannagan, *Riverside Milton* (Boston, 1998), 260, dates it 1646-48. There is, however, no reason to assume (as Shawcross and others do) that the Latin text published by Milton in 1673 is necessarily the text he used at the time of composing his English version. For a convincing rejection of Shawcross's reasons, see *A Variorum Commentary on the Poems of John Milton*, ed. M.Y. Hughes (New York, 1972), II, 502-505. Cf. *ibid.*, 504: "If the style does not resemble that of the early Milton, it does not much resemble that of the later poet either; in fact it is unique."

[41] Gordon Campbell, *A Milton Chronology* (New York, 1997), 214.

[42] *John Milton: Complete Shorter Poems*, ed. S.P. Revard (Wiley-Blackwell, 2009), 308.

this is a school (or university) exercise. Like the *Apologus de Rustico et Hero*,[43] it was published only in 1673 (in this instance with the Latin text subjoined),[44] at a time when Milton seems to have been gathering together his life's work for publication. But more striking is the fact that the methodology governing the piece seems to exemplify that of the "metaphrase," one of the key translational exercises practiced in the early modern classroom.

John Dryden defined "metaphrase" as "turning an author word by word, and line by line, from one language into another."[45] In terms of Renaissance pedagogy it was a rigorously effective means of instilling into a pupil sensitivity to meter and form, to the inflected syntax of the Latin language, and not least to ways in which *Latinitas* could be replicated via creative experimentation in a vernacular translation. For Ascham "Metaphrasis is to take some notable place out of a good poet and turn the same sense into meter or into other words in prose."[46] It demanded of its subject intellectual alertness "because in traveling in it the mind must needs be very attentive and busily occupied in turning and tossing itself many ways and conferrying with great pleasure the variety of worthy wits and judgements together,"[47] and tested the ability to substitute words for words, phrases for phrases, while still retaining the "source message" and structure of the original. Hence an English version of a Latin original might seek to recreate that original through the use of Latinate vocabulary, word-order and syntax. Brinsley in setting forth his own pedagogical recommendations and practice takes pains to emphasize:

> The propriety of the English words, answering to the Latine, in the first and naturall signification, and expressing the force of the Latine words. And where the Latine phrase is somewhat hard or obscure to be expressed in our English tongue, word for word; there I have also expressed that by a more

---

[43] See pages 36-53.

[44] The subjoining of the Latin "original" is interesting in light of Brinsley's recommended pedagogical practice: "Cause them to rule their books both sides at once ... On the first side toward the right hand, in which the English is to be set, to leave a lesse margent: on the other side for the Latine a greater margent; because the Latine may bee written in a lesse space than the English" (*Ludus Literarius*, 150-151).

[45] John Dryden, *Preface to Ovid's Epistles* (London, 1680). Text is that of *The Works of John Dryden*, eds. E.N. Hooker and H.T. Swedenberg Jr (University of California Press, 1956), I, 114.

[46] Ascham, *The Scholemaster*, 93.

[47] Ascham, *The Schlolemaster*, 109-110.

plain phrase. Moreover, where any phrase is over-harsh in our English tongue, to expresse the Latine verbatim … that harsh phrase is also placed in the Margent, over-against the Latine phrase.[48]

And so to Milton:

Horace, *Odes* 1.5

John Milton

Rendered almost word for word without Rhyme according to the Latin Measure, as near as the Language will permit

	Quis multa gracilis te puer in rosa	What slender Youth bedew'd with liquid odours	
	perfusus liquidis urget odoribus	Courts thee on Roses in some pleasant Cave,	
	grato, Pyrrha, sub antro?	Pyrrha for whom bindst thou	
	cui flavam religas comam	In wreaths thy golden Hair,	
5	simplex munditiis? Heu quotiens fidem	Plain in thy neatness; O how oft shall he	5
	mutatosque deos flebit et aspera	On Faith and changed Gods complain: and Seas	
	nigris aequora ventis	Rough with black winds and storms	
	emirabitur insolens,	Unwonted shall admire:	
	qui nunc te fruitur credulus aurea,	Who now enjoys thee credulous, all Gold,	
10	qui semper vacuam, semper amabilem	Who alwayes vacant always amiable	10
	sperat, nescius aurae	Hopes thee; of flattering gales	
	fallacis; miseri, quibus	Unmindfull. Hapless they	
	intemptata nites; me tabula sacer	To whom thou untry'd seem'st fair. Me in my vow'd	
	votiva paries indicat uvida	Picture the sacred wall declares t'have hung	
15	suspendisse potenti	My dank and dropping weeds	15
	vestimenta maris deo.[49]	To the stern God of Sea.	

In terms of its reception through the centuries, it might be remarked that Horace, *Odes* 1.5, with its interconnected themes of love, credulity, betrayal, and retirement from love,[50] is one of the most, if not *the* most,

---

[48] Brinsley, *Ludus Literarius*, 109. At 117-118 he criticizes "interlineal translation" "where the Translation is joyned with the authour, and so they are set together word for word."

[49] Text of both Latin and English is that printed in *Poems &c Upon Several Occasions by Mr John Milton: Both English and Latin &c Composed at Several Times* (London, 1673). I have modernized punctuation.

[50] For studies of the Ode, see E.A. Fredricksmeyer, "Horace's Ode to Pyrrha (*Carm.* 1.5)," *CP* 60 (1965), 180-185; Viktor Pöschl, "Die Pyrrhaode des Horaz (c. 1.5)," *Hommages à J. Bayet*, eds. Marcel Renard and Robert Schilling (*Collection Latomus* 70: Brussels, 1964), 579-586; M.C.J. Putnam, "Horace, *Carm.* 1.5: Love and Death," *CP* 65 (1970), 251-254; Kenneth Quinn, "Horace as a Love Poet: A Reading of *Odes* 1.5," *Arion* 2 (1963), 59-77; J.C. Brown, "The Verbal Art of Horace's *Ode to Pyrrha*," *TAPhA* 111 (1981), 17-22; David Coffta, "Programme and Persona in Horace, *Odes* 1.5," *Eranos* 96 (1998), 26-31; D.W. Thomson Vessey, "Pyrrha's

"translated" of Latin lyrics.[51] This may also have been the case in the early modern classroom. One way into Milton's "translation" is via the headnote he provided, in which, as Clark points out, he seems to show "a very schoolboy pride."[52] It is a pride, it could be argued, that is closely linked to pedagogical practice and to Milton's associated experience and perceptions, both as schoolboy and (by the time he was publishing the version in 1673) as erstwhile schoolmaster. In the following discussion pedagogical methodology (and Milton's consciousness of the same) will be used to support and augment Charles Martindale's reading of the poem as metaphrase.[53]

At the outset it should be emphasized that Milton's provision of headnotes to many of his poems frequently acted as a means of Renaissance self-fashioning—a rather boastful self-advertisement signaling his youthfulness at the time of composition. For example, in the 1645 volume he takes pains to indicate the date or his precise age at the time of his early compositions, and he does so in the instances of "both English[54] and Latin." Indeed very frequently his age translated into Latin is incorporated into the heading or title of a Latin poem.[55] Thus Milton's headnotes may in themselves function as a means of guiding reader response or at the very least as a form of sign-posting for his audience.

Grotto and the Farewell to Love: A Study of Horace, *Odes* 1.5," in *Why Horace? A Collection of Interpretive Essays*, ed. W.S. Anderson (Bolchazy-Cardicci, 1999), 20-30.

[51] See Ronald Storrs, *Ad Pyrrham: A Polyglot Collection of Translations of Horace's Ode to Pyrrha (Book 1, Ode 5)* (London, 1959).

[52] Clark, *John Milton at St Paul's School*, 178.

[53] See Charles Martindale, "Unlocking the Word-Hoard: In Praise of Metaphrase," *Comparative Criticism*, 6 (1984), 47-72, reworked in his *Redeeming the Text*, 75-100 (= Chapter 4: "Translation as Rereading: Symphony in Three Movements").

[54] *On the Morning of Christ's Nativity, Compos'd 1629; A Paraphrase on Psalm 114, This and the following Psalm were done by the Author at fifteen yeers old; On Shakespeare, 1630; Comus, 1634, Lycidas ... 1637.*

[55] *Elegia Secunda, Anno aetatis 17; Elegia Tertia, Anno aetatis 17; Elegia Quarta, Anno aetatis 18; Elegia Quinta, Anno aetatis 20; Elegia Septima, Anno aetatis undevigesimo; Anno aetatis 16: In Obitum Procancellarii Medici; In Quintum Novembris, Anno aetatis 17; Anno aetatis 17: In Obitum Praesulis Eliensis.* The title-page of the second (Latin) section of the 1645 volume has the following heading: *Ioannis Miltoni Londiniensis Poemata Quorum Pleraque Intra Annum Aetatis Vigesimum Conscripsit.* The Latin inscription on the oval framing his portrait in the frontispiece to the 1645 volume proclaims a poet in the twenty-first year of his life. On the engraving (by Marshall) and Milton's sardonic response, see pages 154-155.

What aspects of his "translation" then does Milton highlight? First, he points out that his version is verbally close to the original: it is "rendered almost word for word." As remarked previously, this was perhaps the chief characteristic of the Renaissance metaphrase. Hence Milton is, by implication, revealing himself as mastering that art, so to speak, as excelling in this methodology. Second, he announces that his version does not rhyme. Rhyming translations were criticized by early modern educational theorists, especially if their inclusion was likely to hamper the rendering. To reinforce the point Ascham readily adapts the comments of none other than Quintilian:

> Quintilian in his learned Chapter *de Compositione* ... doth justly inveigh against all rhyming; if there be any, who be angry with me, for misliking of rhyming may be angry ... with Quintilian also for the same thing.[56]

In fact rhymed verse and the metaphrase were viewed as virtually incompatible. Third, Milton draws attention to the fact that his poem seeks to approximate "the Latin measure" of the original. "Measure" here encompasses meter, but also perhaps the stanzaic structure of the whole.[57] The ability of English verse to reproduce the meter of a classical original is discussed by Ascham, who contrasts the respective clumsiness and felicity of English poetry in rendering hexameter and iambic verse.[58] But visually Milton's poem proper (in the number and shape of its stanzas: two iambic pentameters followed by two iambic trimeters) provides in effect a vernacular mirror-image[59] of Horace's meter (third Asclepiad) and line-length.[60] His translation actually *looks* Horatian. Comparable perhaps is Marvell's *An Horatian Ode Upon Cromwell's Return From Ireland*, which like Milton's translation seeks to replicate (on a visual

---

[56] Ascham, *The Scholemaster*, 145-146. Cf. his criticism of "that barbarous and rude rhyming" (145). Contrast his praise of the Earl of Surrey and of Gonsalvo Periz, who "avoided the fault of rhyming" in their translations of Virgil, *Georgics* 4, and Homer's *Odyssey* respectively (147).

[57] Contrast John Hale, *Milton's Languages: The Impact of Multilingualism on Style* (Cambridge, 1998), 71: "even if 'measure' refers only to the metre."

[58] Ascham, *The Scholemaster*, 146: "Although *Carmen Exametrum* doth rather trot and hobble than run smoothly in our English tongue yet I am sure our English tongue will receive *Carmen Iambicum* as naturally as either Greek or Latin."

[59] On possible visual and linguistic mirroring in the 1645 volume, see pages 158-165.

[60] Cf. Martindale, "In Praise of Metaphrase," 54.

level) Horatian stanzaic structure.[61] Fourth, Milton conveys the fact that his translation endeavors to reproduce a Latin original in the English language – or at least "as near as the Language will permit." The headnote as a whole, and the latter phrase in particular, are not very far removed from Brinsley's general precepts concerning translation:

> In all such translating either English or Latine this is carefully to be observed; ever to consider well the scope and drift of the Author and the circumstances of the place; and to labour to express lively, not only the matter, but also the force of each phrase, *so near as the propriety of the tongue will permit.*[62]

Milton's headnote in short seems to display a metalinguistic awareness or "the ability to reflect upon and manipulate spoken and written language"[63] – an ability now recognized as both characteristic and symptomatic of early bilingual experience. Vygotsky argues that the act of rendering the same message in different languages enables "the child to see his language as one particular system among many, to view its phenomena under more general categories, and this leads to awareness of his linguistic operations."[64] Cummins has noted that metalinguistic awareness is more evident in bilingual than in monolingual children.[65] Similarly Baker has highlighted "an analytical attitude towards language" and a "better ability to regulate, manage and control their language processing" as particularly characteristic of bilingual children.[66] Hamers and Blanc provide a useful overview:

> Early bilingual experience seems to promote a number of cognitive and metalinguistic abilities: originality, creativity, divergent thinking, problem solving, symbol substitution, rule discovery, sensitivity to linguistic cues, disambiguation and verbal flexibility.[67]

---

[61] See Haan, *Andrew Marvell's Latin Poetry*, 53-55.

[62] Brinsley, *Ludus Literarius*, 156-157. Italics are mine.

[63] Colin Baker, *The Care and Education of Young Bilinguals* (Clevedon, 2005), 71.

[64] L.S. Vygotsky, *Thought and Language* (Cambridge Mass., 1962), 110.

[65] James Cummins, "Bilingualism, Language Proficiency and Metalinguistic Development," in *Childhood Bilingualism: Aspects of Linguistic, Cognitive and Social Development*, eds. Peter Homel, Michael Palij and Doris Aaronson (New Jersey, 1967), 57-73, at 67.

[66] Baker, *The Care and Education of Young Bilinguals*, 71.

[67] Hamers and Blanc, *Bilinguality and Bilingualism*, 78.

Milton implicitly draws the reader's attention to the essentially Latinate English employed throughout a translation which in turn might be seen to epitomize a highly creative level of linguistic mixing (loan blending) or "borrowing a word from the lexicon of the other language and grammatically adapting it to the language used in the utterance."[68] For Milton linguistic mixing works on both a verbal and a syntactical level: verbally, in terms of his choice of nouns and adjectives,[69] and the preference for English words with Latin roots as a means of rendering their Horatian equivalent: thus "liquid odours"(1)/*liquidis ... odoribus* (2); "admire" (8)/*emirabitur* (8); "credulous" (9)/*credulus* (9); "vacant" (10)/*vacuam* (10); "amiable" (10)/*amabilem* (10). Through such Latinisms the linguistic alterity of Milton's metaphrase also seems to mirror "the alterity of Horace's lyric manner."[70] But if the rendering looks back to Horace, it also looks ahead to the mature vernacular Milton, the poet of *Paradise Lost*, an epic permeated by Latinisms, by English words used in a Latinate sense.[71]

The poem's Latinity operates on a syntactical level also as Milton replicates the inflected word order of the ancient language by postponing verbs until the end of clauses ("complain" [6], "admire" [8], "hopes thee" [11]).[72] He uses enjambment as a means of allowing his vernacular

---

[68] Hamers and Blanc, *Bilinguality and Bilingualism*, 36.

[69] Archie Burnett, "The Fifth Ode of Horace, *Lib*. I, and Milton's Style," *MQ* 16 (1982), 68-72, remarks on the high frequency of adjectives in Milton's version.

[70] Martindale, *Redeeming the Text*, 79.

[71] A few examples will suffice: "abject" (from *abicio-ere* [to cast down]): "so thick bestrewn/Abject and lost lay these, covering the flood" (*PL* 1. 311-312); "reluctant" (from *reluctor-ari* [to struggle]): "till supplanted down he fell/A monstrous serpent on his belly prone,/Reluctant, but in vain" (*PL* 10. 513-515); "involved" (from *involvo-ere* [to roll/wrap around]): "Satan involved in rising mist" (*PL* 9. 75). See also Chapter 6 herein. All quotations are from *Milton: Paradise Lost*, ed. Alastair Fowler (London and New York, 2006).

[72] On the "hopes thee ..." construction, Hale, *Milton's Languages*, 71, remarks: "[Milton's] English, forced into the Latin word-order, cannot make clear who is 'credulous' and who is 'amiable' nor what 'vacant' means. What inflection can clarify readily, English fails to: the syntax crumples into nonsense." Contrast Louis MacNeice: "Much better than most translations. If only because of the word-order. 'Who always vacant, always amiable, hopes thee.' Keeping the hopes to the end is much more dramatic, you see. And here Milton's following Horace. Though of course it's much easier in an inflected language." (*Carpe Diem*, written and produced by Louis MacNeice, Third Programme, Monday 8th October 1956, 7.30-8.15 p.m.). See A.J. Peacock, "Louis MacNeice: Transmitting Horace," *Revista Alicantina de Estudios Ingleses* 5 (1992), 119-130, and especially 124: "There is ... a constant

rendering (like its Horatian equivalent) to cut across stanzaic division.[73] As in Horace, he holds back the *simplex munditiis* phrase to enable it to open the second stanza,[74] and he replicates the repetition of *qui ... qui* (9-10) in "who ... who" (9-10) and of *semper ... semper* (10) in "always ... alwayes" (10). His emphatically positioned "me" at the beginning of the final clause (13) balances its precise Latin equivalent *me* (13), thereby achieving complete verbal (and indeed visual) assimilation,[75] and he reproduces the archaism of the accusative with infinitive construction: *me .../... indicat.../suspendisse* (13-15) in "me ... /... declares t'have hung" (13-14).

One question remains to be answered: is anything lost in translation in terms of Milton's metaphrastic rendering? Perhaps the reader is left wondering how different the final product would have been had Milton adopted (or been asked to adopt?) a more liberal approach both verbally and syntactically—one epitomizing Brinsley's rather minimalist recommendation:

> For translating any Latine Author into English, only to expresse the sense and meaning of it; the sense and drift of the Latine Author is principally to be observed, and not the phrase nor propriety of the tongue to be so much sought to be expressed or stucken onto.[76]

Milton's poem by contrast is marked by a degree of artificiality that ensues as a consequence of its excessive fidelity to the "phrase" and the "propriety" of the Latin "tongue," and by a tone that is at times overly puritanical. For example, the difficult phrase *simplex munditiis*[77] is

---

tension, in translations from the Latin, between the resources of an inflected and an uninflected language."

[73] Cf. Martindale, "In Praise of Metaphrase," 54; *Redeeming the Text*, 79.

[74] Cf. Martindale, "In Praise of Metaphrase," 54; *Redeeming the Text*, 79.

[75] Cf. the visual and quasi-aural assimilation effected by Milton's choice of "all gold" (9) to render Horace's *aurea* (9) and "flattering" (11) to render Horace's adjective *fallacis* (12). For potential Latin/English aural assimilation in *Paradise Lost*, see pages 174-180 and 190-198.

[76] Brinsley, *Ludus Literarius*, 157.

[77] R.G.M. Nisbet and Margaret Hubbard, *A Commentary on Horace Odes Book I* (Oxford, 1970), 75, state: "*munditiis* does not make an oxymoron with *simplex* but points in the same direction."

A young lover's credulity (*credulus* [9]), his lack of knowledge (*nescius* [11]) of future betrayal, have become for both Adam and Eve ("our *credulous* mother" [9.644]),[89] an essentially transient present in which prelapsarian ignorance is bliss:

> Sleep on
> Blest pair; and O yet happiest if ye seek
> No happier state, and know to know no more (*Paradise Lost* 4. 773-775)[90]

1.3 *Paraphrasis*: "Awake, Arise, or Be For Ever Fall'n"[91]

The Miltonic injunction that Adam and Eve should enjoy sleep equates the state of sleepfulness ("sleep on" [*PL* 4.773]) with the absence of a quest for knowledge ("know to know no more" [*PL* 4.775]), the latter conveyed via appropriately somnolent and punningly hypnotic repetition: "know," "know," "no."[92] The reverse of this was the case in the early modern classroom. In fact the command to dispel sleep and to rise early served both as a behavioral maxim for young schoolboys in quest of knowledge, and also as the basis of Latin exercises in *paraphrasis*.

The popularity of the theme of early rising[93] manifests itself in a variety of ways, not least via a Latin proverb: *diluculo surgere saluberrimum est*, which was regularly included in Latin grammars and textbooks,[94] as indeed it would later be by Milton in his own *Latin*

---

[89] Italics are mine.

[90] Cf. "Can it be sin to know,/Can it be death? And do they only stand/By ignorance, is that their happy state" (4. 517-519).

[91] *Paradise Lost* 1.330.

[92] Cf. Shakespeare, *Macbeth* 4.1.118: "Seek to know no more."

[93] For a later essentially moralistic appropriation of the theme, see John Wesley, *The Duty and Advantage of Early Rising* (London, 1786), especially 12: "If you were to rise early every morning, as an instance of self-denial ... it would constantly keep it in your mind, that softness and idleness were the bane of religion. It would teach you to exercise power over yourself, and to renounce other pleasures and tempers, that war against the soul."

[94] See *A Variorum Commentary on the Poems of John Milton: Volume I: The Latin and Greek Poems*, ed. Douglas Bush (New York, 1970), 333.

*Grammar.*⁹⁵ That the proverb was more than familiar to any Renaissance schoolboy is attested by Shakespeare's *Twelfth Night*, in which the aristocratic Sir Toby Belch offers the following authoritative reproach to his gull Sir Andrew Aguecheek:

> Approach, Sir Andrew; not to be abed after midnight, is to be up betimes; and *diluculo surgere* thou knowest—(*Twelfth Night* 2.3.1-3).⁹⁶

Here the familiar educational maxim is quoted by heart albeit in a partial and somewhat lighthearted manner by one whose "joy is in the jest as well as in the bottle."⁹⁷ It is not without significance that the maxim is completely unfamiliar to Aguecheek, whose very name is "suggestive of cowardice,"⁹⁸ a temerity that may be reflected in his apparent resistance to second-language acquisition. Sir Toby's statement elsewhere that Aguecheek "speaks three or four languages word for word without book" (1.3.26-27) signifies, as Draper notes, that he has merely "memorized odds and ends from a popular phrase book."⁹⁹ In effect he has taken an all too conveniently careless shortcut by bypassing the rigor of linguistic training central to the early modern pedagogical system. Aguecheek's rejoinder to Sir Toby's reproach not only betrays his inability to construe this familiar Latin phrase, but also turns the whole upon its head as if in a parodic inversion of the Socratic tutor/pupil relationship: "Nay, by my troth, I know not: but I know, to be up late, is to be up late" (2.3.4-5)–with that repetition of "know," ("no[t],") "know" perhaps even inspiring the Miltonic injunction "and *know* to *know no* more" (4.775).¹⁰⁰

And if the proverb offered a useful maxim for the schoolboy, so too could its Latin syntax be teased out to serve a specifically grammatical purpose. It is thus invoked by William Lily in his hugely influential Latin Grammar:

---

⁹⁵ *CM* 6, 330.

⁹⁶ Text is that of *Twelfth Night*, eds. J.M. Lothian and T.W. Craik (Arden Shakespeare: London, 2003). On Milton's habitual practice of not retiring to bed before midnight, see his comment in *Defensio Secunda* cited in note 14.

⁹⁷ J.H. Summers, "The Masks of *Twelfth Night*," in *Shakespeare: Twelfth Night: A Casebook*, ed. D.J. Palmer (Macmillan, 1980), 86-97, at 92.

⁹⁸ J.W. Draper, *The Twelfth Night of Shakespeare's Audience* (New York, 1975), 41.

⁹⁹ Draper, *The Twelfth Night of Shakespeare's Audience*, 57.

¹⁰⁰ Italics are mine.

> Heere note also, that somtime the Infinitive mode of a verb, or els a whole clause afore going, or els some membre of a sentence, may be the nominative case to the verb: as *Diluculo surgere, saluberrimum est*, To arise betime in the morning, is the most holsome thing in the worlde.[101]

And a Latin poem by Lily included in the same work lauds inter alia the benefits of early rising. Entitled *Carmen de Moribus* and cast in elegiac couplets, it urges the *discipulus* to flee his bed quickly in the morning and to shake off idle sleep, after which he should go to church and worship God:

> Qui mihi discipulus puer es, cupis atque doceri,
>   Huc ades, haec animo concipe dicta tuo.
> Mane citus lectum fuge, mollem discute somnum:
>   Templa petas supplex, et venerare Deum.[102]

Rather similar instructions are issued by Ioachim Camerarius in Latin elegiac verses incorporated by Erasmus in his educational tractate *De Civilitate Morum Puerilium Libellus*. Here, however, the tone is marked by a greater sense of urgency as though the *suasoria* of a poetic description of dawn coupled with associated birdsong can in itself serve as an enticingly compelling exhortation to get up out of bed:

> Sic tamen exsurgens discusso mane sopore,
>   Commendare Deo te studiumque potes:
> Nunc iterum nos iucundum das cernere lucem,
>   Eque pater tenebris sancte videre diem.
> Nox abiit, splendor circum se tollit Olympum,
>   Stellave vicini praevia lucis adest.
> Et nunc rara nitent, Phoebea lampade pulsa,
>   Quaeque nitent modicum sidera lumen habent.
> Iam nos e stratis excivit mollibus ales,
>   Quae tacitum nullum tempus abire sinit.[103]

---

[101] William Lily, *A Shorte Introduction of Grammar*, intro. J. Flynn (New York: Scholars' Facsimiles and Reprints, 1945), Cv^r.

[102] *Guilielmi Lilii ad Suos Discipulos Monita Paedagogica, seu Carmen de Moribus*, 1-4, in Lily, *A Shorte Introduction of Grammar*, D^v.

[103] *Praecepta Honestatis atque Decoris Puerilis. Auctore Ioachimo Camerario*, in Erasmus, *De Civilitate Morum Puerilium Libellus* (Frankfurt, 1547) 34^v-35^r.

In 1874 two short Latin poems (cast in elegiacs and asclepiads, respectively) and an accompanying Latin prose essay, all on the theme of early rising, were discovered by Alfred Horwood at Netherby Hall, Longtown, Cumbria, among the papers of Sir Frederick Graham. The MS leaf was loose in the same box as Milton's *Commonplace Book*. Bearing his name, it is also quite possibly in a young Miltonic hand.[104] Not included in either the 1645 or 1673 editions, the three pieces were first printed by Horwood in 1876.[105] As Clark has convincingly shown, Milton's Latin prose essay follows the scheme of the *Sententia* or "Proverb,"[106] an exercise prescribed, described and exemplified in the *Progymnasmata* of Aphthonius, a fourth-century AD grammarian and teacher of rhetoric in Antioch.[107] This textbook on theme-writing had assumed pride of place in the early modern classroom largely on account of its accessibility and hence popularity via a Latin translation compiled and edited by Reinhard Lorich in 1542. Recommended by both Erasmus and Hoole, and regarded by Brinsley as difficult but essential, Aphthonius's *Progymnasmata* via Lorich was even prescribed by statute in several Renaissance schools.[108] One of the great merits of this text was its provision of a wealth of *exempla* of the themes in question, and a clear exposition of the associated exercises. The *Sententia* constituted a brief dictum or proverb of general import intended to persuade, dissuade or to edify:

> Sententia est oratio brevi complexu aliquid quod ad hortandum dehortandumve pertinet, explicans. Sententiarum vero alia exhortans, alia dehortans, elia enuntians.[109]

---

[104] However, Campbell, *A Milton Chronology*, 24, remarks that "the handwriting does not resemble mature examples of JM's hand such as the supplicat of 1629."

[105] A.J. Horwood, *A Commonplace Book of John Milton* (London, 1876; rev. 1877), 61-63. The manuscript is now among the holdings of the Humanities Research Center, University of Texas, Austin: Shelfmark Pre-1700 MS127.

[106] Clark, *John Milton at St Paul's School*, 234-237. See also Maurice Kelly, "Grammar School Latin and John Milton," *CW* 52.5 (1959), 133-136.

[107] See F.R. Johnson, "Two Renaissance Textbooks of Rhetoric: Aphthonius' *Progymnasmata* and Rainolde's *A Booke Called the Foundation of Rhetorike*," *HLQ* 6 (1943), 427-444, at 437; G.A. Kennedy, *Greek Rhetoric* (Princeton, 1963), 54-56.

[108] See Clark, *John Milton at St Paul's School*, 230-231.

[109] *Aphthonii Progymnasmata, Partim a Rodolpho Agricola, Partim a Ioanne Maria Catanaeo Latinitate Donata cum Scholiis R. Lorichii* (London, 1596), 100.

oritur, tepidi fulcra relinque tori).[124] A reading of the elegiacs and asclepiads alongside Milton's associated Latin prose theme indicates moreover that they are not discrete or alternative verse experimentations on the given theme, but that they follow upon each other consecutively in logical fulfilment of the prerequisites of the prescribed exercise. Brinsley urges that pupils "turne the prose of the Poets into the Poets owne verse, with delight, certainty and speed, without any bodging."[125] As argued here, the relationship beween Milton's "two" Latin poems and his Latin prose *Sententia* is that of a single poetic self-paraphrase:

> Surge, age surge, leves, iam convenit, excute somnos,
>   Lux oritur, tepidi fulcra relinque tori
> Iam canit excubitor gallus praenuntius ales
>   Solis et invigilans ad sua quemque vocat
> Flammiger Eois Titan caput exserit undis   5
>   Et spargit nitidum laeta per arva iubar
> Daulias argutum modulatur ab ilice carmen
>   Edit et excultos mitis alauda modos
> Iam rosa fragrantes spirat silvestris odores
>   Iam redolent violae luxuriatque seges   10
> Ecce novo campos Zephyritis gramine vestit
>   Fertilis, et vitreo rore madescit humus
> Segnes invenias molli vix talia lecto
>   Cum premat imbellis lumina fessa sopor
> Illic languentes abrumpunt somnia somnos   15
>   Et turbant animum tristia multa tuum
> Illic tabifici generantur semina morbi
>   Qui pote torpentem posse valere virum
> Surge, age surge, leves, iam convenit, excute somnos,
>   Lux oritur, tepidi fulcra relinque tori   20

The opening hexameter urging the addressee to arise and to shake off sleep (*surge, age surge*,[126] *leves, iam convenit, excute somnos*),[127] corresponds to the definition of the *Paraphrastico* provided by Lorich whereby the pupil should explain the meaning of the proverb in

---

[124] See Horwood, 63.

[125] Brinsley, *Ludus Literarius*, 107.

[126] Cf. Milton, *In Quintum Novembris* 97: *surge, age, surge piger, Latius quem Caesar adorat*. The injunction is addressed to the pope by Satan disguised as a Franciscan.

[127] Both here and in line 19 Milton originally wrote *arcere somnos*. His substitution of *excute* for *arcere*, while occasioned no doubt *metris causa*, is interesting given the injunction *mollem discute somnum* in Lily's Latin poem on the subject (line 3). See page 27.

a simple exposition (*simplici expositione explicabis sententiam*),[128] and exemplified by Milton's prose *surge igitur, surge deses nec semper teneat te mollis lectus*.[129]

Lines 2-12 correspond to the Aphthonian *Causa*[130] classified by Clark as "pleasant,"[131] thereby paralleling the prose theme's emphasis on the pleasures of dawn. In both, these pleasures are multisensory, progressing from 1) the visual (the rising sun: *lux oritur* [2], *Titan caput exserit* [5]//*aspice solem purpureo colore orientem*; verdant fields: *laeta per arva* [6] *novo campos ... gramine* [11]//*herbescentem agrorum viriditatem* and a variety of flowers: *rosa* [9], *violae* [10], *florum omnium viriditatem*) to 2) the aural (birdsong: *daulias argutum modulatur ab ilice carmen/edit et excultos mitis alauda modos* [7-8]//*audi argutos avium concentus*), and then to 3) the olfactory (the fragrance of flowers: *iam rosa fragrantes spirat silvestris odores/iam redolent violae* [9-10]/*non satiari possis suavitate odorum qui e floribus efflantur*).[132]

Lines 13-18 correspond to the Aphthonian *Causa* classified by Clark as "profitable,"[133] emphasizing that early rising has salutary effects upon one's health. The elegiacs convey this by describing the opposite scenario: the consequences of oversleeping (15-16) and the ensuing onset of disease (*illic tabifici generantur semina morbi* [17]); the prose version states that early rising is conducive to a strong constitution and is most suited to study (*quippe summo mane cubitu surgere ad firmam corporis valetudinem non parum conducit studiis vero aptissimum est*).[134] After a repetition of the *paraphrastico* Milton has recourse to a different meter:

---

[128] *Aphthonii Progymnasmata*, ed. Lorich, 125.

[129] Cf. Wesley, *The Duty and Advantage of Early Rising*, 9: "For sleep thus indulged gives a softness and idleness to all our tempers, and makes us unable to relish any thing but what suits with an idle state of mind, as sleep does ... Now he that turns sleep into an idle indulgence does as much to corrupt his soul as the epicure does."

[130] *Causa: Debet enim praeses semper vigilare, et subditorum suscipere curam, quam somnus aufert et officii reddit immemorem* (*Aphthonii Progymnasmata*, ed. Lorich, 125).

[131] Clark, *John Milton at St Paul's School*, 235.

[132] Milton's Latin prose version explicitly highlights the sensory via a series of rhetorical questions: *oculos delectare cupis? ... aures iuvare velis? ... naribus placebis?* Text of the Latin prose theme is that of Horwood. See note 105.

[133] Clark, *John Milton at St Paul's School*, 236.

[134] Cf. Wesley, *The Duty and Advantage of Early Rising*, 12: "If you were to rise early every morning, as an instance of self-denial ... it would constantly keep it in your

> Ignavus satrapam dedecet inclytum
> Somnus qui populo multifido praeest.
> Dum Dauni veteris filius armiger
> Stratus purpureo procubuit thoro
> Audax Euryalus, Nisus et impiger   25
> Invasere cati nocte sub horrida
> Torpentes Rutilos castraque Volscia
> Hinc caedes oritur clamor et absonus.[135]

This metrical shift occurs at a significant point in the exercise as *Causa (pleasant), Causa (profitable)* now give way to a *Comparatio*. Just as his prose version draws a comparison with a good king who should not sleep all day, but should instead plan for the commonwealth both night and day (*praeterea boni regis est non somno immodico corpus saginare et vitam feriatam et laboris vacuam transigere, at reipublicae cum nocte tum die consulere*) so the asclepiads stress that lazy sleep ill-becomes a distinguished governor of his people (21-22). The *Comparatio* is in turn succeeded by the customary *Testimonio veterum* presented explictly in the prose version with mention of an injunction against deep sleep in Theocritus[136] and the rebuke provided by the Dream to Agamemnon in Homer.[137] The verse equivalent also presents a *testimonio veterum* but it does so subtextually and intertextually by turning (23-28) not to Homer, but to Virgil, *Aeneid* 9, and to an episode that comes to function as the piece's *Conclusio*. Where the prose version states that enemies have been slaughtered when overwhelmed by sleep,[138] the verses *illustrate* the truth of this by citing an epic case in point: the fatal consequences of Turnus's sleeping, during which Nisus and Euryalus made their way through the

---

mind, that softness and idleness were the bane of religion. It would teach you to exercise power over yourself, and to renounce other pleasures and tempers, that war against the soul."

[135] Consecutive line numbering is mine as a means of signaling the continuity between the two "halves" vis-à-vis Milton's recourse to and paraphrase of the Latin prose theme/*Sententia*.

[136] See Theocritus, *Idyll* 18. 9-12.

[137] Homer, *Iliad* 2.23-25: "'You sleep, son of battle-minded Atreus, tamer of horses. A man that is a counselor must not sleep the whole night through, one to whom an army has been entrusted, and on whom rest so many cares.'" (Homer, *Iliad*, trans. A.T. Murray, rev. W.F. Wyatt [Cambridge Mass.: Loeb Classical Library, 1999]).

[138] *multi enim, hostes somno gravi pressos et quasi sepultos adorti occisione occiderunt et tantam stragem ediderunt ut aut visu aut auditu miserabile sit.*

enemy camp, causing huge slaughter and destruction (*hinc caedes oritur* [28]).[139]

As noted previously, Milton's Latin verses (and variations) on the theme are characterized by the contrast between the benefits of early rising (*Causa Pleasant*) and its corollary (*Comparatio*), namely, the public dangers of slothfulness. It is a contrast that recurs in an inverted form in *Paradise Lost* 1 and 5. In book 1 Satan, ironically assuming perhaps the vociferously imperious stance of the early modern schoolmaster ("He called so loud" [314]) in a now infernal classroom, rebukes his sleeping crew ("for the ease you find/To slumber here" [320-321]), censuring their "abject posture" [322] and issuing, as it were, a vernacular *paraphrasis* of the *surge, age surge* imperative: "Awake, arise, or be for ever fall'n" [330])—itself appropriately followed by a Miltonic roll-call of sorts (376ff.). In accordance with the *Comparatio*'s application of the whole to a public sphere, the authorial voice appropriates via a simile the *ignavus ... somnus* theme to a military and political domain. On this occasion, however, the guilty party constitutes not the illustrious ruler (the *satrapa ... inclytus*) but fallen angels now resembling sleeping sentinels suddenly discovered by "whom they dread":

> They heard, and were abashed, and up they sprung
> Upon the wing, as when men wont to watch
> On duty, sleeping found by whom they dread,
> Rouse and bestir themselves ere well awake. (*Paradise Lost* 1. 331-334)

This vernacular *Comparatio* seemingly gives way to a vernacular *Causa (Pleasant)* in *Paradise Lost* 5 but with an important difference. For now Satan's dominating and domineeringly magisterial loud voice is displaced by the "voice/mild" (15-16) of Adam, which whispers a most gentle version of the school maxim to an atypically female pupil, as it were—the sleeping Eve:

> Awake
> My fairest, my espoused, my latest found,
> Heaven's last best gift, my ever new delight,
> Awake, the morning shines, and the fresh field

---

[139] On the Nisus and Euryalus episode, traditionally regarded by scholars as one of the epic's heroic yet tragic episodes, see, among others, G.J. Fitzgerald, "Nisus and Euryalus: A Paradigm of Futile Behavior and the Tragedy of Youth," in *Cicero and Virgil: Studies in Honour of Harold Hunt*, ed. J.R.C. Martyn (Amsterdam, 1972), 114-137; L.F. Pizzolato, "'Fortunati ambo': per Niso ed Eurialo," in *Studia Classica Iohanni Tarditi Oblata* (Milan, 1995), 1.265-283. For a more balanced reading, see Sergio Casali, "Nisus and Euryalus: Exploiting the Contradictions in Virgil's 'Doloneia,'" *HSCP* 102 (2004), 319-354, who emphasizes (like Milton) their "massacre of sleeping men" (345), and draws attention to the ambiguities inherent in the episode.

> Calls us, we lose the prime, to mark how spring
> Our tended plants, how blows the citron grove,
> What drops the myrrh, and what the balmy reed,
> How nature paints her colours, how the bee
> Sits on the bloom extracting liquid sweet. (*Paradise Lost* 5. 17-25)

The repetition of "awake" (17, 21) has a rhetorical effect not dissimilar to the *surge ... surge* injunction. But this injunction is couched in language of gentle ownership (the fourfold "my" [17-18]) and praise (19). The threefold "how" (21, 22, 24) enticingly conveys the multisensory benefits of early rising: the visual, the aural and the olfactory.[140] But the ostensibly pleasant *causae* of the prelapsarian Eden into which Eve is awakened are disturbingly at odds with her sleeping world, which, it emerges, has been infiltrated by a lurkingly ominous master or *magister* of sorts.[141] For as if to exemplify the pejorative statement in the *Carmina Elegiaca* that sleep can only bring with it dreams (*somnia* [15]) and associated sorrows that disturb the mind (*et turbant animum tristia multa tuum* [16]), Eve has had a dream, "of offence and trouble, which my mind/Knew never till this irksome night" (5.34-35). It is a dream moreover that contains in effect a grossly distorted *paraphrasis* of the *surge, age surge* maxim and its pleasant cause.[142] This time "with gentle voice" (37) Satan seeks to beguile Eve by means of a paraphrastic rendering of the early rising theme:

> Why sleepst thou Eve? Now is the pleasant time,
> The cool, the silent, save where silence yields
> To the night-warbling bird, that now awake
> Tunes sweetest his love-laboured song; now reigns
> Full orbed the moon, and with more pleasing light
> Shadow sets off the face of things. (*Paradise Lost* 5. 38-43)

This theme within a theme, this dream within a dream, is uttered in a cunningly disguised Satanic voice that on the surface seems to conform to

---

[140] Cf. *Song of Solomon* 2.10.3: "Rise up, my love, my fair one, and come away. For ... the fig tree putteth forth her green figs, and the vines with the tender grape give a good smell ..."; *Song of Solomon* 7.12: "Let us get up early to the vineyards; let us see if the vine flourish, whether the tender grape appear, and the pomegranates bud forth." Translation is that of the *King James Version*.

[141] Satan is, after all, the *fraudumque magister* (*In Quintum Novembris* 17) and "artificer of fraud" (*PL* 4.121).

[142] See in general Howard Schultz, "Satan's Serenade," *PQ* 27 (1948), 17-26.

and replicate aspects of the Latin verse exercise on the subject.[143] It does so both rhetorically and structurally. The threefold repetition of "now" (38, 40, 41) is comparable perhaps with the repetition of *iam* in Milton's Latin verse exercise (3, 9, 10).[144] And here too the speaker highlights via the *causa (pleasant)* features of the natural world whose benefits are lost to the sleeper. But all through a glass darkly. The result is nothing more than a "travesty,"[145] a perversion of the *sententia* on early rising as night usurps day, and the daytime sun, birds and the dawn chorus of birdsong are displaced by the moon, and by a nightingale ominously warbling amid silent stillness. In a surreal inversion of the *surge, age surge* motif, the sleeping Eve dreams that she awakes, that she rises "I rose as at thy call" (5.48), and that she arrives at "the Tree/Of interdicted knowledge" (5.51-52). In a dream that is both macabre and parodic the injunction to wakefulness is tellingly associated with the quest for knowledge.[146] Crucially, however, this knowledge is "interdicted": its source, the fruit of the forbidden tree itself.

1.4 "The Turning of Verses": Milton's *Apologus de Rustico et Hero*

An apple tree and the alluring enticement of its fruit lie at the heart of Milton's *Apologus de Rustico et Hero*. Not included in the 1645 volume, this short Latin fable was published for the first time in 1673. Because of this fact some scholars have inferred that it was composed between these two dates.[147] More probably the piece is a further example of a school exercise pertaining to Milton's years at St Paul's School. The model for the poem is in this instance Christian rather than pagan; Renaissance rather than classical: a fable by Giovanni Baptista Mantuanus (1488-

---

[143] On the distortedly convoluted *Latinitas* of the Satanic vernacular voice, see pages 180-183.

[144] Cf. the heightened repetition of *iam* in Milton, *Elegia Quinta* (on the arrival of spring), lines 2, 4, 15, 25, 31, 35.

[145] Alastair Fowler, ed. *Paradise Lost*, ad loc.

[146] Contrast the association of sleep with the absence of a quest for knowledge in *PL* 4 773-775, discussed at pages 25-26.

[147] See, for example, Leigh Hunt, who has suggested that the poem has some topical and political significance (*Literary Examiner*, 6 Sept 1823). Bush, *Variorum*, I, 152, suggests that no such explanation is needed, and rightly points out that *At A Vacation Exercise* and the *Fair Infant* were likewise first printed in 1673.

1516),[148] also known by the more familiar appellation "Mantuan."[149] Mantuan's Latin verse was widely read both on the continent and in England during the early modern period.[150] Significantly it also took its place in the Renaissance classroom alongside classical models for school exercises in imitation, translation and original Latin verse-composition:

> *Facile precor gelida quando pecus omne sub umbra*
> *Ruminat* and so forth. Ah! good old Mantuan!
> I may speak of thee as the traveller doth of Venice:
> > Venetia, Venetia,
> > Chi non ti vede, non ti pretia.
> Old Mantuan, old Mantuan! Who understandeth thee
> not, loves thee not.
> (Shakespeare, *Love's Labour's Lost*, 4.2.92-98)[151]

This trilingual outburst is voiced by the Shakespearean schoolmaster Holofernes, whose name appropriately reflects his tyrannical biblical counterpart.[152] One can perhaps imagine an early modern teacher rigorously drilling his schoolchildren in Latin syntax, prosody and grammar, and citing a Latin verse to exemplify a grammatical nicety or to set his trembling victims a model for translation or imitation. But the ironic point here is that even the schoolmaster gets the Latin quotation wrong! He does so by misquoting *facile* for *Fauste*[153] in a paradox of

---

[148] See H.F. Fletcher, "Milton's *Apologus* and its Mantuan Model," *JEGP* 55 (1956), 230-233.

[149] See the index to Baldwin, *Shakspere's Small Latine and Lesse Greeke*. See also W.P. Mustard, *The Eclogues of Mantuan* (Baltimore, 1911), Introduction, passim.

[150] See, for example, E.S. Leedham-Green, *Private Libraries in Renaissance England* (New York, Binghamton, 1994), 96, 122, 220; see also her *Books in Cambridge Inventories: Book-Lists From Vice-Chancellors' Court Probate Inventories in the Tudor and Stuart Periods* (Cambridge, 1986), II, 522. Cf. A.F. Johnson and Victor Scholderer, *A Short-Title Catalogue of Books 1470-1600* (New York, 1964), III, 282. Included here are references to editions of Mantuan's *Adulescentia* (1649, 1652, 1655, 1669, 1679) and *Bucolics* (1656). Mantuan's pastoral and religious verse was frequently reworked, echoed and to some degree "translated" by subsequent English authors. See Lee Piepho's comprehensive discussion in "Versions by Thomas, Lord Fairfax of Some Poems by Mantuan and Other Neo-Latin Writers," *RR* 8 (1984), 114-120.

[151] Text is that of *Love's Labour's Lost*, ed. Richard David (Arden: Methuen, 1951).

[152] See *Book of Judith*, passim.

[153] The allusion is to the opening lines of Mantuan's first Latin eclogue. The quotation proved the center of an erudite quarrel between Gabriel Harvey and Thomas Nashe. In

sorts for, rather like *diluculo surgere saluberrimum est*, this was "the one tag that even the worst of Grammar School dunces might be expected to remember."[154] It is tempting to suggest that the less talented pupil, unable to "understand" "good old Mantuan," would *not* have loved this author, and would not have found such exercises "easy."

Scholarship is divided as to whether Mantuan was prescribed at St Paul's School. Some critics have assumed a negative viewpoint,[155] with the two most thorough investigations into this field by Clark[156] and Fletcher[157] finding no conclusive evidence that he was ever studied at St Paul's or even among the holdings of the school library. Nevertheless Clark is happy to speculate: "In spite of lack of evidence he may have been used as an author when Milton was at St Paul's."[158] An examination of general educational systems current in sixteenth- and seventeenth-century schools indicates that Mantuan *was* studied and that he was in fact prescribed by statute at St Paul's in 1518. Colet recommends "Lactantius, Prudentius and Proba and Sedulius and Juvencus and Baptista Mantuanus."[159] Hoole states that he was one of the authors read by boys of the fourth form: "For after-noon lessons, they read Terence two dayes, and Mantuan two dayes."[160] It is highly likely moreover that in addition to Mantuan's pastoral verse, his religious and moral poetry was included in the St Paul's curriculum, a suggestion first posited by

---

his *Four Letters* (1593) Harvey stated: "The summe of summes is, he lost his imagination a thousand waies, and I believe searched every corner of Grammar-Schoole witte (for his margine is as deeplie learned, as *Fauste precor gelida*) to see if he could finde any meanes to relieve his estate." Text is that of *The Works of Gabriel Harvey*, ed. A.B. Grosart (London, 1884), I, 195.

[154] David, ed. *Love's Labour's Lost*, 85.

[155] See Kathleen Hartwell, *Lactantius and Milton* (Cambridge Mass: Harvard University Press [1929]), viii.

[156] Clark, *John Milton at St Paul's School*, passim.

[157] Fletcher, *The Intellectual Development of John Milton*, passim.

[158] Clark, *John Milton at St Paul's School*, 125.

[159] See Lupton, *Life of Dean Colet*, 279.

[160] Hoole, *A New Discovery* as quoted by Clark, *John Milton at St Paul's School*, 123-124.

Piepho.[161] As will be argued, this is further substantiated by Milton's *Apologus*.

The model for Milton's poem occurs as one of only two fables (*Apologi*) included in the fourth book of Mantuan's *Sylvae*, a collection of miscellaneous verse of both secular and religious content. According to Fletcher, Milton's reworking of Mantuan exemplifies the "double translation system."[162] Recommended by a whole stream of Renaissance educators, this exercise required that the pupil translate a piece from one language into another; then, without looking at the original, translate his own version back into the original language, finally comparing his version with that original. Or as expressed in terms of modern linguistic theory: a source message composed in L_A was transposed into a written form in the target language L_B, which was in turn converted once again back to L_A. This methodology was applied to, for example, Greek into Latin and vice versa; Latin into English and vice versa. It is usefully summarized by Ascham, who offers the following advice as to how Cicero should be double translated:

> The childe must take a paper booke, and sitting in some place, where no man shall prompt him, by him self, let him translate into Englishe his former lesson. Then shewing it to his master, let the master take from him his Latin booke, and pausing an houre, at the least, then let the childe translate his own Englishe into Latin againe, in an other paper booke. When the childe bringeth it, turned into Latin, the master must compare it with *Tullies* book, and lay them both together.[163]

Ascham turns to Pliny the younger to reinforce his argument that translating into and out of one language greatly facilitates the acquisition of grammar, syntax, and much more:

> Ye perceive, how Plinie teacheth, that by this exercise of double translating, is learned, easely, sensiblie, by litle and litle, not onelie all the hard congruities of Grammar, the choice of aptest words, the right framing of wordes and sentences, cumlines of figures and formes, fitte for verie matter, and proper for everie tong, but that which is greater also, in marking dayly, and following diligentlie thus, the steppes of the best Authors, like invention

---

[161] See Lee Piepho, "Mantuan's Religious Poetry in Early Tudor England: Humanism and Christian Latin Verse," *MH* 20 (1993), 65-83.

[162] See Fletcher, "Milton's *Apologus* and its Mantuan Model," passim.

[163] Ascham, *The Scholemaster*, 26. Cf. Clark, *John Milton at St Paul's School*, 172-173.

of Argumente, like order in disposition, like utterance in Elocution, is eselie gathered up.[164]

Brinsley reveals that the exercise could and did operate on an oral as well as a written level: "whether reading out of the Author into the translation, or out of the translation into the Author, or doing it by pen."[165] How then did this work in practice? Perhaps the whole is most eloquently exemplified by Milton's future friend and contemporary, Andrew Marvell, albeit from the other side of the desk, so to speak. For Marvell, as for Milton, bilingualism and pedagogy were to become inextricably intertwined. In such bilingual companion pieces as *Ros*/"On a Drop of Dew"; *Hortus*/"The Garden" Marvell, through "translating" his own neo-Latin into an experimental vernacular, simultaneously enhanced that vernacular.[166] This he achieved by means of quasi-Baroque wordplay manifested in a series of puns, macaronic and otherwise, appropriated from one language and poem into its vernacular equivalent.[167]

Can the same be said of the young Milton? Clark certainly thinks so, speculating that "Milton must have done a great deal of translating as well as keeping up of paper books at school – translation from Latin into English, from English into Latin, from Greek into English and into Latin, from Hebrew into English and into Latin."[168] Linguistically, however, the situation is much more complex than either Clark or Fletcher would concede, since Milton's *Apologus* seems to engage with both a Latin original and a vernacular rendering. Hence it may present a unique example of early modern bilingual pedagogy in practice.

---

[164] Ascham, *The Scholemaster*, 94-95.

[165] Brinsley, *Ludus Literarius*, 108.

[166] It was probably while acting as tutor to Mary Fairfax at Nun Appleton House that Marvell produced these parallel neo-Latin and vernacular poems. See Haan, *Andrew Marvell's Latin Poetry*, 57-94. In so doing he may well have been composing his own "originals," so to speak, his pseudo-classical models, which he then seems to have reworked into English verse, perhaps as a means of illustrating the system to his young pupil.

[167] The very language, rhetoric, form and subject matter of Marvell's celebrated English poems would be altogether very different were it not for the fact that he had composed these works in Latin first. Gordon Campbell, ed., *Andrew Marvell* (London: Everyman, 1997), xii, usefully compares this practice to that of Samuel Beckett, who "disciplined his dramatic prose by writing his plays in French and then translating them into English."

[168] Clark, *John Milton at St Paul's School*, 177.

Milton appears to draw not only upon Mantuan's Latin poem,[169] but also upon a Latin prose version of the fable that occurs in the left margin of the poem in an edition of Mantuan's *Opera* published in Paris in 1513.[170] Furthermore he also seems to have had access to an English phonetic rendering of the fable by William Bullokar, who in his *Aesop's Fables in True Orthography* (London, 1585) offers both a metrical and prose version. There is ample testimony to the fact that Aesop (who was among authors recommended by Ascham, Brinsley and Hoole), was studied at St Paul's.[171] The inclusion of texts such as Bullokar's in the school's curriculum would certainly have accorded with the well-attested phonetical and philological interests of Alexander Gil the Elder, high master of the School when Milton was a pupil.[172] Bullokar's incorporation of a fable by Mantuan (and indeed a variety of fables by other authors) under the collective title *Aesop's Fables in True Orthography* conforms to the early modern practice of printing thematic volumes in which extracts from a wide range of authors were assembled under certain moral headings.[173] Milton's version thus seems to find its origins in bilinguality itself—and more than that for, as argued here, it conflates features from a Latin original and a vernacular rendering.

---

[169] For general links between Mantuan and Milton (selected lines from *Lycidas* and *Paradise Lost*), see Mustard, ed. *The Eclogues of Mantuan*, 52. For parallels with *On the Morning of Christ's Nativity*, see A.F. Leach, "Two Notes on Milton," *MLR* 2 (1906-7), 121-128; "Milton as Schoolboy and Schoolmaster," 311.

[170] *Primus (Secundus, tertius) Operum B. Mantuani Tomus in quo sunt Commentariis Murrhonis, Brantii et Ascensii Haec Illustrata* (Paris, 1513).

[171] For example, Robert Langham, a student of St Paul's, while describing festivities in Kenilworth in 1575 states: "I went to Scool forsooth both at Pollz, and allso at saint Antoniez: in the fifthe foorm, past Esop fabls iwys, red Terens, *Vos istec intro auferte*, and began with my Virgill *Tytire tu patulae*." Text is that of *A Letter*, ed. R.J.P. Kuin (Leiden, 1983), 79. Piepho correctly identifies the unnamed references to Terence's *Andria* and Virgil's *Eclogues*, and proceeds to remark on "Langham's failure to mention Mantuan's eclogues." This, however, may not be significant in that Langham is naturally being selective and could not really have been expected to provide a full reading list of all the authors whom he had studied. John Ogilby refers to "Aesop, whose Apologs this day are read and familiar with Children in their first Schools" (*The Fables of Aesop Paraphras'd in Verse* [London, 1651], A2^V [Dedicatory Epistle]).

[172] Alexander Gil the Elder (1565-1635) promoted a phonetic system of English in his *Logonomia Anglica* (London, 1619; rev. 1621).

[173] J. Baldius Ascensius, for example, produced in 1492 a thematic collection of extracts from Virgil, Horace and also from the *Sylvae* of Mantuan. These were arranged according to subject with an extensive commentary.

I (a) MANTUAN

Apologus alter ad eundem[174]

Rusticus ex malo dulcissima poma legebat,
  unde dare urbano sola solebat hero.
Ast herus illectus frugum dulcedine malum
  transtulit in laribus proxima rura suis.
At quia malus erat senior, translata repente   5
  aruit et proles cum genitrice obiit.
"Heu male transfertur senio cum induruit arbor!"
  inquit herus. "Fuerat carpere poma satis."
Qui nimium cupiunt atque inconcessa sequuntur
  desipiunt. Cohibet qui sua vota sapit.   10

Another Fable to the Same

A peasant used to pick the sweetest apples from an apple-tree. From this he used to give single apples to his master from the city. But the master, enticed by the sweetness of the fruit, transplanted the apple-tree into the fields next to his own dwelling. But because the apple-tree was very old, it suddenly withered when transplanted, and the fruit together with the tree which had borne it perished. The master said: "Alas, it is a bad thing to transplant a tree when it has grown hard with old age. It was sufficient to pick the apples." Those who desire too much and follow things that are forbidden are foolish. He who restrains his desires is wise.

(b) MILTON

Apologus de rustico et hero

Rusticus ex malo sapidissima poma quotannis
  legit et urbano lecta dedit domino.
Hic incredibili fructus dulcedine captus
  malum ipsam in proprias transtulit areolas.
Hactenus illa ferax, sed longo debilis aevo,   5
  mota solo assueto, protinus aret iners.
Quod tandem ut patuit domino, spe lusus inani,
  damnavit celeres in sua damna manus
atque ait, "Heu, quanto satius fuit illa coloni
  (Parva licet) grato dona tulisse animo!   10
Possem ego avaritiam frenare gulamque voracem:
  Nunc periere mihi et foetus et ipsa parens."

The Fable of the Peasant and His Master

Every year a peasant picked the most sweetly-tasting apples from an apple-tree and gave them, when picked, to his master from the city. The latter, captivated by the unbelievable sweetness of the fruit, transplanted the apple-tree itself to his own garden. Up to this point it had been productive, but weakened by old age and moved from its accustomed soil, it instantly withered and became barren. When this at last became evident to the master, deluded by vain hope, he cursed the hands whose haste had brought him loss, and said: "Alas, how much better it would have been to have accepted with gratitude those gifts from my tenant, small though they were! I could have curbed my greed and devouring gluttony: now I have lost both the offspring and the mother as well."[175]

II Latin Prose Version

<u>Rusticus ex Malo</u>. Festiviore apologo docet immodicam cupiditatem reprimendam, quia saepe illis qui eo quid satis est contenti non sunt, dum superflua quaerunt, necessaria desunt. Quae res aperitur hic aviditate cuiusdam civis, qui cum ex arbore pomifera suavissima mala a vilico suo quotannis reciperet, non contentus fructu malum in hortum suum transtulit, ubi quia vetula erat aruit, et sic nec fructum nec arborem amplius habuit.

---

[174] Text: *Opera* (Paris, 1513) 194ᵛ. I have modernized spelling and punctuation. Fletcher, "Milton's *Apologus* and its Mantuan Model," ad loc, misreads the abbreviation *uñ* of line 2 (in the 1513 text) as the unmetrical *unum* (which in any case does not make sense in the context, given that *dare* already has the neuter plural *sola* as object). The correct reading is *unde* (as is confirmed by its occurrence in other editions of the poem which do not employ abbreviations).

[175] Here, as elsewhere, all translations of Latin are mine.

Rusticus ex Malo: In this livelier fable he teaches that immoderate greed ought to be restrained because often those people who are discontented with what is sufficient lack those things which are necessary while they seek those which are superfluous. This fact is evident here in the greed of a certain citizen who, although he received every year from his tenant the sweetest apples from an apple-tree, was not content with the fruit, but transplanted the apple-tree into his own garden where, because it was old, it withered and thus he no longer possessed either the fruit or the tree.

III WILLIAM BULLOKAR

A Fabl takn out-of Mantuan.[176]

A certein contry-man gathered very-savery aplz of an apl-tre which he had in a very-ner litl feld, he gav' gathered or chozn] aplz too hiz maister being a townz-man, whoo being entyced with an uncredibl swetnes of the aplz, at-length remooved the apl-tre untoo him-self: the apl-tre being very-old withered, and thaer the aplz and apl-tre' waer lost toogether or a-lyk.] Which when it waz told too the good-man of the hows, he sayth, alas how hard a thing iz it too plant or set] an old tre' in an-other plac. I had ynowh and spar, if I had known too lay brydlz on my covetoosnes, and too gather the frut from the bow. Mantuan rehaerceth this fabl, thus:

> A contry-man riht-swet aplz did gather from a tre,
> Whaer-of he waz wont too gev giftz too townish maister fre:
> But the maister enticed with the swetnes of the frut,
> Re-moovd the tre' intoo the groundz, next too hiz-own hows sett:
> But bycaus it waz over-old, re-mooved soon did dy,
> And the encraec' with the bredor did perish-utterly.
> It waz ynowh, sayth the maister, aplz too tak, alas,
> Il iz re-moovd a tre' when it waxth hard with ag long past.
>   The moral.
> They that be' too-wyz, and folow things un-grantabl, ar foolz: he that iz
> wyz restraineth hiz desyrz.

It is hardly surprising to discover that Milton's *Apologus* owes a much greater debt to the Latin of Mantuan than to the English of Bullokar. In fact it is the close affinity between these two Latin poems that suggests the particular type of school exercise which Milton's version represents. All evidence seems to point not to the double translation scheme identified by Fletcher, but to another exercise: "the turning of verses" eloquently described by Brinsley, who enjoins the schoolmaster as follows:

> Cause them to turne the verses of their Lecture into other verses, either to the same purpose, which is easiest for young beginners, or turne to some other purpose, to express some other matter; yet ever to keepe the very phrase of the Poet, there or in other places, onely transposing the words or phrase, or changing some word or phrase, or the numbers or persons, or applying them to matters which are familiar, as they did in imitating Epistles. This may be practised, each to bring first a verse or

---

[176] Text is that of *Aesop's Fables in True Orthography* (London, 1585). See Max Plessow, *Geschichte der Fabeldichtung in Englan bis zu John Gay (1726); nebst Neudruck von Bullokars "Fables of Aesop" 1585*, in *Palaestra* 52 (1906), 48-49.

two thus changed, either being given at eleven to be brought at one, or at evening to be brought in the morning, or both.[177]

He cites examples of this pedagogical methodology:

> For turning of verses divers waies, M. Stockwood his Progymnasma scholasticum is instar omnium, to direct and to incourage young Schollers. In which booke towards the end of it, you shall have one Disticke or couple of Verses, varied 450. wayes. The verses are these:
> 1. Linque Cupido iecur; cordi quoque, parcito: si vis
>   Figere, fige alio tela cruenta loco.
> 2. Parce meo iecori; intactum mihi linquito pectus:
>   Omnia de reliquo corpore membra pete.
> 3. Caece puer, &c.[178]

The practice is well described by Clark:

> The exercise depends in part on the relative indifference of Latin elegiac verse to word order so long as the meter is kept regular. So the boys were set to transpose words in a given distich without destroying the meter. Or they might vary the phrase or in some other way express the thought of the original, in different words or in different word order but in correct even though uninspired meter.[179]

The affinity between the two fables is apparent from the titles. In both instances the poem is entitled *Apologus*, a genre that, according to Aphthonius via Lorich, had a rhetorically persuasive force.[180] Mantuan's is the second of two: *Apologus alter ad eundem*;[181] Milton has *Apologus de rustico et hero*. The *herus* of Milton's title is the only instance of its occurrence in the poem. Where Mantuan cites the noun three times (lines 2, 3 and 8), Milton substitutes *dominus* throughout, employing it in lines 2 and 7. Thus the unique *herus* of the title seems to signal the poem's debt to Mantuan as the two protagonists are described via the same term. Striking too is the identical opening phrase *Rusticus ex malo*, providing

---

[177] Brinsley, *Ludus Literarius*, 194.

[178] Brinsley, *Ludus Literarius*, 197.

[179] Clark, *John Milton at St Paul's School*, 181.

[180] *sunt autem Apologi maxime compositi ad popularitatem atque vim persuasionis.* (*Aphthonii Progymnasmata*, ed. Lorich, 12).

[181] The *eundem* of Mantuan's title is Gioffredo Caroli (*Iaffredus Carolus*), to whom the preceding *Apologus* on a frog is addressed. He is also the addressee of the first poem of *Sylvae* bk IV, where he is described as *Delphinatus praesidem et Mediolani Vicecancellarium*. On Caroli, see *Dizionario Biografico degli Italiani* (Rome: Istituto della Enciclopedia Italiana, 1977), sv.

what is virtually an alternative title (or short title), as is suggested by its occurrence at the beginning of the Latin prose account (II). In both Mantuan and Milton lines 1-2 describe the same situation: the picking of delicious apples by a peasant (*rusticus*), who in turn gives these to his master from the city (*urbanus*). This dichotomy between country and city is characteristic of the early modern *Apologus*. Aphthonius via Lorich cites as an *exemplum Apologi* the story of the town mouse and the country mouse,[182] a fable that he appropriately traces back to Horace.[183]

Where Mantuan has the superlative *dulcissima* to describe the fruit (1), Milton substitutes the superlative *sapidissima*, thereby avoiding the repetition in Mantuan of *dulcissima* (1) and *dulcedine* (3). Milton's *sapidissima* is more effective because of its extra sibilant, which is felt when read in connection with the sibilants in line 1 as a whole:

> Rusticus ex malo sapidissima poma quotannis

The hissing sibilants aptly convey the enticing juices of the apples, a linguistic technique that would come to be appropriated on a vernacular level in *Paradise Lost* 9. There Satan describes the scent and juices of the apple in a speech that is in itself a verbally hypnotic *oratio sapidissima*, indulgingly luxuriant in its recourse to sibilants:

> Till on a day roving the field, I chanced
> A goodly tree far distant to behold
> Loaden with fruit of fairest colours mixed,
> Ruddy and gold: I nearer drew to gaze;
> When from the boughs a savoury odour blown,
> Grateful to appetite, more pleased my sense
> Than smell of sweetest fennel, or the teats
> Of ewe or goat dropping with milk at even,
> Unsucked of lamb or kid, that tend their play.
> To satisfy the sharp desire I had
> Of tasting those fair apples, I resolved
> Not to defer; hunger and thirst at once,
> Powerful persuaders, quickened at the scent
> Of that alluring fruit, urged me so keen. (*Paradise Lost* 9. 575-588)

---

[182] *Aphthonii Progymnasmata*, ed. Lorich, 19-20: *mus rusticus urbanum hospitio excepit, et amicum quibus potuit cibis exquisitis refecit. Urbanus agrestia fastidiens obsonia, rusticum in urbem secum duxit. Ineunt, quod opipare fuit instructum, convivium. Inter epulandum auditur strepitus in sera, et latratus canum. Ambo trepidare et fugitare, rusticus maxime, qui viarum ignarus aegre se tueri. Sed ad sese reversus, ait: "malo cum securitate meam inopiam quam istam cum tali anxietate copiam."*

[183] *Aphthonii Progymnasmata*, ed. Lorich, 20: *exemplum eiusdem dilatati apud Horatium*. Cf. Horace, *Satires* 2.6.

Likewise the hissing alliteratives of a Miltonic vernacular alluringly seduce the reader,[184] as they convey the power of the scent of the apples over Eve:

> Meanwhile the hour of noon drew on, and waked
> An eager appetite, raised by the smell
> So savoury of that fruit, which with desire,
> Inclinable now grown to touch or taste,
> Solicited her longing eye. (*Paradise Lost* 9. 739-743)

The Miltonic *sapidissima* develops the more straightforward *sapit* (Mantuan 10) to embrace and suggest the twofold meaning of the Latin verb *sapio-ere* ("to taste"/"to be wise").[185] In so doing, it anticipates the association of the word "sapience" in *Paradise Lost* with "wisdom in matters determined by the sense of taste."[186] Hence Adam proclaims: "Eve, now I see thou art exact of *taste,*/And elegant, of *sapience* no small part" (*PL* 9.1017-1018).[187]

Milton's Latin verses contain the adverb *quotannis* (1), which, while absent from Mantuan's poem, occurs in the Latin prose version (II): *mala ... quotannis reciperet*. Where Mantuan employs the imperfect tense (*legebat* [1] and *solebat* [2]), Milton substitutes the perfect tense (*legit* and *dedit* [2]) and achieves a virtual *figura etymologica* between *legit* and *lecta* (2).[188] The past participle *lecta*, although absent from Mantuan, finds a vernacular parallel in Bullokar's prose version: "he gav' *gathered or chozn* aplz."[189]

Lines 3-4 of both poems describe the master's enticement by the fruit and the transplanting of the actual apple tree. Where Mantuan has merely *frugum dulcedine* (3), Milton adds an emphatic qualifying adjective "incredible" (*Hic incredibili fructus dulcedine captus* [3]).[190]

---

[184] See Stanley Fish, *Surprised by Sin: The Reader in Paradise Lost* (Macmillan, 2nd ed., 1997), passim.

[185] See *OLD* sv.

[186] L.E. Lockwood, *Lexicon to the English Poetical Works of John Milton* (New York, 1907; rpt 1968), ad loc.

[187] Italics are mine.

[188] For a vernacular equivalent perhaps, cf. Bullokar's "gev giftz."

[189] Italics are mine.

[190] As noted by Bush (*Variorum*, I, 153), *dulcedine captus* is a stock phrase: e.g. Virgilian *Culex* 126; Ovid, *Metamorphoses* 1.709; 11.170; Juvenal 7.84; Statius,

Again it is in Bullokar's English prose version (III) that a parallel can be found: "entyc'ed with an *un-credibl* swe'tnes of the aplz."[191] But Milton's inclusion of the adjective anticipates another fateful seduction by fruit—this time in a vernacular epic—and the heightened and heightening sensations that the sweet juices seem to cause. Central to the success of Satan's temptation-speech in *Paradise Lost* is his fallaciously alluring description and re-creation of that "strange alteration" (*PL* 9. 599), that incredible metamorphosis both intellectually and linguistically, which (he says) he experienced as a result of eating the apple (*PL* 9. 594-605).[192] The same is true of Eve's reaction to tasting the juices of the apple as she deceives herself into thinking that she has surmounted her human condition and attained the divine (*PL* 9. 785-790).[193] And when Adam partakes of the fruit, they are "as with new wine intoxicated both" (*PL* 9. 1007) and "fancy that they feel/Divinity within them breeding wings/ Wherewith to scorn the earth" (*PL* 9. 1009-1011).

In the *Apologus* Milton conveys the audacity of the transplanting through an emphatic *ipsam* (*malum ipsam* [4]), which does not occur in Mantuan. Given the later Milton's predilection for punning,[194] it is likely that he is playing on *malum-i* (n) (evil) and *malus -i* (f) (apple-tree).[195] Such word play is also discernible in iconographical representations of the Fall. The equation of apple-eating with evil as evinced by symbolic

---

Thebaid 10. 79; Castiglione, *Carmina* 4.9; Vida, *Christiad* 4. 869; *De Arte Poetica* 1.184; 1.288; Campion, *Umbra* 319.

[191] Italics are mine.

[192] "Amid the tree now got, where plenty hung/Tempting so nigh, to pluck and eat my fill/I spared not, for such pleasure till that hour/At feed or fountain never had I found./Sated at length, ere long I might perceive/Strange alteration in me, to degree/Of reason in my inward powers, and speech/Wanted not long, though to this shape retained./Thenceforth to speculations high or deep/I turned my thoughts, and with capacious mind/Considered all things visible in heaven,/Or earth, or middle, all things fair and good" (*PL* 9. 594-605).

[193] "for Eve/Intent now wholly on her taste, naught else/Regarded, such delight till then, as seemed,/In fruit she never tasted, whether true/Or fancied so, through expectation high/Of knowledge, nor was godhead from her thought" (*PL* 9. 785-790).

[194] Cf., for example, *Paradise Lost* 1.1-2: "Of mans first disobedience, and the fruit/ Of that forbidden tree," where "fruit" means both the apple and the consequence. For an excellent study of Miltonic puns, see E.S. Le Comte, *A Dictionary of Puns in Milton's English Poetry* (New York, 1981).

[195] Cf. Mantuan: *Heu male transfertur* (7). For classical precedent, cf. Plautus *Amphitryo* 723: *enim vero praegnati oportet et malum et malum dari ut quod obrodat sit, animo si male esse occeperit.*

interpretations of the fruit has been usefully examined by Schippers,[196] who discusses the use of apple-symbolism in works by authors of the Hebrew Andalusian school. Here the apple was seen as a symbol not only of love, but also of misfortune. Educated people were frequently depicted as shrinking from eating apples.[197] A bite into the fruit signified a kiss,[198] whereas the unbitten apple represented virginity.[199] This is not unrelated to the Fall. As Colebrook has pointed out, in *Paradise Lost* evil and its effect upon fallen beings are frequently associated with the act of eating in which "what is devoured can corrupt and even consume the self."[200] It is only after tasting the apple that the shamefulness of carnal desire manifests itself to both Adam and Eve—as though *malum* (evil) and *malus* (apple tree) are now indistinguishable. Comparable perhaps is a statement in the work of Abu Nuwas (750-815):

> May God punish the man who eats an apple;
> may God afflict him in his mouth
> Or that the man admits his insufficiency,
> with the exception of you whose name I do not want to mention.[201]

And as Adam laments the Fall, the equation of evil and of fruit is emphasized via a possible macaronic pun:

> ... since our eyes
> Opened we find indeed, and find we know
> Both good and *evil*, good lost, and *evil* got,
> *Bad fruit* of knowledge, if this be to know. (*Paradise Lost* 9.1070-1073)[202]

---

[196] Arie Schippers, "Hebrew Andulasian and Arabic Poetry: Descriptions of Fruit in the Tradition of the 'Elegants' or Zurafa," *Journal of Semitic Studies* 33.2 (1988), 219-232.

[197] Schippers, "Descriptions of Fruit," 223.

[198] Schippers, "Descriptions of Fruit," 222.

[199] Schippers, "Descriptions of Fruit," 228. For the link between "fruit" and sexual debasement, see *Paradise Lost* 4. 766-767: "Of harlots, loveless, joyless, unendeared/ Casual fruition ..."

[200] Claire Colebrook, *Milton, Evil and Literary History* (London, 2008), 46. Milton's depiction of Sin and Death is couched in imagery of self-consumption. Cf. *ibid.*, 45: "eating is a profoundly important figure in the axiology of good and evil."

[201] Schippers's translation, "Descriptions of Fruit," 223.

[202] Italics are mine.

The appropriately juxtaposed adjective "bad" (*malus-a-um*) and noun "fruit" (*malus* [apple tree]) may hint at their virtual synonymity. It is noteworthy that the noun "malice" (with its possible pun on *malum/malus*) is seen as originating in Satan himself and in language suggestive of a horticultural setting: "for whence,/But from the author of all ill *could spring*/So deep a *malice*, to confound the race/Of mankind *in one root*" (*PL* 2.380-383).²⁰³

Lines 5-6 of both poems describe the ill-consequences of the transplanting of the tree, which, since it is already old, immediately withers and dies. Whereas Mantuan has a causal clause beginning with *At quia*, followed by a past participial phrase and a clause beginning with *et*, Milton relies on the skillful juxtaposition of phrases that reach a sudden climax in the decay of the tree. Furthermore his lines highlight a stark contrast between the tree as it was and the tree as it became, a point not fully emphasized by Mantuan. This contrast between *hactenus illa ferax* at the beginning of line 5 and *protinus aret iners* at the end of line 6 works on two levels: first, between the adverbs (*hactenus*, describing the condition of the tree up to the present stage, and *protinus*, depicting the sudden reversal as the tree rapidly withers and dies) and, second, between the adjectives (*ferax*, describing the tree's fertility, and *iners*, conveying lifelessness and decay). In between these two phrases occur the reasons for this sudden disintegration: the tree has been weakened by old age (*longo debilis aevo*),²⁰⁴ an elaboration of Mantuan's *At quia malus erat senior* (5) and, perhaps, the *quia vetula erat* of the prose account. Much more explicit in Milton is the injury done to the tree as a consequence of its transplantation from its usual soil (*mota solo assueto* [6]). The concept of the detrimental effect of transplantation, or at least removal, from one's "native soil" is a virtual leitmotif of *Paradise Lost*. The fallen Satan laments his expulsion from Heaven as follows:

> Is this the region, *this the soil*, the clime,
> Said then the lost archangel, this the seat
> *That we must change* for heaven, this mournful gloom
> For that celestial light?   (*Paradise Lost* 1. 242-245)²⁰⁵

---

²⁰³ Cf. "... how all his *malice* served but to *bring forth*/Infinite goodness" (*PL* 1.217-218). Italics are mine.

²⁰⁴ Bush, *Variorum*, I, 153, compares Lucretius, *De Rerum Natura* 5.832: *aevo debile*; Seneca, *Medea* 258: *senio trementem debili atque aevo gravem*.

²⁰⁵ Italics are mine.

Adam and Eve, having eaten the forbidden fruit, are themselves "transplanted," as it were, from their "native soil." Michael informs Adam that he is to be expelled from Paradise:

> But longer in this Paradise to dwell
> Permits not; *to remove thee* I am come,
> And send thee from the garden forth to till
> The ground whence thou wast taken, *fitter soil* (*Paradise Lost* 11. 259-262).

Having partaken of evil (*malum*), they have themselves become synonymous with a transplanted tree (*malus*), uprooted and displaced from the garden in which they were originally planted.[206] Thus does Adam lament:

> Must I *thus leave thee Paradise? thus leave*
> *Thee native soil!*   (*Paradise Lost* 11. 269-270)

Milton proceeds to convey the withering of the tree as a consequence of its transplantation, substituting the historic present *aret* for Mantuan's *aruit*. This contrast between former fertility and sudden decay as a result of human transgression recurs in *Paradise Lost* in the deterioration of the world of nature as a consequence of the picking and eating of an apple ("Earth felt the wound, and nature from her seat/Sighing through all her works gave signs of woe,/That all was lost" [9. 782-784])—a deterioration mirrored in the fading roses on the garland woven by Adam for Eve (9.888-893).[207]

The subsequent lines in the two Latin poems are noteworthy in that Milton inserts a two-line transitional passage that does not occur in Mantuan, where lines 7-8 constitute a statement by the master and 9-10 an account of the moral of the whole. Milton will develop these features, yet perhaps he felt the transition from narrative to direct speech rather too abrupt in Mantuan, as indeed it may be. At any rate, he inserts two lines

---

[206] On planting as image and metaphor in *Paradise Lost*, cf. "therein plant/A generation" (1.652-653); "there plant eyes" (3.53); "Paradise ... in the east/Of Eden planted" (4.208-210); "not to taste that only tree/Of knowledge, planted by the tree of life" (4.423-424); "whose dwelling God hath planted here in bliss" (4.884); "this garden, planted with the trees of God" (7.538); "A circuit wide, enclosed, with goodliest trees/Planted" (8.304-305). On transplanting, cf. "them who ... live in thee transplanted" (3.291-293); "light .../Transplanted from her cloudy shrine" (7.359-360). See in general K.L. Edwards, *Milton and the Natural World: Science and Poetry in Paradise Lost* (Cambridge, 2005).

[207] "On th'other side, Adam, soon as he heard/The fatal trespass done by Eve, amazed,/Astonied stood and blank, while horror chill/Ran through his veins, and all his joints relaxed;/From his slack hand the garland wreathed for Eve/Down dropped, and all the faded roses shed" (*PL* 9. 888-893).

that, apart from extending the poem by an additional elegiac couplet, can be viewed as an authorial intervention to keep the whole in balance:

> Quod tandem ut patuit domino, spe lusus inani,
> damnavit celeres in sua damna manus. (7-8)

Milton actually *describes* the revelation—a feature only implicit in Mantuan. The syntactical phraseology of *Quod tandem ut patuit* finds a general parallel in Bullokar's "Which when it waz told." Milton also goes further than Mantuan by punning on the etymological link between *damnavit* and *damna*.[208] The phrase *spe lusus inani* (7)[209] is an authorial comment upon the vain hope that has deluded the master, in lines that convey a vivid sense of the anger and regret felt as he curses the hands which have been so swift to cause his loss. Comparable perhaps is the "rash hand" of Eve in *Paradise Lost*, which similarly results in loss: "that all was lost" (*PL* 9. 780-784).[210] Furthermore Milton's *in sua damna manus* (8) introduces a quasi-suicidal undercurrent not present in Mantuan's version. The more mature Milton would have the despairing Eve suggest that she and Adam seek death "with our own hands" (*PL* 10. 1002).[211]

Both Mantuan and Milton use the exclamatory *heu* to convey the master's regret (*heu male transfertur* [Mantuan 7]/*heu quanto satius fuit* [Milton 9]). Milton's comparative phrase is a development of Mantuan's *fuerat carpere poma satis* (8). He proceeds to stress the contrast between the former state when the master enjoyed the apples, even though this was

---

[208] Cf. references to "damnation" at *Paradise Lost* 1.215; 2.482; 2.496; 2.597; 4.392.

[209] Cf. *Paradise Lost* 11. 124-125: " ... and all my trees their prey,/With whose stolen *fruit* man once more to *delude*."

[210] "So saying, her *rash hand* in evil hour/Forth reaching to the fruit, she plucked, she ate:/Earth felt the wound, and nature from her seat/Sighing through all her works gave signs of woe,/*That all was lost*" (*PL* 9. 780-784). Italics are mine.

[211] "Let us seek death, or he not found, supply/*With our own hands* his office on our selves;/Why stand we longer shivering under fears,/That show no end but death, and have the power,/Of many ways to die the shortest choosing,/Destruction with destruction to destroy" (*PL* 10. 1001-1006). The hand motif is a recurring leitmotif of *Paradise Lost*. Milton establishes a contrast between virtuous and evil "hands", between God the Father, at whose "right hand" sits the son, (and who can also use his hand to wield thunder) and the "fatal hands" of the demonic crew (2. 712). Adam and Eve are frequently depicted as "hand in hand" as a symbol of their union, even at the very point of their expulsion from Paradise. See pages 194-198.

a small gift[212] (*parva licet* [10]), and the present when he has absolutely nothing—a fact conveyed by the forceful *nunc* and the contracted perfect *periere* (12) expressing the harsh finality of the whole (*nunc periere mihi et foetus et ipsa parens*). The image of the parent and its offspring expands upon Mantuan's *aruit et proles cum genitrice obiit* (6), but develops the element of personification to suggest a mother dying along with her embryo[213] — foetus in the modern sense of the word, as well as its literal meaning of fruit/offspring. Here the pun on "fruit" seems fully exploited.[214]

This contrast between past joys and present sorrow creates what is almost a tragic sense of loss, which in Milton's lines, as opposed to Mantuan's, is distinctly personal. Whereas Mantuan has *qui* in the third person plural and singular (9-10), Milton has the first person *ego* whereby the moral and sense of loss are personalized and become, not a general statement, but part of the master's inner feelings:

> Possem ego avaritiam frenare gulamque voracem.
> Nunc periere mihi et foetus et ipsa parens. (11-12)

As *possem*, *ego* and *mihi* suggest, the emphasis is upon the individual's recognition of his voracious greed. Milton's metaphor of the bridle (*avaritiam frenare* [11]) may owe some debt to Bullokar's "if I had known to lay brydlz on my covetoosnes." He develops Mantuan's *qui nimium cupiunt* (9) (itself balanced in the Latin prose version by *immodicam cupiditatem*) into the more graphically guttural *gulamque voracem* (11). The theme of gluttony will play a central role in the depiction of the Fall of both Adam and Eve. Thus: "Greedily she engorged without restraint,/And knew not eating death" (*PL* 9.791-792); "greedily they plucked/The fruitage fair to sight" (*PL* 10.560-561).[215] Milton, unlike Mantuan, highlights the self-awareness of the master, his

---

[212] Milton's use of the gift motif (*dona* [10]) finds a parallel in Bullokar's verse adaptation "too gev giftz too townish maister fre" (3).

[213] On Milton's recourse to the foetal metaphor in *Paradise Lost*, cf., for example, (of thoughts) "To perish rather, swallowed up and lost/In the wide womb of uncreated night,/Devoid of sense and motion" (2.149-151). Cf. also the depiction of the embryonic state of the uncreated world: "The earth was formed, but in the womb as yet/Of waters, embryon immature involved,/Appeared not" (7.276-278). See in general Louis Schwartz, *Milton and Maternal Mortality* (Cambridge, 2009).

[214] Contrast *Paradise Lost* 5.388-391: "Hail mother of mankind, whose *fruitful* womb/Shall fill the world more numerous with thy sons/Than with these various *fruits* the trees of God/Have heaped this table." Italics are mine.

[215] See Colebrook, *Milton, Evil and Literary History*, 45-46.

recognition of the loss he must endure, and his tragic acknowledgment of the harsh reality of the present as opposed to the now squandered benefits of the past. Again it is possible to look ahead—to the powerfully rhetorical and highly personalized speech uttered by the fallen Adam ("How shall *I* behold the face/Henceforth of God or angel ... Oh might *I* here/In solitude live savage ... cover *me* ye pines,/Ye cedars, with innumerable boughs/Hide *me*, where *I* may never see them more" [*PL* 9. 1080-1090]).[216] That contrast between former happiness and the *nunc* of present loss underlies his bitter reproach to Eve for wandering away from his side ("we had *then*/Remained still happy, not as *now*, despoiled/Of all our good, shamed, naked, miserable." [*PL* 9. 1137-1139]).[217] For our fallen parents the *malus* (apple tree) will bear not apples, but "bad fruit" (*PL* 9.1073). *Malus* and *malum* will ultimately become interchangeable in a punningly bilingual assimilation. As Stubbs remarks:

> Languages are not incompatible. We can translate between them. And bilinguals speak different languages, but they do not perceive the world differently when they switch from one language to another.[218]

---

[216] Italics are mine.

[217] Italics are mine.

[218] Michael Stubbs, "Language and the Mediation of Experience: Linguistic Representation and Cognitive Orientation," in *The Handbook of Sociolinguistics*, ed. Florian Coulmas (Oxford, 1997), 358-373, at 359.

Chapter 2

Bilingualism and Biculturalism: Cambridge and Beyond

>   ... in contempt,
> At one slight bound high overleaped all bound
> Of hill or highest wall, and sheer within
> Lights on his feet.   (*Paradise Lost* 4.180-183)

The verbal flexibility characteristic of the young bilingual[1] and exemplified by the Milton of St Paul's School came to manifest itself much more profoundly during his Cambridge years and beyond. In seventeenth-century Cambridge Latin functioned as the University's public voice, an "official, institutionalized language."[2] As such it would seem to fit the definition of "exogenous language" were it not for one important fact. Although it is certainly true that Latin constituted the formal linguistic medium of, for example, encaenia, graduation, and university anthology,[3] it also possessed a role that was in effect much more creatively pervasive than that typically assumed by an exogenous language. Crucially it was a language of performance, indeed a language *in* performance. For now a classical medium became revitalized as a vibrantly active and proactive neo-Latin voice, transcending the merely functional to assume a central place in a Cambridge speech community.

That Milton took his place upon a Cambridge stage that was both performative and essentially public is attested by his anonymous biographer, who proclaims:

---

[1] See Meuter, "Language Selection in Bilinguals"; Michael and Gollan, "Becoming Bilingual"; Hamers and Blanc, *Bilinguality and Bilingualism*, 78.

[2] Hamers and Blanc, *Bilinguality and Bilingualism*, 11.

[3] See J.W. Binns, *Intellectual Culture in Elizabethan and Jacobean England: The Latin Writings of the Age* (Leeds, 1990), 40-43; Hale, *Milton's Cambridge Latin: Performing in the Genres 1625-1632* (Cambridge, 2005), 6.

> At about eighteen yeers of age hee went to Christs College in Cambridge; where for his diligent study, his performance of public exercises, and for choice Verses, written on the occasions usually solemniz'd by the Universities, as well as for his virtuous and sober life, hee was in high esteem with the best of his time.[4]

In fact Milton's "public exercises" constituted, in the words of John Hale, "speech-acts"[5] whereby the young undergraduate contributed to a wide variety of Cambridge genres, both performative and literary. And he did so by participating in Latin debates and disputations, by writing "act verses,"[6] and by composing "voluntaries."[7] But, as Edward Jones has noted, "participation ... is not the same thing as approval or endorsement."[8] It is an important point, which can and should be taken further. For despite their superficial conformity to recognized academic convention, despite their apparent fulfillment of the formalities attendant upon university occasion, Milton's Cambridge Latin compositions are far from conformist. Hale has acknowledged that Milton "did at times overgo the required, by doing new things or modifying a set genre,"[9] but on the whole he tends to underestimate and hence to underplay ways in which the unimaginative rigidity of the university curriculum functioned somewhat paradoxically as a rather liberating experience for the "Lady of Christ's College."[10] Furthermore it is precisely and consistently through the medium of Latin that Milton seeks to transgress, to "overleap" established boundaries. This he achieves by means of overt interrogation and possible parody of established university practices, by his Latin poetry's imaginatively creative engagement with *both* Latin and

---

[4] Text is that of *Early Lives*, ed. Darbishire, 18-19.

[5] Hale, *Milton's Cambridge Latin*, 4.

[6] See Hale, *Milton's Cambridge Latin*, 33-65.

[7] See Hale, *Milton's Cambridge Latin*, 123-145.

[8] Jones, "'Ere Half my Days,'" 9.

[9] Hale, *Milton's Cambridge Latin*, 185. See in particular the excellent discussion of the "salting" and Milton's reworking of same (195-219). See also pages 88-89 and 122-123.

[10] For the term, see *Prolusion* 6.18: *a quibusdam, audivi nuper "Domina."* Cf. Aubrey, *Life*, ed. Darbishire, 3: "he was so faire that they called him the Lady of Christ's Coll." See also David Masson, *The Life of John Milton: Narrated in Connexion with the Political, Ecclesiastical, and Literary History of his Time* (Cambridge, 1859-94), I, 260.

vernacular intertexts,[11] by linguistic experimentation, and by the adoption of a tone that never fails to surprise. In all of this he seems to rejoice in an individualism that is not only unconformist, but audaciously irreverent at times.

For the Milton of Cambridge moreover the composition of neo-Latin verse, "the most intertextual poetry known to Europe,"[12] and a not insignificant way to "gain attention and consequent preferment"[13] within a university community becomes an exploratory means of self-interrogation central to an evolving self-fashioning that is bicultural in essence. In a re-invention of Clark's phrase, John Milton the Englishman "become[s] a Roman ... of sorts,"[14] not only because he employs the language of that ancient city and civilization,[15] but also and especially because he uses it frequently to attack and to satirize an English institution and everything that that institution represents. In this respect he can be seen to exhibit a balanced biculturalism, which, as Hamers and Blanc note, "often goes hand in hand with a balanced bilinguality."[16] The fact that all but two of his undergraduate compositions are in Latin is particularly insightful, and merits consideration in relation to recent conclusions that bilingual development "can ... lead a person to renounce the cultural identity of his mother-tongue group and adopt that of the second-language group."[17] Technically then Latin does indeed take its place as a second language within a university speech community, but for the Cambridge Milton it also becomes a first language of sorts, his *preferred* linguistic medium of communication and of composition. The result is a paradox that is bicultural in essence: it is in the language of ancient Rome that Milton articulates and replicates experiences (both private and public) associated with an English world (and sometimes

---

[11] See pages 58-60, 67-74, 76-79, and 84-88. For a general survey, see Estelle Haan, *John Milton's Latin Poetry: Some Neo-Latin and Vernacular Contexts* (PhD thesis, The Queen's University of Belfast, 1987).

[12] Hale, *Milton's Languages*, 12.

[13] Hale, *Milton's Languages*, 4. For fuller discussion, see Binns, *The Latin Writings*, passim.

[14] Clark, *John Milton at St Paul's School*, 172. Cf. page 13.

[15] Cf. Hale, *Milton's Cambridge Latin*, 9: [the Cambridge genres] "resuscitate the Latin lexis of Rome."

[16] Hamers and Blanc, *Bilinguality and Bilingualism*, 11.

[17] Hamers and Blanc, *Bilinguality and Bilingualism*, 11.

indeed its vernacular writings). Milton's re-creation of that world via a neo-Latin voice that embraces things English on both a contextual and intertextual level is perhaps thus describable (in the words of the 1645 volume) as "both English and Latin."[18]

2.1 Bicultural Self-Fashioning: Both Londoner and Roman

Sometimes physical distance from the immediacy of a community can afford a useful lens through which to view that absent world. In terms of the Latin Elegies associated with his Cambridge years the youthful student seems to be proactive in his quest to embrace a cultural alterity. Whether at London or at Cambridge, Milton frequently employs Latin and the rich intertextuality of classical literature to fashion himself as the other. Thus his imaginative engagement with the poets of classical Rome comes to serve as a self-conscious means of attracting attention to a Miltonic *différence* that seems to set him apart (and that sometimes quite literally) from the academic world which he is describing.

For example, the speaker of *Elegia Prima*, supposedly "rusticated" from Cambridge[19] to London, presents himself as a second Ovid,[20] but with one important difference: he can rejoice in his expulsion and consequent exile. It is a difference that is all the more forceful precisely because it is being voiced in Latin, the language of Ovid.[21] Latin verse both engenders and facilitates a whole series of "cross-comparisons" between Milton's own situation and that of the Roman poet (and his

---

[18] For discussion of the volume, see Chapter 5.

[19] The references to *vetiti ... laris* (*El*.1.12) and *exilium* (*El*.1.17, 20) have led scholars to argue that Milton was temporarily rusticated from Cambridge University. It is not impossible, however, that the poem merely alludes to the university vacation now presented as a metaphorical exile. See Carey, ed. *Complete Shorter Poems*, 19. However, that Milton had some sort of dispute with his tutor William Chappell is evident from a number of factors. See note 42.

[20] Cf. Buchanan, *Elegy* 1. 93-94: *exul Hyperboreo Naso proiectus ad axem,/exilium Musis imputat ille suum*, although in that instance the equation is between the teacher and Ovid. Text is that of Buchanan, *Poemata Quae Extant* (Amsterdam, 1687). See in general Estelle Haan, "Milton and Buchanan," *HL* 46 (1997), 266-278.

[21] See John Hale, "Milton Playing with Ovid," *MS* 25 (1982), 115-130; Hale, *Milton's Languages*, 33-37. More generally, see D.P. Harding, *Milton and the Renaissance Ovid* (Urbana, 1946).

poetry).²² The speaker can enjoy in the London metropolis *to* which he has been banished literary and quasi-amatory pleasures reminiscent of those celebrated by Ovid as pertaining to Rome, the city *from* which he was exiled: the theater, reading, the sight of pretty girls, all now described in terms ironically yet daringly reminiscent of the *Ars Amatoria*,²³ the poem that was probably responsible at least in part for Ovid's banishment.²⁴ And yet despite the poem's unquestionable *Romanitas*, there may be something essentially "English" about the theatrical experiences described (reflecting in all probability both Milton's attendance at plays and his private reading of comedy and tragedy). *Sinuosi pompa theatri* (27)²⁵ may, as Burbery has suggested, refer to the curve of the Blackfriars' auditorium,²⁶ a suggestion rendered all the more plausible in view of Gordon Campbell's uncovering of the Miltons' connections with the Blackfriars Theatre.²⁷ And although the catalogue of stock dramatic characters (29-34) is undoubtedly suggestive of Roman comedy,²⁸ *catus ... senior* (29), *prodigus haeres* (29) and *miles* (30) may allude to Pennyboy Canter, Pennyboy Junior and Captain Sunfield in Ben Jonson's *The Staple of News*.²⁹ Noteworthy too in Milton's catalogue is the somewhat surprising inclusion of the barrister thundering forth his barbaric words (*sive decennali foecundus lite patronus/detonat inculto barbara verba foro* [31-32]). This may, as Warton suggested,³⁰ allude to

---

²² See R.W Condee, "Ovid's Exile and Milton's Rustication," *PQ* 37 (1958), 498-502, reworked in his *Structure in Milton's Poetry: From the Foundation to the Pinnacles* (Pennsylvania, 1974), 22-27.

²³ See in particular *Elegia Prima* 51-76, and Bush, *Variorum*, I, ad loc.

²⁴ At *Tr.* 2.1.207 Ovid cites as reasons for his exile an unidentified *carmen et error*.

²⁵ Cf. Ovid, *Ars Amatoria* 1.89: *sed tu praecipue curvis venare theatris*; Propertius, *El.* 4.1.15: *nec sinuosa cavo pendebant vela theatro*.

²⁶ T.J. Burbery, "John Milton, Blackfriars Spectator?: 'Elegia Prima' and Ben Jonson's *The Staple of News*," *Ben Jonson Journal* 10 (2003), 57-76, reworked in T.J. Burbery, *Milton The Dramatist* (Pennsylvania, 2007), 6-17, at 9.

²⁷ Gordon Campbell, "Shakespeare and the Youth of Milton," *MQ* 33 (December 1999), 95-105. Cf. Herbert Berry, "The Miltons and the Blackfriars Playhouse," *MP* 89 (1992), 510-514.

²⁸ See Bush, *Variorum*, I, ad loc.

²⁹ As suggested by Burbery, *Milton The Dramatist*, 11-14.

³⁰ *Poems upon Several Occasions ... by John Milton*, ed. Thomas Warton (London, 1791), ad loc.

an Anglo-Latin drama composed by one of Milton's Cambridge Fellows, George Ruggle (Clare College). Although there is no evidence of a performance in London of Ruggle's *Ignoramus* (famously acted before King James, and to the king's unqualified delight, at Cambridge in 1615, though unpublished until 1630), it is not inconceivable that Milton had to hand a manuscript copy of the play. Bush's comment that Milton's "description does not fit Ruggle's burlesque lawyer"[31] is unduly dismissive.[32] Alternatively the depiction of the barrister may constitute yet another allusion to Jonson's *The Staple of News*, in this instance, to the legalistic Picklock.[33] Likewise the oxymoronic juxtaposition of a young girl's ignorance and passion (35-36)[34] is reminiscent of Princess Pecunia in that same play.[35] If so, Latin has now become the medium of a description of vernacular and in particular Jonsonian drama.

Similarly Milton's allusion to tragedies that include the *puer infelix* (41) leaving joys untasted and succumbing to death,[36] and a fierce avenger of crime returning from the darkness and crossing the Styx (43-44)[37] may embrace not only classical but also such Shakespearean drama as *Romeo and Juliet*, *Richard III*, *Hamlet* or *Macbeth*. Bush's speculation that "in a Latin poem ... a young scholar might have thought it doubtfully decorous to allude to English plays"[38] is misleadingly reductivist. The very opposite of this may have been the case (after all, Milton will have no qualms in describing in Latin [*Elegia Sexta*] his own vernacular work

---

[31] Bush, *Variorum*, I, 51.

[32] Throughout the play the language of the character Ignoramus, marred by its coarseness, crudity, and tainted hybridity, is certainly describable as *barbara verba* in an *inculto foro*. See George Ruggle, *Ignoramus* (London, 1630), passim.

[33] As argued by Burbery, *Milton The Dramatist*, 13.

[34] *saepe novos illic virgo mirata calores/quid sit amor nescit, dum quoque nescit, amat* (*El.* 1.35-36). Cf. Ovid, *Met.* 4.329-330 (Hermaphroditus): *pueri rubor ora notavit/(nescit enim, quid amor), sed et erubuisse decebat*.

[35] Cf. 2.5.50-53: "That youth .../I have so oft contemplated and felt/Warm in my veins and native as my blood"; cf. 2.5.57: "But how it came to pass I do not know." See Burbury, *Milton the Dramatist*, 14.

[36] *seu puer infelix indelibata reliquit/gaudia, et abrupto flendus amore cadit* (*El.* 1.41-42).

[37] *seu ferus e tenebris iterat Styga criminis ultor/conscia funereo pectora torre movens* (*El.* 1. 43-44).

[38] Bush, *Variorum*, I, 52.

On the Morning of Christ's Nativity).³⁹ And all with a telling paradox: Milton uses Latin to encapsulate a national and vernacular dramatic heritage, the privilege of which he can enjoy in London. It is a heritage that rivals that of the ancient world in general and of Ovid's Rome in particular.⁴⁰

If London can both replicate and surpass the pleasures of Ovid's lost Rome, Cambridge by contrast comes to function as a second Tomis inconducive to the poet and his art–with its anti-pastoral *arundiferus ... Camus* (11),⁴¹ its *nuda ... arva* (13), its *duri ... minae ... magistri* (15)⁴² symbolizing a rigidity, a dearth and death of creativity, the latter conveyed in the equation of the university with marshy swampland reminiscent of a Stygian mire. And as the poem nears its conclusion the phraseology of *iuncosas Cami remeare paludes* (89)⁴³ suggests a migrating sea-bird's return to mere marshland.⁴⁴ Indeed the harshly consonantal language implicitly associates the *raucae murmur ... Scholae* (90)⁴⁵ with frogs croaking in that reedy swamp in a pseudo-Aristophanic

---

³⁹ *Elegia Sexta* 81-88. See pages 84-88.

⁴⁰ Likewise in *Mansus* 30-34 he will describe and celebrate in Latin his own nation's literary and poetic heritage via the metaphor of swans singing upon the Thames. See pages 124-125.

⁴¹ Cf. *Lycidas* 103-104: "Next Camus, reverend sire, went footing slow,/His mantle hairy, and his bonnet sedge." See also Ovid, *Tr.* 3.10.71-78; 3.12.13-16; *Epistulae ex Ponto* 1.3.51-52.

⁴² The threats of a stern tutor about which Milton complains here may allude to William Chappell, Milton's Cambridge tutor, from whom (according to Christopher Milton) Milton received "some unkindness." Aubrey adds "he whipped him" (Darbishire, ed. *Lives*, 10). Whether or not this was the case, it is evident that his relationship with Chappell was a difficult one, and may be linked to his purported rustication from the university. Upon his return to Cambridge he would be assigned to a new tutor, Nathaniel Tovey. Milton, however, may also be echoing Buchanan, *El.* 1, on which see Haan, "Milton and Buchanan."

⁴³ Cf. *arundiferum ... Camum* (11).

⁴⁴ Cf. Var., *R.R.* 3.5.7: *cum [coturnices] ex Italia trans maria remeant*. For Milton's later avian self-fashioning in the Latin poetry associated with his Italian journey, see pages 119-120, 124-125, and 135-136.

⁴⁵ In contrast to the *placidae ... Musae* (25) of London, Cambridge is equated with frog-like croaking, symbolizing the garrulous, logistic intricacies of a sterile curriculum. Cf. *Prolusions* 1 and 3. Hale, *Milton's Cambridge Latin*, 127, interestingly suggests that *raucae ... Scholae* may allude to the Cambridge disputations.

comedy of academic manners.⁴⁶ But it is a comedy to which must return the exile who is not an exile, the Ovid who is not Ovid, the Londoner who is also Roman. And all to good effect. For by virtue of a paradoxical truth shared by both Ovid and Milton, that frequently lamented Tomis or Cambridge *did* in fact prove an important source of poetic inspiration.

2.2   Tricultural "Cross-Comparison": Milton, Ovid, Young

Another type of "cross-comparison" with Ovid underlies *Elegia Quarta*⁴⁷ addressed to Milton's former tutor, the Scotsman Thomas Young, who was serving as chaplain to the English merchants in Hamburg.⁴⁸ Here through a subtly complex engagement with *Tristia* 3.7 Milton once again establishes a series of autobiographical parallels with the Roman poet, but in this instance he subsequently transfers and applies the equation with Ovid to his addressee, Young himself. In both poems the speaker issues a series of injunctions to the letter, imagining it finding its recipient (Perilla [Ovid's stepdaughter];⁴⁹ Thomas Young) either sitting with a member of his or her family or engaged in some form of literary activity. Thus Ovid anticipates that his letter will find the poetess Perilla sitting with her "sweet mother" or amidst books and the Muses (*Tr.* 3.7.3-4).⁵⁰ Milton in

---

[46] Cf., for example, the croaking Chorus of frogs at Aristophanes, *The Frogs*, 229-235: "That is right, Mr. Busybody, right! For the Muses of the lyre love us well; And hornfoot Pan who plays on the pipe his jocund lays; And Apollo, Harper bright, in our Chorus takes delight; For the strong reed's sake which I grow within my lake To be girdled in his lyre's deep shell. Brekekekex, ko-ax, ko-ax." Translation is that of B.B. Rogers, *Aristophanes: Frogs* (Cambridge Mass.: Loeb Classical Library, 1950). Kenneth Dover, commenting on τρέφω (234), remarks: "the frogs speak as if reeds are a crop which they cultivate" (*Aristophanes: Frogs*, ed. Kenneth Dover [Oxford, 1993], 225). Contrast Virgil, *Georgics* 1.378: *veterem in limo ranae cecinere querelam*.

[47] Hale, while shedding light on the Ovidian dimension of Milton's Latin poetry, gives *Elegia Quarta* a very general treatment: "the Ovidian theme of exile emphasizes the contrast in gravity of the issues underlying the exile, which are Milton's own choice of issues. The contrast is handled adeptly" (*Milton's Languages*, 36).

[48] On Young, see page 3.

[49] For the argument that Perilla was Ovid's stepdaughter (and daughter of his third wife), see A.L. Wheeler, "Topics from the Life of Ovid," *AJP* 46 (1925), 26-28.

[50] *aut illam invenies dulci cum matre sedentem/aut inter libros Pieridasque suas* [*Tr.* 3.7.3-4]).

a homely expansion imagines the letter finding Young sitting with his "sweet wife" (Rebecca Young), nursing his children on his knee and poring over either the writings of the Holy Fathers or the Bible, or else inspiring his children with religious fervor (*El*. 4.41-46).[51] The expansion is replicated linguistically and syntactically as the Ovidian *sedentem* is developed to embrace three further present participles: *mulcentem* (42), *versantem* (44) and *saturantem* (45). But as the poem proceeds it is Young who eventually comes to approximate the exiled Ovid. By the same token the speaker comes to assume the role of an Ovidian stepdaughter of sorts in a rather daringly gendered inversion befitting perhaps the "*Lady* of Christ's College."[52] Thus do Ovidian roles fluctuate and oscillate as both speaker and addressee are at different times *both* Ovid and Perilla.[53]

Just as Ovid complains that he has been bereft of country, family and home (*Tr*. 3.7.45),[54] so Young is depicted as a refugee, deprived of his native *penates* and forced to eke a living in a foreign land (85-86)[55] as though betrayed by his *patria dura parens* (*El*. 4.87). This intertextual shift facilitates other types of equations. The tone of *Tristia* 3.7 is frequently paternal. The speaker, having praised Perilla's *ingenium* (14),[56] recalls in a wistful flashback how he was the first (*ego ... primus*) to direct that intellect towards the waters of the Muses as a means of preserving her inspirational powers (*Tr*. 3.7.15-16),[57] powers that he was

---

[51] *invenies dulci cum coniuge forte sedentem,/mulcentem gremio pignora chara suo,/forsitan aut veterum praelarga volumina patrum/versantem, aut veri biblia sacra Dei,/caeleste animas saturantem rore tenellas,/grande salutiferae religionis opus* (*Elegia Quarta* 41-46).

[52] Italics are mine. See note 10.

[53] For my argument that a similar methodology of intertextual oscillation may be discernible in the closing lines of *Paradise Lost*, see pages 190-198.

[54] *en ego, cum caream patria, vobisque domoque* (*Tr*. 3.7.45). Cf. *Epistulae ex Ponto* 4.4.7: *ecce domo patriaque carens oculisque meorum*.

[55] *et, tibi quam patrii non exhibuere penates/sede peregrina quaeris egenus opem* (*El*. 4.85-86).

[56] For the poem's intratextual parallelism between the learning and *ingenium* possessed by Perilla and Ovid, respectively, see B.R. Nagle, *The Poetics of Exile: Program and Polemic in the Tristia and Epistulae ex Ponto of Ovid* (Collection Latomus 170: Brussels, 1980), 150-151.

[57] *hoc ego Pegasidas deduxi primus ad undas,/ne male fecundae vena periret aquae* (*Tr*. 3.7.15-16).

the first to recognize in her tender years (*Tr.* 3.7.17).[58] Milton, however, reviews his *own* earliest years while enjoying Young's tutelage, stating that it was under his tutor's guidance that he as protégé first (*primus ego* [29]) drank of inspirational waters on mount Parnassus, thereby receiving a quasi-religious form of poetical initiation (29-32).[59] Ovid recalls how he used to read Perilla's compositions, describing himself as both her judge and teacher (*saepe tui iudex, saepe magister eram* [24]). In Milton, the teacher/pupil relationship works on a more formal level. But now the roles are reversed: the *magister* is *not* the speaker but the poem's addressee, Young himself, a tutor more cherished than such famous classical instructors as Socrates, Aristotle, Phoenix and Chiron (23-28).[60] One of the lessons that Ovid aims to convey to Perilla is that of the value of composing poetry. The letter is to ask her if she is absorbed in the act of composition (11-12)[61] and to tell her not to be dissuaded by the fact that it was his poetry that caused Ovid harm (27-28). The speaker urges her not to be afraid, and encourages her to return to the art of composing poetry (29-32). As Ovidian roles are reversed once more, Milton hopes that Young has time for the Muses in the midst of the surrounding civic disturbances in Hamburg (51). Nonetheless in a series of encouraging imperatives he urges him not to lose hope amid civic turmoil and personal danger.[62]

In both instances, however, the so-called "exile" in which Ovid and Young find themselves can be alleviated and in a sense redeemed albeit in different ways. Thus both poems conclude with a *consolatio*. Ovid proclaims that even if he is killed by the sword, the powers of his *ingenium* will enable him to live on after his death, thereby rendering him immortal (49-50).[63] In Milton's poem *ingenium* is replaced by the protective power of God. Thus even though Young is surrounded by the

---

[58] *primus id aspexi teneris in virginis annis* (*Tr.* 3.7.17).

[59] *Primus ego Aonios illo praeeunte recessus/lustrabam, et bifidi sacra vireta iugi,/ Pieriosque hausi latices, Clioque favente,/Castalio sparsi laeta ter ora meo.* (*Elegia Quarta* 29-32). The lines suggest a form of poetic baptism in language that is appropriately religious given Young's Puritanism.

[60] Cf. page 3.

[61] *"tu quoque" dic "studiis communibus ecquid inhaeres,/doctaque non patrio carmina more canis?"* (*Tr.* 3.7.11-12).

[62] *at tu sume animos* (*El.* 4.105); *et tu ... sperare memento* (*El.* 4.123).

[63] *quilibet hanc saevo vitam mihi finiat ense,/me tamen extincto fama superstes erit* (*Tr.* 3.7.49-50).

inutilis is *exactly* how the office of Beadle was viewed by the purported mourner and speaker, who, like *Mors* herself perhaps, *officio nec favet ipsa suo* (4)! Ridding moreover is rather comically presented as no more than a minion of an Apollonian Vice-Chancellor (*et celer a Phoebo nuntius ire tuo* [12]). Stylistically too, the combination of paired vowels (*a-a*) in the second hemistich of 19-24[77] and associated internal rhyme (*telis ista petenda tuis* [20])[78] has a rather jovial effect of lilting celebration that seems very much at odds with the poem's closing exhortation to weep and to mourn. Tone, rhetoric, and mythological allegory serve to belie the piece's superficial conformity to occasion and linguistic medium. It is not difficult to imagine a somewhat gleefully mischievous Milton pinning these verses to the hearse-cloth.[79] After all, this act functioned as an important form of self-display for the budding poet,[80] and at the very least for a student who clearly wanted to attract attention.

Complementing the poem's essential *Latinitas* is its potential engagement with vernacular intertexts. The depiction of the usurpation of the Cambridge *praeco* by *Mors*, who is the *ultima praeconum* (3), who is "cruel," and whose grim summons is issued and symbolized by a metaphorical mace, may owe some debt to a vernacular tradition most famously encapsulated perhaps in Hamlet's dying words ("as this fell sergeant death,/Is strict in his arrest" [*Hamlet* 5.2. 347-348]). Here, as Rebecca Pitts has argued, Death is presented as a "grim police officer who will not be resisted,"[81] "the bailiff of the Almighty."[82] Citing a parallel in Sylvester's *Du Bartas* ("And Death, drad Serjant of th'eternall Judge,/Comes very late to his sole-seated Lodge"),[83] she traces both

---

[77] As noted by Stanley Koehler, *Milton and the Roman Elegists: A Study of Milton's Latin Poems in their Relation to the Latin Love Elegy* (Unpublished dissertation: Princeton, 1941), 149.

[78] As noted by F.R.B. Godolphin, "Notes on the Technique of Milton's Latin Elegies," *MP* 37 (1939-40), 351-356, at 355.

[79] Hale, *Milton's Cambridge Latin*, 129, notes that "it was usual for an *individual* to pin his tribute to the pall."

[80] See Binns, *Latin Writings*, 34; Hale, *Milton's Cambridge Latin*, 129.

[81] R.E. Pitts, "'This Fell Sergeant, Death,'" *ShQ* 20.4 (1969), 486-491, at 487.

[82] Pitts, "'This Fell Sergeant, Death,'" 488.

[83] Joshua Sylvester, trans., *Du Bartas, His Divine Weekes and Workes* (London, 1605), 112 (*The Third Day of the First Week*).

phrases back to a common tradition exemplified by a medieval treatise (c. 14/15 cent.) entitled *The Lamentation of the Dying Creature*:

> *The Dying Creature enset with Sickness incurable sorrowfully Complaineth him thus*: "Alas that ever I sinned in my life. To me is come this day the dreadfullest tidings that ever I heard. Here hath been with me a sergeant of arms whose name is Cruelty, from the King of all Kings, Lord of all Lords, and Judge of all Judges; laying on me the mace of His office, saying unto me: 'I arrest thee and warn thee to make ready.... The Judge that shall sit upon thee, He will not be partial, nor He will not be corrupt with goods, but He will minister to thee justice and equity ...'"[84]

As in *Hamlet*, Death is a "sergeant" whose name is Cruelty (the latter likewise conveyed by Shakespeare's adjective "fel") and who undertakes an "arrest."[85] In *Elegia Secunda* "cruel" death (*saeva/Mors* [3-4]) may justifiably be regarded as assuming a rather similar role. Of particular relevance to Milton's poem moreover is the metaphor of the mace ("laying on me the *mace* of his *office*")[86] in light of the *baculum* (1) as the instrument of both Beadle and Death, who significantly *officio nec favet ipsa suo* (4). Hamlet's words, as Pecheux has pointed out, can also be situated in relation to the tradition of the Dance of Death. This is best epitomized by John Lydgate's translation of the Parisian *Danse Macabre in Cimetière des Innocents*,[87] itself inspired in all likelihood by the grim fatalities caused by a medieval plague. Here as Pecheux notes:

> In every form of the Dance (really a procession) personages from all walks of life, high and low, are accosted by Death, who is represented as an authoritative figure whose word of command cannot be resisted.[88]

This is vividly conveyed in Lydgate's translation, which provides an interesting vernacular context not only for *Elegia Secunda*, but also for

---

[84] BL MS.Harl.1706, f. 96. See Pitts, "'This Fell Sergeant, Death,'" 489-490.

[85] Pitts, "'This Fell Sergeant, Death,'" 490.

[86] Italics are mine.

[87] Mother M. Christopher Pecheux, "Another Note on 'This Fell Sergeant,'" *ShQ* 26.1 (1975), 74-75. Lydgate's poem may have been composed to accompany an image depicted on the cloister walls of St Paul's Cathedral, destroyed in 1549, but described in John Stow's 1598 *Survey of London*, 264, as "artificially and richly painted ... Death, leading all estates." See Amy Appleford, "John Carpenter, John Lydgate, and the Daunce of Poulys," *Journal of Medieval and Early Modern Studies* 38.2 (2008), 285-314.

[88] Pecheux, "Another Note," 74.

completely subverted by a very unsubtle engagement with Ovid's erotic verse. Hale's assessment that Milton's treatment of the bishop is "Christian" rather than "secular"[98] is misleadingly overstated. The speaker's yearning for such dream visions (*talia contingant somnia saepe mihi* [68]) is linguistically evocative of Ovid's wish for repetitive midday love-making sessions with Corinna (*Amores* 1.5).[99] Bush regards this as a "notorious instance" of "the radical and even violent change" that the classical original or "ancient jewel" has undergone in Milton's hands.[100] Indeed the whole seems to come full circle. The poem's final quasi-Ovidian wish invites a re-reading of its opening declaration *moestus eram* (1) as a possible parodic echo and appropriation of the opening words of Ovid's poem: *aestus erat* (1). And as the speaker places his limbs upon the bed (*membra cavo posui refovenda cubili* [35]) the language recalls the Ovidian speaker doing something similar (*adposui medio membra levanda toro* [*Am*. 1.5.2]) yet different: for his reclining was greeted not by a dream, but by a waking vision of the semi-naked Corinna. Both evocative and provocative, the poem's engagement with an Ovidian intertext sets into ironic relief its earlier description of the sainted bishop now somewhat uncomfortably equatable with a disrobed and naked femininity. *Defluxit* (55), describing the bishop's white robe "flowing down" to his ankles, is ironic given the description of Corinna as *tunica velata recincta* (*Am*. 1.5.9) followed by her forceful disrobing (*deripui tunicam* [*Am*. 1.5.13]) by the Ovidian speaker, who proceeds to hymn her nakedness.[101] Forever alert to an academic readership, which was in turn alert to classical allusion, Milton's recourse to the Latin language functions as a frequently rebellious statement targeting the institutional norms (academic and ecclesiastical) of seventeenth-century England. This is also achievable (and achieved) by more subtle engagement with vernacular poetry.

If the Ovidian ending of *Elegia Tertia* invites re-reading, so too does the poem's possible engagement with a Chaucerian[102] and more

---

[98] Hale, *Milton's Cambridge Latin*, 133.

[99] Ovid, *Amores* 1.5.26: *proveniant medii sic mihi saepe dies!* Cf. E.S. Le Comte, "Sly Milton: The Meaning Lurking in the Contexts of His Quotations," *ESC* 1 (1976), 1-15.

[100] Bush, *Variorum*, I, 14.

[101] The potentially erotic subtext of Milton's lines is reinforced perhaps by the description of Aurora as the mistress of Cephalus (*Cephaleia pellice* [67]).

[102] Milton's earliest knowledge of Chaucer's poetry may have come to him via the work of his father's close friend John Lane (fl. 1620), who in 1615 completed in

specifically a Macrobian tradition of the medieval dream vision.[103] Upon close study of the poem's language and structure it becomes apparent that aspects of the speaker's pre-dreaming sorrow—his sad memories, his sense of melancholic solitude, his associated diatribe against death—recur in a transmuted form in the dream proper (35-66). Indeed to some extent the experience might be regarded as exemplifying an *insomnium*, which, according to the Macrobian definition, was equivalent to the Greek τρέϕτ οϼ, a nightmarish fantasy caused by physical or emotional distress, and reflective of the dreamer's waking concerns.[104] Thus, states Macrobius, the love-lorn man might dream of either enjoying or being

---

manuscript Chaucer's unfinished *Squire's Tale*. This adds ten cantos to the original. Milton pointedly alludes to the incomplete status of Chaucer's *Squire's Tale* in *Il Penseroso* 109-115. In an unpublished piece, *Triton's Trumpet* (1621), Lane praises the elder Milton's skill in music. Milton's *Commonplace Book* refers to Chaucer no fewer than four times. In all instances the page references are to the second edition of Chaucer's works by Thomas Speght (1602). *Elegia Septima* recounts the speaker's spurning of and subsequent punishment by Cupid in language rather reminiscent of Chaucer, *Troilus and Criseyde* 1. Like the speaker of *El.* 7 (*atque tuum sprevi maxime numen, Amor* [4]), Troilus had ridiculed the power of love: "I have herd told, pardieux, of your lyvynge,/Ye loveres, and youre lewed observaunces" (1.197-198); "O veray fooles, nyce and blynde be ye!" (1.202). As in *El.* 7.11-12, Cupid's anger is thereby aroused: "At which the God of Love gan looken rowe/Right for despit, and shop for to be wroken" (1.206-207). Both poems present a carefree, skeptical youth wandering at a leisurely pace amidst a throng of beautiful ladies. The Latin phrase *et modo ... / et modo* (51-52) merits comparison with "Now here, now there ..." (1.187). Both depict love as perceived through the eyes, and as a chance occurrence (*lumina luminibus male providus obvia misi/neve oculos potui continuisse meos./unam forte aliis supereminuisse notabam ...* [59-61]/"And upon cas bifel that thorugh a route/His eye percede ..." [1. 271-272]). Text is that of Chaucer, *Works*, ed. F.N. Robinson, reproduced in *The Riverside Chaucer* (Oxford, 1991).

[103] See among others S.R. Fischer, "Dreambooks and the Interpretation of Medieval Literary Dreams," *Archiv für Kutturgeschichte* 65 (1983): 1-20; Alison Peden, "Macrobius and Medieval Dream Literature," *Medium Aevum* 54 (1985): 59-73; Josephine Bloomfield, "'The Doctrine of These Olde Wyse': Commentary on the Commentary Tradition in Chaucer's Dream Visions," *Essays in Medieval Studies* 20 (2003): 125-133.

[104] According to Macrobius, Commentary on Cicero's *Somnium Scipionis* 1.3.4, the *insomnium* (nightmare): *est enim τρέϕτ οϼ quotiens cura oppressi animi corporisve sive fortunae, qualis vigilantem fatigaverat, talem se ingerit dormienti*. Text is that of *Ambrosii Theodosii Macrobii Commentarii In Somnium Scipionis*, ed. Iacobus Willis (Leipzig, 1970).

> A dream is nothing else but a bubbling scum or froth of the fancy, which the day hath left undigested; or an after-feast made of the fragments of the imaginations ... our thoughts intentively fixed all the daytime upon a mark we are to hit, are now and then overdrawn with such force, that they fly beyond the mark of the day into the confines of the night.[116]

Read ironically as a pseudo-Chaucerian/Macrobian *insomnium*, Milton's *Elegia Tertia* may in effect present the nightmarish fantasy of a youthful "imaginacyoun." In its surreal fusion of the secular and the Christian it may suggest that it is only in the subconscious mind of a dreamer (a dreamer who is both Miltonic and melancholic) that a bishop could ever make his way into heaven!

2.4 "Both Latin and English"? *Naturam Non Pati Senium*

Milton's seeming conformity to and simultaneous lack of conformity to university occasion manifest themselves in other ways that evince a flexibility that is at times intertextual, at times interlingual—at times, both.

In September 1629 the University Chancellor, Henry Rich, Earl of Holland, and the French Ambassador, Charles de l'Aubespine marquis de Chateauneufare, visited Cambridge. In contribution to philosophical disputations held in honor of the occasion Milton ghost-wrote *Naturam Non Pati Senium*. These verses, commissioned by John Forster, a Fellow of Christ's College, and delivered by Forster during the public debate, were printed and circulated on 24 September 1629. Important manuscript evidence in Lambeth Palace Library[117] and the British Library[118] attesting to these facts has recently been unearthed by Sarah Knight.[119] The LPL MS lists as one of the topics to be disputed: *Natura non patitur senium*, and specifically mentions Milton,[120] thereby corroborating Hale's acute suggestion that both this poem and *De Idea Platonica* began life as

---

[116] Thomas Nashe, *The Terror of the Night* (London, 1594), C3^v.

[117] Lambeth Palace Library MS 770.

[118] British Library MS Harley 7038. Masson, *Life*, I, 186, mentions this manuscript but fails to associate it with Milton's poems.

[119] See Sarah Knight, "Milton's Student Verses of 1629," *N&Q* 255.1 (2010), 37-39.

[120] It does so beneath the heading *In Philos.*, and under Forster's name.

Cambridge "act-verses" which were later developed.[121] Although conspicuously longer than the typical Cambridge act-verse,[122] Milton's poem conforms to that miniature genre in its balanced rhetoric, its scientific/cosmological subject, and related reliance on Ovid and Lucretius.[123] Sessions sees the *Naturam* as following the standard format of the *disputatio*, consisting of an *exordium* (1-7), a *reprehensio* (8-32), a *confirmatio* (33-65), with a *propositio* in the first four lines and a *peroratio* (65-69).[124] The twofold division of the poem moreover, embracing a negative response to a question followed by a full proposition and positive exposition, parallels perhaps the use of contrasting opposites in the companion picces *L'Allegro* and *Il Penseroso* and in itself reflects that use of subdivision so beloved of Ramist logic.[125] The poem achieves a sense of balance through the repetition of key words at the beginning of a line. Thus *Heu* (1, 16); *ergo* (8, 19). These are counterbalanced by the respondingly emphatic *At* (33), conveying the omnipresent forethought of God (*At pater omnipotens fundatis fortius astris/consuluit rerum summae* [33-34]).

The prerequisite of Latin as linguistic medium combined with the hexameter as chosen meter enables the *Naturam* to interact in a special way with Lucretius's *De Rerum Natura*. Lucretius depicts *Natura* as a life-bringing force in the universe, and establishes intratextual points of contact between her irradiating powers and the illuminating force of Epicurus and ultimately of the poet himself. By their light all can disperse the darkness; all can bring forth some form of birth. All in short share a creative power that is essentially positive. Through subtle echoes of Lucretian phraseology and sentiment[126] Milton conveys all the more emphatically the absurdity of the concept of nature's decay.

The poem's subject matter, however, seems inextricably linked to a near contemporary vernacular debate concerning the question of nature's

---

[121] See Hale, *Milton's Cambridge Latin*, 33-50. Most notably, the LPL MS attests that the version of *Naturam* printed in 1645 and 1673 contains thirteen extra lines: *in prioribus pauxilla variatio ab illis, quae spargebantur in Comitiis additis item 13 versiculis* (LPL MS 770, 238-239).

[122] As noted by Knight, "Milton's Student Verses of 1629," 39.

[123] See Hale, *Milton's Cambridge Latin*, 33-50.

[124] W.A. Sessions, "Milton's *Naturam*," *MS* 19 (1984), 53-72, at 54.

[125] Sessions, "Milton's *Naturam*," 54.

[126] For examples of verbal echoes, see Bush, *Variorum*, I, ad loc.

decay,¹²⁷ a debate exemplified by two works in particular. The year 1616 had seen the publication of Godfrey Goodman's *The Fall of Man or the Corruption of Nature, Proved by the Light of Our Naturall Reason*, arguing that nature as encompassing man, all living creatures, the earth, and the heavens is liable to decay. In response George Hakewill composed *An Apologie of the Power and Providence of God in the Government of the World, Or an Examination and Censure of the Common Errour Touching Natures Perpetuall and Universall Decay* (1627). This cogently presented refutation of Goodman's thesis argued that the very concept of decay necessarily undermines the power and providence of God in the universe.[128] Hitherto scholars have been skeptical about possible links between the two works. Parker, for example, assumes a negative stance, stating that the *Naturam* "owes absolutely nothing to Hakewill's book unless it be the general subject,"[129] and Bush states: "There seems to be no sufficient evidence for either a negative assertion like Parker's or for a positive one."[130] But, as I have suggested elsewhere, Milton's poem may indeed provide such evidence as the speaker ironically adopts a Goodwinian stance, only to refute it by apparent recourse to Hakewill's treatise.[131]

Of particular relevance to Milton's interlingual flexibility is the section (lines 33-65) vindicating the permanence and incorruptibility of nature. This seems in effect to proffer a bilingual dialogue of sorts: a Miltonic answer (in Latin) to a passage from Arnobius's *Adversus Gentes* cited by Hakewill (in translation only) in support of his argument:

> His Latine, because the allegation is long and in some places it savours of the Affrican harshnes, I will spare, and onely set downe the English.[132]

Arnobius, in Hakewill's version, discusses the supposed relaxation in the cosmic order by presenting a series of ironic questions:

---

[127] See Victor Harris, *All Coherence Gone* (Chicago, 1949).

[128] The second edition (1630) of Hakewill's work would contain an account of a phlebotomy performed by Theodore Diodati, father of Milton's close friend Charles.

[129] Parker, *Biography*, ed. Campbell, 2, 773.

[130] *Variorum*, I, 214.

[131] See Estelle Haan, "Milton's *Naturam Non Pati Senium* and Hakewill," *MH* 24 (1997), 147-167.

[132] *An Apologie of the Power and Providence of God in the Government of the World* (Oxford, 1627), 55. Cf. Milton, *An Apology Against a Pamphlet*: "the gay ranknesse of Apuleius, Arnobius, or any moderne fustianist" (*CM* 3, 347).

Is the frame of this engine and fabricke which covereth and incloseth us all in any part loosed or dissolved? Hath this wheeling about of Heaven swarving from the rule of its primitive motion either begun to creepe more slowly, or to be carried with headlong volubilitie? Doe the Stars begin to raise themselves up in the West, and the Signes to incline towards the East?[133]

Milton's lines indicate that this is not the case. There is no relaxation in the fixed order of the universe since God has commanded all things to retain their normal course (35-36).[134] He emphatically dismisses Arnobius's speculations about the possible retardation or acceleration in the movement of the planets by describing the behavior of Saturn and Mars (37-40).[135] He even seems to answer Arnobius's question about the movement of the stars by asserting that God has firmly established them in their fixed places (*fundatis fortius astris* [33]), and by alluding to the morning and evening stars (45-48).[136] Both discuss at some length the behavior of the sun and moon. Arnobius speculates about the possible diminution in the sun's powers:

> The Prince of Stars the Sun whose light clotheth, and heat quickneth all things, doth hee cease to be hot, is he waxen cooler, and hath he corrupted the temper of his wonted moderation into contrary Habits?[137]

Again Milton implies the answer "no" as he states that the sun is always bright and youthful and does not deviate from its normal course (41-44).[138] And where Arnobius asks: "Those first Elements, whereof it is

---

[133] *Apologie*, 55.

[134] *atque ordine summo/singula perpetuum iussit servare tenorem* (*Nat*. 35-36).

[135] *Volvitur hinc lapsu mundi rota prima diurno,/raptat et ambitos socia vertigine caelos./Tardior haud solito Saturnus, et acer ut olim/fulmineum rutilat cristata casside Mavors* (*Nat*. 37-40).

[136] *surgit odoratis pariter formosus ab Indis/aethereum pecus albenti qui cogit Olympo/mane vocans, et serus agens in pascua coeli,/temporis et gemino dispertit regna colore* (*Nat*. 45-48).

[137] *Apologie*, 55.

[138] *Floridus aeternum Phoebus iuvenile coruscat,/nec fovet effoetas loca per declivia terras/devexo temone deus; sed semper amica/luce potens eadem currit per signa rotarum* (*Nat*. 41-44). In both instances there is a reference to the waxing and waning of the moon. Arnobius wonders whether this has ceased to occur ("Hath the Moone left off to repaire herselfe, and by continuall restoring of new to transforme herselfe into her old shapes?" [*Apol*., 55]), a speculation rejected by Milton (*Fulget, obitque vices alterno Delia cornu,/caeruleumque ignem paribus complectitur ulnis* [*Nat*. 49-

agreed that all things are compounded, are they changed into contrary qualities?"[139] Milton replies: *nec variant elementa fidem* ... (51).[140] Both allude to the behavior of winds. Where Arnobius questions their strength: "Have the winds breathed forth their spirits as having spent their blasts?"[141] Milton confidently describes winds which are as powerful as ever (53-55).[142] And in response to the Arnobian speculations about the fertility or otherwise of the earth,[143] Milton states (60-63) that *Terra* is not lacking in strength. On the contrary, flowers continue to blossom and retain their fragrance and beauty.[144] Blossoming also is a Miltonic *lingua Latina* in contrapuntal engagement with a vernacular rendering.

50]). Milton's lines may also echo in a general sense Hakewill's discussion of the movement of the planets, in a passage that likewise mentions Saturn, Mars, the sun and the moon, and dismisses the concepts of retardation and acceleration: "The proper motion of Saturne was by the Ancients observed, and is now likewise found, by our moderne Astronomers, to be accomplished within the space of thirtie yeares, that of Jupiter in twelve, that of Mars in two, that of the Sunne in three hundred sixty five dayes and allmost six howers, that of Venus and Mercury in very neere the same space of time, that of the Moone in twentie seven dayes and all most eight howres: Neither do we find that they have either quickned or any way slackned these their courses, but that in the same space of time they allwayes run the same races which being ended, they bring them againe as freshly as the first instant they set forth" (*Apol.*, 81).

[139] *Apologie*, 55.

[140] This is in full accordance with Hakewill, two of whose headings are: "That the Elements are still in number foure, and still retaine the ancient places and properties" (*Apol.*, 102); "That the Elements still hold the same proportions each to other, and by mutuall exchange the same dimensions in themselves" (*Apol.*, 106).

[141] *Apologie*, 55.

[142] *Nec per inane furit leviori murmure Corus,/stringit et armiferos aequali horrore Gelonos/trux Aquilo, spiratque hiemem, nimbosque volutat* (*Nat.* 53-55).

[143] "Doth the Earth refuse to receive the seeds cast into her? Will not trees budde forth? Have fruites appointed for food by the burning up of their moisture changed their tast?" (*Apol.*, 55).

[144] *sed neque Terra tibi saecli vigor ille vetusti/priscus abest, servatque suum Narcissus odorem,/et puer ille suum tenet et puer ille decorem/Phoebe tuusque et Cypri tuus* (*Nat.* 60-63). The theme occurs in two of Hakewill's headings: "Touching the pretended decay of the Earth, together with the Plants, and beasts, and minerals" (*Apol.*, 128); "That there is no decrease in the fruitfulnesse, the quantities or virtues of plants" (*Apol.*, 139).

2.5 Bipartite and Bilingual Signifiers: *Elegia Sexta*

Interlingual flexibility manifests itself on rather different levels in *Elegia Sexta*, for here it is matched by a fusion of the secular and the Christian. Although the piece has received scholarly attention in terms of Renaissance poetical theory (Fink),[145] the nativity tradition (Pecheux),[146] and its internal unity (Low),[147] its role as bipartite and bilingual signifier has largely gone unnoticed.

Milton's poem is a reply to a now lost communication from Charles Diodati,[148] which had apologized for the poor quality of his own writing, citing as an excuse his convivial surroundings and the festivities of the Christmas season. Milton replies by praising Diodati's description:

> Quam bene sollennes epulas, hilaremque Decembrim
>   Festaque coelifugam quae coluere Deum,
> Deliciasque refers, hiberni gaudia ruris,
>   Haustaque per lepidos Gallica musta focos. (9-12)

The lines seem to equate Diodati with all that is secular, pagan, joyful and celebratory, peppered, as they are, with such adjectives as *hilaris*, *lepidus*, and such nouns as *epulae*, *festa*, *deliciae* and *gaudium*.[149] The characteristics highlighted here likewise permeate the Diodati/Milton correspondence. Diodati's two surviving Greek letters to Milton[150] are noteworthy for their "exuberant pastoralism."[151] In one he imagines a shared sunshine holiday amid dancing and laughter;[152] in the other he

---

[145] Z.S. Fink, "Wine, Poetry, and Milton's *Elegia Sexta*," *ES* 21 (1939), 164-165.

[146] Mother M. Christopher Pecheux, "The Nativity Tradition in Milton's *Elegia Sexta*," *MS* 23 (1987), 3-19.

[147] Anthony Low, "The Unity of Milton's *Elegia Sexta*," *ELR* 11 (1981), 213-223.

[148] On Diodati, see pages 132-134.

[149] Diodati is likewise associated with feasting (this time on a celestial level) in the closing lines of *Epitaphium Damonis*, on which see page 134.

[150] BL Add.MS 5016 ff. 5 and 71.

[151] Gordon Campbell, "Imitation in *Epitaphium Damonis*," *MS* 19 (1984), 165-177, at 165.

[152] "... and the air and the sun and the river and trees and birds and earth and men will celebrate the holiday with us, and laugh with us, and join in the dance with us" (trans. Campbell, "Imitation in *Epitaphium Damonis*," 165).

extols the beauties of the countryside[153] with a quasi-Romantic sensitivity as if in anticipation of Dorothy Wordsworth.[154] It is Diodati's joyful company, laughter, wit and charm that Milton will particularly miss, as stated in his Latin pastoral lament (*Epitaphium Damonis*) on the premature death of his closest friend since boyhood.[155]

Inherent in the aforementioned passage are a number of tensions that merit closer investigation. The lines combine oxymoronic statements (the "feasts" are "solemn");[156] they fuse the pagan and the Christian: the *festa* in celebration of the Christian God, who is described in pagan terms as *coelifuga*, as an exile from heaven. Hale regards this as a "splendid epithet,"[157] and both Bush and Hale suggest that it is a Miltonic coinage.[158] The word, however, does have neo-Latin precedent, occurring in a Latin version of Theocritus, *Idyll* 15 by Helius Eobanus Hessus (1531), where it appears, albeit in an adjectival form, to qualify (as in Milton) a divinity. In this instance the divinity is the goddess Persephone, queen of the pagan underworld. And the context may not be without (ironic) relevance to Milton's poem. Theocritus's Idyll, a mime set in Alexandria, involves two female protagonists (Gorgo and Praxinoa) as they make preparations to attend a festival. On this occasiona, however, the festival is a pagan one–that of Adonis,[159] which occurs every twelve

---

[153] "the pathways are in bloom, and embellished and teeming with leaves, on every branch there is a nightingale or goldfinch or other song-bird seeking delight with its chirpings" (trans. Campbell, "Imitation in *Epitaphium Damonis*," 165).

[154] See, for example, *Grasmere Journal*: 15 April 1802: "A few primroses by the roadside–woodsorrel flower, the anemone, scentless violets, strawberries, and that starry, yellow flower which Mrs. C. calls pile wort"; 16 April 1802: "The sun shone, the wind had passed away, the hills looked chearful, the river was very bright as it flowed into the lake" (*Journals of Dorothy Wordsworth*, ed. Ernest De Selincourt [London, 1941], I, 131-132).

[155] *quis mihi blanditiasque tuas, quis tum mihi risus,/Cecropiosque sales referet, cultosque lepores?* (*Ep. Dam.* 55-56).

[156] Cf. "Hast thou no verse, no hymn, or solemn strain" (*Nativity*, 17).

[157] *John Milton, Latin Writings: A Selection*, ed. J.K. Hale (Arizona, 1998), 73.

[158] See Bush, *Variorum*, I, 116: "*Coelifugam* has not been observed elsewhere and may be a Miltonic coinage"; cf. Hale, "Notes on Milton's Latin Word-Formation in the *Poemata* of 1645," *HL* 43 (1994), 405-410, at 406.

[159] Thus Gorgo exhorts Praxinoa to accompany her to the palace of King Ptolemy and participate in the festival of Adonis which is in preparation: *ibimus, ut pulchro quae pulchra paravit Adonidi/Adsimus pompae*. Text is that of *Theocriti Syracusani Idyllia Triginta Sex, Latino Carmine Reddita, Helio Eobano Hesso Interprete* (Basle, 1531),

months.¹⁶⁰ When asked by one of the bystanders to stop shouting out, Gorgo proclaims her identity, asserting her right to freedom of speech and, more specifically, to articulating her words in Doric Greek.¹⁶¹ In response Praxinoa reaffirms this by uttering an invocation to Persephone as the *coelifuga umbrarum regina silentum*, and uttering what is in effect an exasperated plea for linguistic freedom:

> Prax.: Ne sine coelifuga umbrarum regina silentum
> Ut quisquam imperitet nobis nisi fortior unus
> Non metuo ne mensura tibi ludar inani.

It is not inconceivable that the now lost communication by Diodati, himself noted for his "pastoralism,"¹⁶² had ironically appropriated aspects of the pastoral Theocritean festival of Adonis in its account of another annual, this time, Christian feast,¹⁶³ perhaps in terms reminiscent of pagan festivities. Evocation of a festival of love would be interestingly apposite given the inherent eroticism¹⁶⁴ and implicit homoeroticism¹⁶⁵ of the Milton/Diodati correspondence. Did perhaps Diodati write in Greek, his favorite linguistic medium,¹⁶⁶ thereby employing and articulating his own

---

1F1ᵛ. See *The Poetic Works of Helius Eobanus Hessus*, ed., trans., and annotated by Harry Vredeveld (Binghamton, 2004).

¹⁶⁰ *Adonim/mense duodecimo tibi deduxere reversum/mollipedes ac tardigradae plus omnibus Horae.*

¹⁶¹ *Dorica verba loqui cum simus Dores opinor/possumus, et nobis, nisi fallunt omnia, fas est.*

¹⁶² See notes 152 and 153.

¹⁶³ Low, "The Unity of Milton's *Elegia Sexta*," 221, cautiously speculates that "several lines suggest that he [Diodati] had written an elegy whose chief connection with Christmas or with other matters religious or epic was to celebrate the conviviality of a high occasion, as an elegy normally would."

¹⁶⁴ See, for example, the opening lines of *Elegia Prima*.

¹⁶⁵ See in particular J.T. Shawcross, "Milton and Diodati: An Essay in Psychodynamic Meaning," *MS* 7 (1975), 127-163; R.F. Gleckner, *Gray Agonistes* (London, 1997), passim; Matthew Curr, *The Consolation of Otherness: The Male Love Elegy in Milton, Gray and Tennyson* (London, 2002), 1-44.

¹⁶⁶ Of Diodati's surviving compositions all but one (a Latin elegy on the death of William Camden, published in *Camdeni Insignia* [1624] and Diodati's only published poem) are composed in Greek. See D.C. Dorian, *The English Diodatis: A History of Charles Diodati's Family and His Friendship with Milton* (New Brunswick, 1950), 108-109.

Dorica verba, as it were? That this may have been the case is suggested by the contrast in line 3 between Diodati's Greek *Musa* and Milton's Roman *camoena*[167] (*at tua quid nostram prolectat musa camoenam*).[168] Speculation aside, what is evident is that Milton's lines are colored by their fusion of the secular and the Christian. As Bush points out, "editors suggest that Milton had in mind the Roman Saturnalia as well as the month of Christmas,"[169] and Low correctly observes that "one need not read the poem as wholly Classical in spirit."[170] The potential compatibility of the classical and the Christian may likewise have shone through Diodati's description of the Christmas festivities. Though couched in pagan terms, Milton's phrase *coelifugam ... Deum* is the infant Christian God, whose annual feast, like that of Adonis, has come around. But the elegy presents other sorts of contrasts and comparisons: between different types of poets, and interestingly between different types of languages, most notably in its climactic self-paraphrase in Latin of the vernacular *On the Morning of Christ's Nativity*.

Languages are twinned, languages are contrasted in what is in effect a twin poem of sorts. Divided into two sections, *Elegia Sexta* strikes a contrast between the elegiac poet who is inspired by wine and who writes light themes, and the heroic bard who is inspired by the divine,[171] who is a chaste priest of the gods and whose theme is much more serious. As such it seems to display that Miltonic predilection for pairing and contrasting perhaps best epitomized by the "companion pieces" *L'Allegro* and *Il Penseroso* and in all likelihood a consequence of the rigorously scholastic balance that was a prerequisite of the successful Cambridge disputation.[172] And perhaps more than that. For, it could be argued, this Latin elegy contains a vernacular play within a play, so to

---

[167] On *Camoena*, see *OLD* sv: "One of the Roman goddesses, prob. Orig. water-deities connected especially with a grove outside the Porta Capena ... Identified with the Muses, especially in Roman contexts. See Horace, *Odes* 1.12.39; 2.16.38."

[168] As noted by Bush, *Variorum*, I, 115.

[169] Bush, *Variorum*, I, 116.

[170] Low, "The Unity of Milton's *Elegia Sexta*," 216.

[171] On the contrast between wine and the divine as inspirational forces, see Minturno, *De Poeta* (1559; rpt. Munich, 1970), 72; Scaliger, *Poetices Libri Septem* (Geneva, 1561), 5. See also Z.S. Fink, "Wine, Poetry, and Milton's *Elegia Sexta*," passim; J.M. Steadman, "Chaste Muse and *Casta Iuventus*: Milton, Minturno and Scaliger on Inspiration and the Poet's Character," *Italica* 40 (1963), 28-34.

[172] See Hale, *Milton's Cambridge Latin*, 15-31.

speak, or poems within a poem: a l'allegro and il penseroso encased within and engaging with its own *Latinitas*.

For example, both the elegiac poet and l'allegro are associated with Bacchus and Venus. In the Latin poem these two deities are among the gods who assist the composition of elegy (*Liber adest elegis, Eratoque, Ceresque, Venusque* [51]), parents of Mirth, who is invoked in *L'Allegro* as one "whom lovely Venus at a birth/With two sister Graces more/To ivy-crowned Bacchus bore" [14-16]). Both poems describe merry-making as manifested respectively in the festivities of the Christmas season (*El.* 6.9-12) or in the catalogue of jovial personifications attendant upon Mirth (*L'Allegro* 25-32).[173] Both describe music and the dancing of young maidens although there is a contrast between the respective settings— indoors in the Latin (*El.* 6. 37-40) and outdoors in the English (*L'Allegro* 93-98). In both, the elegiac poet/l'allegro is contrasted with one of a much more serious nature: the heroic bard/il penseroso. The secular is displaced by the religious in terms of tone and imagery as a solemn note is struck. The heroic bard must be temperate (*parce ... /vivat* [59-60]) in food; he must drink only "sober draughts" from a pure stream (*sobriaque e puro pocula fonte bibat* [62]); he must be free from crime, morally upright, and possessed of a *casta iuventus* (63). In short, he is a priest of the gods (*Diis etenim sacer est vates, divumque sacerdos,/spirat et occultum pectus, et ora Iovem* [77-78]).[174] This *sacerdos* finds a parallel in the "pensive Nun" (Melancholy) of *Il Penseroso*, who is "devout and pure,/*Sober*, steadfast, and demure" (31-32).[175] Both the heroic poet and il penseroso sing a more elevated and solemn theme than the elegiac poet/l'allegro. The Latin poem's epicist sings of war, the gods, heroes, and the upper and lower worlds (55-58). Il penseroso sings of the upper, middle and lower realms (90-94) and his subject matter embraces Orphic song and Chaucerian and Spenserian Romance (103-120).

But the vernacular dimension of *Elegia Sexta* manifests itself in another way. For the poem's concluding lines offer a unique self-paraphrase in Latin[176] of *On the Morning of Christ's Nativity*:

---

[173] "Haste thee nymph, and bring with thee/Jest and youthful Jollity,/Quips and cranks, and wanton wiles,/Nods, and becks, and wreathed smiles,/Such as hang on Hebe's cheek,/And love to live in dimple sleek;/Sport that wrinkled Care derides,/And Laughter holding both his sides" (*L'Allegro* 25-32).

[174] Cf. Vida, *De Arte Poetica* 1.561-563: *ipse tuae egregios audax nunc laudis honores/ingredior, vates idem, superumque sacerdos,/sacraque dona fero teneris comitatus alumnis*; 2.3-4: *... templa ipse in vestra sacerdos/sacra ferens*.

[175] Italics are mine.

[176] On paraphrase and Miltonic self-paraphrase, see pages 25-36.

> Paciferum canimus caelesti semine regem,
>   Faustaque sacratis saecula pacta libris,
> Vagitumque Dei, et stabulantem paupere tecto
>   Qui suprema suo cum patre regna colit.
> Stelliparumque polum, modulantesque aethere turmas,   85
>   Et subito elisos ad sua fana deos.
> Dona quidem dedimus Christi natalibus illa,
>   Illa sub auroram lux mihi prima tulit.
> Te quoque pressa manent patriis meditata cicutis,
>   Tu mihi, cui recitem, iudicis instar eris.   90

Woodhouse alludes to what he sees as a "sudden transition" from the main body of the poem to these concluding lines.[177] Martz views them as "a clean break with the previous discussion of elegy and epic,"[178] and Pecheux rather naively asks: "Why do the details in the description not correspond exactly with those in the English poem?"[179] These points might be answered by the argument that Milton's self-paraphrase serves in effect a twofold purpose: it is a succinct summary of an English poem, but a summary whose details are upon closer inspection selectively appropriate to the elegy's preceding lines.

The speaker's announcement is couched in imagery of birth: he is singing of a king begotten of heavenly seed (*caelesti semine regem* [81]); his vernacular poem is a gift in honor of Christ's nativity (*Christi natalibus* [87]). In the course of the elegy Milton had praised Diodati as a writer of elegy, stating that it is hardly surprising that three gods have combined their divine powers, and have *given birth* (*peperisse*) to his poetry:

> Scilicet haud mirum tam dulcia carmina per te
> Numine composito tres peperisse deos (35-36)

Thus Diodati's *carmina* have been engendered by a divine trinity of sorts. This pagan trinity of Bacchus, Apollo and Ceres is, in Milton's *Nativity*, something very different: the "trinal unity" (11) of Father, Son and Holy Spirit, begotten by his own vernacular *carmen*.

The succinct nature of the Latin synopsis should not detract from its significance. Milton in effect reads and paraphrases Milton, highlighting in concise yet insightful terms key aspects of the English poem. Christ as king is "peace-bearing" (*paciferum* [81]). This carefully

---

[177] A.S.P. Woodhouse, *The Heavenly Muse: A Preface to Milton* (Toronto, 1972), 36.

[178] L.L. Martz, "The Rising Poet, 1645," in *The Lyric and Dramatic Milton*, ed. J.H. Summers (New York, 1965), 3-33, at 23.

[179] Pecheux, "Nativity Tradition," 3.

chosen adjective (applied to the olive by Virgil)[180] encapsulates a leitmotif of the vernacular piece ("And with his Father work us a perpetual peace" [7], "the meek-eyed Peace" [46], "universal peace" [52], "peaceful was the night" [61], "reign of peace" [63]). And, as in the English ("For so the holy sages once did sing" [5]), Christ's birth is the fulfillment of Old Testament prophecy (*faustaque sacratis saecula pacta libris* [82]). But then not without some disparity Milton announces that his poem proclaims *vagitumque Dei, et stabulantem paupere tecto* (83). Parker notes that the vernacular equivalent does not record the infant cry of God.[181] Martz suggests that "Milton is emphasizing the poem's allegiance to the naïve tradition of the Christmas carol,"[182] and Pecheux usefully cites parallels in Fortunatus[183] and, most notably, in Prudentius: *vagitus ille exordium/vernantis orbis prodidit*.[184] The latter was interpreted by Erasmus as signaling the rebirth of all who are baptized in Christ,[185] and by Fabricius as denoting the beginning of consolation and serving to presage the rejuvenation of the world.[186] But the *vagitus* of the infant Christ child may also operate on an intratextual level as it seems both to Christianize and to counter the essentially pagan bacchic wailing of the Muses described earlier in the poem: *saepius Aoniis clamavit collibus Euoe/mista Thyonea turba novena choro* (17-18). And now infant wailing and the child's cradling in a poor stable are contrasted with his heavenly abode (*qui suprema suo cum patre regna colit* [84]) just as in the English poem Christ "Forsook the courts of everlasting day,/And chose with us a darksome house of mortal clay" [13-14]).

Bush perceptively states that lines 85-86 are almost a summary of the three main themes or movements of the vernacular piece.[187] Milton

---

[180] Cf. *Aen*. 8. 116.

[181] Parker, *Biography*, ed. Campbell, I, 69: "Milton here emphasizes—as his ode does not—the infant wails and humble roof of the Christ-child." Note, however, "All meanly wrapped in the rude manger lies" (*Nativity* 31).

[182] Martz, "The Rising Poet," 24.

[183] Fortunatus, *Hymn to the Cross*, 13: *vagit infans inter arta conditus praesepia*.

[184] Prudentius, *Cathemerion* 11. 61-62.

[185] *in Christo ... vagitus indicabat mundum renasci quandoquidem qui baptizantur in Christum, per illum renascuntur* (Erasmus, *Prudentii Opera* [London, 1824], 1001-2).

[186] *vagitus in aliis hominibus miseriae exordium est, in puero Christo initium solatii, et orbis quasi iuvenescentis praesagium* (Fabricius, *Prudentii Opera Omnia* 2.1135).

[187] Bush, *Variorum*, I, 125.

describes the pole as giving birth to stars in his famously (or infamously) coined adjective *stelliparum* (85). Salmasius would complain: "He calls the sky *stelliparum*, as if it would produce stars."[188] Pecheux, while remarking that "the combination of 'stella' and 'pario' does seem to be Milton's innovation," notes the theological and lexical implications of *pario* and suggests that the sound of the word may have links with the musical devices of Christian hymnody.[189] One might add that the Miltonic coinage achieves a further effect in that the sky giving birth to stars appropriately mirrors on a cosmic level the nativity of Christ (*Christi natalibus* [87]), and, as noted previously, the depiction of a pagan trinity as having given birth (*peperisse* [36]) to Diodati's poetry. Juxtaposed with the *stelliparumque polum* are the *modulantesque aethere turmas* (85). The starry sky with its squadrons (*turmae*) both fuse and move beyond their vernacular equivalent ("And all the spangled host keep watch in squadrons bright" [21]),[190] for the squadrons of the Latin paraphrase constitute angelic hosts producing music. In so doing they encapsulate a recurring leitmotif of the vernacular poem: "And join thy voice unto the angel quire" (27), "When such music sweet" (93), "Divinely-warbled voice/Answering the stringed noise" (96-97). They may also function intratextually as a Christianized version of the Thracian lyre celebrated earlier in *Elegia Sexta* as the elegiac poet's instrument (37-38).[191] Noteworthy is Milton's synopsis of the displacement of pagan deities from their conventional shrines (*et subito elisos ad sua fana deos* [86]) or, as the vernacular poem puts it: "Peor, and Baalim,/Forsake their temples dim" (198-199), "And sullen Moloch fled" (205). In a sense *Elegia Sexta* has done precisely that as pagan deities are replaced by a climactic celebration of Christ (87). The Latin poem gifted to Diodati (whose name, after all, means "god-given")[192] both embraces and gives

---

[188] *stelliparum coelum appellat, qui stellas pariat* (Salmasius, *Ad Ioannem Miltonum Responsio* [London, 1660], 5). See J.M. French, *The Life Records of John Milton* (New York, 1966), IV, 345-347.

[189] Pecheux, 16.

[190] Cf. "The stars with deep amaze/Stand fixed in steadfast gaze" (69-70).

[191] *nunc quoque Thressa tibi caelato barbitos auro/insonat arguta molliter icta manu* (37-38).

[192] On Milton's acknowledgment of the punning meaning of Diodati's name, cf. *Ep. Dam.* 210-211: *Diodotus, quo te divino nomine cuncti/caelicolae norint*. On the pun, cf. John Owen, *Epig.* 7.65, addressed to Dr Theodore Diodati, the father of Charles: *Ad Theo-dorum Deo-datum, Medicum: Nomine tu Graio Theodorus es atque*

way to a vernacular *donum* given by Milton to God (*Deo datum*)—to the Christ child on his birthday (*dona quidem dedimus Christi natalibus illa* [87]),[193] thereby paralleling perhaps "Say heavenly Muse, shall not thy sacred vein/Afford a *present* to the infant *God*?" (15-16).[194] It is a poetic gift composed at the approach of dawn (*illa sub auroram lux mihi prima tulit* (88).[195] The birth of day and the birth of Christ are united here and are uniquely paraphrased in a Latin tongue, which both announces and celebrates another type of birth: the birth of a vernacular poem.

2.6 "Overleaping" Linguistic Walls

The intersection of Latin and the vernacular, and the associated birth of an English poem lie at the heart of *Prolusion 6*. Here Milton's self-fashioning is that of a playful, rather recalcitrant student, finding fault with his university's curriculum and crossing linguistic boundaries. And more than that: here is a unique instance of a bilingual author in bilingual performance, delivering in turn Latin prose (an *Oratio* and a *Prolusio*), English verse (*At A Vacation Exercise*) and English prose (now lost); a performative speaker proffering what Hale has discerningly termed "a bilingual medley in a bizarre bunch of registers and modes."[196] The whole demonstrates what Hamers and Blanc have described as a bilingual's "capacity to call on either language,"[197] a capacity likewise acknowledged by Michael and Gollan: "both of a bilingual's languages are always active to some degree."[198]

Latino;/Arte potens Phoebi, Ter-Theodorus eris (*Ioannis Audoeni Epigrammatum*, ed. J.R.C. Martyn [Leiden, 1978], 2, 83).

[193] Cf. Ambrose, *Christe Redemptor Omnium* 23-24: *ob diem natalis tui/Hymnum novum concinimus*.

[194] Italics are mine.

[195] Cf. *Ante lucem nuntiemus Christum regem saeculo/galli cantus, galli plausus proximum sentit diem* (Hilary of Poitiers as cited in Walpole, *Early Latin Hymns*, 5-15).

[196] Hale, *Milton's Cambridge Latin*, 205.

[197] Hamers and Blanc, *Bilinguality and Bilingualism*, 11-12.

[198] Michael and Gollan, "Being and Becoming Bilingual," 390.

The Latin prose exercise pertains to the academic genre of the "salting."[199] Designed as a public test for first-year undergraduates, this lively, frequently raucous occasion demanded of its victims the performance of a Latin speech before their fellow-students. If the student won the approval of the audience he was rewarded by beer. If he incurred his audience's disapproval he was punished in the form of salted beer. This punishment was supposed to cure the student's inadequacies by giving him more salt or wit as denoted by the twofold meaning of the Latin noun *sal*. Milton's *Prolusion* is metaphorically seasoned, as it were, by bilingual puns on *sal* and salt,[200] on Latin words beginning with *sal* (e.g. *salio* "I leap"),[201] and on Latin words resembling the English word "salt" (e.g. *salto* "I dance").[202] But as he draws the Latin to an end this Miltonic Master of Ceremonies announces something rather daring:

> nunc Leges Academicas veluti Romuli muros transiliens e Latinis ad Anglicana transcurro. (Milton, *Prolusio* 6. 26)

The whole performance is colored by a rich metalinguistic awareness characteristic of the bilingual, who may possess "an enhanced ability to focus on the important content and meaning of language, rather than its external structure or sound."[203] But as he announces his transition from Latin to English (*e Latinis ad Anglicana transcurro*), Milton's self-fashioning is ironically Roman: he is a second Remus, who, according to tradition, leapt over the wall of Rome constructed by his brother, Romulus, scorning it because it was mean and low, and eventually meeting his end, slain by Romulus, who had cried out: "Thus shall every man perish that shall dare to leap over my walls."[204] University

---

[199] See Hale's excellent discussion at *Milton's Cambridge Latin*, 195-219. See in general, Roslyn Richek, "Thomas Randolph's Salting (1627): its text, and John Milton's Sixth *Prolusion* as Another Salting," *ELR* 12 (1982), 102-131.

[200] For Miltonic punning on *sal*, cf., for example, such phrases as *Quod ad sales meos ... salsamentarii filius; tunc enim sales mihi essent ad unguem; vos etiam sale ita pulchre defricatos dimitterem* (*Prolusio* 6. 22). All quotations are from Hale's edition in *Milton's Cambridge Latin*.

[201] Cf. *muros transiliens* (*Prolusio* 6. 26).

[202] Cf. *naturae vividae, vegetae, et saltaturientes* (*Prolusio* 6. 11).

[203] Baker, *The Care and Education of Young Bilinguals*, 70.

[204] Cf. Livy, *De Urbe Condita* 1.7: *Volgatior fama est ludibrio fratris Remum novos transiluisse muros; inde ab irato Romulo, cum verbis quoque increpitans adiecisset,*

regulations and linguistic barriers are virtually synonymous. And Milton rejoices in "overleaping" them both (*muros transiliens*).

As the current *Prolusion* gives way to the *Vacation Exercise*, it emerges that "overleaping" linguistic walls is something that Milton dares and loves to do. In what follows he leaps over Latin into English; he leaps over prose into poetry, signaling that transition in lines which upon their publication were self-consciously headed: "The Latin Speeches Ended, the English thus Began." Here is the beginning of that beginning:

> Hail native language, that by sinews weak
> Didst move my first endeavouring tongue to speak,
> And mad'st imperfect words with childish trips
> Half unpronounced, slide through my infant lips,
> Driving dumb silence from the portal door,
> Where he had mutely sat two years before:
> Here I salute thee and thy pardon ask,
> That now I use thee in my latter task:
> Small loss it is that thence can come unto thee,
> I know my tongue but little grace can do thee.
> Thou need'st not be ambitious to be first,
> Believe me I have thither packed the worst. (*At a Vacation Exercise* 1-12)

In terms of the traditional academic vacation exercise these lines signal something of a Miltonic différence: that self-conscious highlighting of a linguistic shift; that recourse to verse rather than to prose; that delineation and salutation of the speaker's linguistic origins. It is, after all, the vernacular, not Latin, that has instructed Milton in his first attempts at articulated speech. Hamers and Blanc note that "in the case of early consecutive bilinguality the child first develops a language representation in which there is only one language,"[205] and Sebastián-Gallés and Bosh argue that "during the first year of life, human beings acquire a remarkable ability to process the sound system of the maternal language."[206] Lyon by contrast has remarked on the fact that children spend a long time at the single-word stage.[207] Instruction in his native language (L_A) has, according to Milton, been imparted to lips that are "infant" (4). And they are thus not just because they belong to an infant,

---

"Sic deinde, quicumque alius transiliet moenia mea", *interfectum*. Text is that of *Titi Livi, Ab Urbe Condita*, ed. R.M. Ogilvie (Oxford, 1974), I, 10.

[205] Hamers and Blanc, *Bilinguality and Bilingualism*, 75.

[206] Sebastián-Gallés and Bosch, "Phonology and Bilingualism," 68.

[207] Lyon, *Becoming Bilingual*, 19.

but because in the adjective's Latinate origin they are *infans* (*in* + *forfari*), incapable of the power of speech,[208] an adjective typically applied to a newborn child's attempts at utterance. Despite its "imperfect words," which are "half unpronounced," despite those "childish trips," language possesses a cognitive power of its own. Brinsley emphasizes the importance of "pronunciation, being that which either makes or mars the most excellent speech. For all speeches are usually esteemed even as they are uttered or pronounced."[209] Wells stresses that a child must develop "an enhanced awareness of the symbolic properties of linguistic representations: the realization that the meaning and implications of a message depend upon the precise linguistic formulation of that message."[210]

Nonetheless Milton's lines are governed by a telling irony couched in oxymoronic expressions.[211] In terms of the exercise in question Latin has indeed given way to the vernacular, now exhorted not to be "ambitious to be first" (11) since in the Latin speech Milton has "thither packt the worst."[212] Still, that the vernacular should follow upon the Latin was indeed the performative norm.[213] However, in terms of the Miltonic voice and the Miltonic autobiographical experience the reverse of this is the case. John Brinsley had proclaimed: "What they are not able to utter in Latine, remember to cause them first to utter in English."[214] For the young Milton it was the vernacular (L_1) that pre-existed Latin (L_2), a vernacular that is here saluted in terms suggestive of an inspirational Muse, whose primary and primal utterance constitute perhaps a linguistic

---

[208] See Lucretius, *De Rerum Natura* 5.1031; Claudian, *Carm. Min.* 30.103, and note 216.

[209] Brinsley, *Ludus Literarius*, 211.

[210] C.G. Wells, *Learning through Interaction: The Study of Language Development* (Cambridge, 1981), 252.

[211] See M.A. Radzinowicz, "To Play in the Socratic Manner: Oxymoron in Milton's *At a Vacation Exercise in the College*," *University of Hartford Studies in Literature* 17 (1985), 1-11.

[212] The comment of Woodhouse and Bush, *Variorum*, II.1, 141, that "Milton either contrasts Latin unfavourably with English, or his skill in Latin unfavourably with his skill in English" fails to grasp the self-deprecating mock modesty of the phrase.

[213] Hale, *Milton's Cambridge Latin*, 214, remarks: "he is playfully apologizing to a personified mother tongue for using her after Latin," and proceeds to point out that this was in fact the "expected order" (215).

[214] See page 6.

anticipation of that "Spirit" of *Paradise Lost* invoked as an aid to speech itself ("that .../I may assert" [*PL* 1. 24-25]):

> Instruct me for thou knowst; thou *from the first*
> Wast present, and with mighty wings outspread
> Dovelike satst brooding on the vast abyss
> And mad'st it pregnant (*Paradise Lost* 1.19-22)

Paradoxically the celebratory announcement[215] of the transition to a vernacular voice looks back to a classical Latin poem, Lucretius's *De Rerum Natura*, whose discussion of the origins of primitive spoken language draws a rather surprising analogy with a contemporary infant child's inability to speak, or, as Lucretius puts it, his *infantia linguae*:

> At varios linguae sonitus natura subegit
> mittere et utilitas expressit nomina rerum,
> non alia longe ratione atque ipsa videtur
> protrahere ad gestum pueros infantia linguae,
> cum facit ut digito quae sint praesentia monstrent.
>   (Lucretius, *De Rerum Natura* 5.1028-1032).[216]

The very first humans were actually born with instantaneous vocal abilities that constituted their instinctive form of communication just as the newborn child resorts to gestural communication. Lucretius had earlier highlighted attempted vociferation as an instinct common to man and beast. Thus animals do not need rattles or the broken prattle of a nurse:

> At variae crescunt pecudes armenta feraeque
> Nec crepitacillis opus est nec cuiquam adhibendast
> Almae nutricis blanda atque infracta loquella
>   (Lucretius, *De Rerum Natura* 5. 228-230)

---

[215] James Holly Hanford's albeit overly sentimentalized remark is worth quoting: "There is no reason to suppose that these enthusiasms do not go back to the early years of Milton's schooling. They are, like the born artist's love of color, his initial gift as a poet" (*The Youth of Milton* [Michigan, 1925], 117-118).

[216] Text is that of *De Rerum Natura* V, ed. C.D.N. Costa (Oxford, 1984). On *infantia linguae*, cf. Bailey, ed. *De Rerum Natura*, ad loc: "*infantia*: in its literal sense: 'the incapacity of the tongue to speak.' It is because this is the characteristic of babyhood that *infans* obtains its normal meaning." Costa, ed., 121, glosses the phrase as "inability to speak," noting that it recurs in Claudian, *Carm. Min.* 30. 103 in the sense of "childish tongue."

Is perhaps this rejection of rattles and baby talk[217] mirrored and appropriated in the Miltonic dismissal of: "those *new-fangled toys*, and trimming slight/Which takes our late fantastics with delight" (19-20)?[218] The Lucretian child, however, differs from both animal and primitive human in that he or she must acquire language only gradually. And yet that Lucretian first human will find a parallel of sorts in the newly created Adam, whose acquisition of language is seemingly instantaneous:

> to speak I tried, and forthwith spake,
> My tongue obeyed and readily could name
> Whate're I saw.   (*Paradise Lost* 8. 271-273)

The lines in the *Vacation Exercise*, lines spoken by the child turned orator, are in the words of John Hale "a bilingual passage on the subject of a bilingual's choice,"[219] addressing a topic that is subsequently described as "some graver subject,"[220] announcing a transition to English yet engaging with a Latin intertext. The passage is strikingly symptomatic of Milton's interlingual verbal flexibility. Some ten years later in his Latin letter to the Florentine Benedetto Buonmattei,[221] he praises the man whose aim it is to establish in maxims and rules the method and habit of speaking and writing. Such merits fortification by means of a wall, which in turn merits protection against overleaping by means of a law only short of that of Romulus.[222] Milton's post-Cambridge years would see him scaling walls (*muros transiliens*) of language, culture and nationality only to discover in the process the permanence and immutability of an acquired *Latinitas*.

---

[217] Bailey, ed. *De Rerum Natura*, ad loc, glosses the Lucretian *infracta loquella* (230) as "broken talk," "baby talk." He compares Porphyrion on Horace, *Sat.* 1.3.47: *blandientes infantibus infingere linguam solent ut quasi eos imitentur*.

[218] Italics are mine.

[219] Hale, *Milton's Languages*, 5.

[220] *At A Vacation Exercise*, 30.

[221] See pages 104-118.

[222] *qui loquendi scribendique rationem et normam probo gentis saeculo receptam, praeceptis regulisque sancire adnititur, et veluti quodam vallo circummunire, quod quidem ne quis transire ausit, tantum non Romulea lege sit cautum* (*CM* 12, 30).

Chapter 3

Both Latin and Tuscan:
Milton and the Italian Academies

>—if Vertue feeble were
>Heaven it selfe would stoope to her
>*Coelum non animum muto, dum trans mare curro*

Thus reads a bilingual entry in the autograph book of a certain Camillo Cardoini.[1] The date is 10 June 1639 and the signature is that of John Milton, who on the verge of completing his Grand Tour, stopped off at Geneva. The inscription marries the vernacular to Latin as the closing lines of *Comus* are followed by an adaptation of a verse from Horace.[2] Although the statement proclaims some sort of intransigence (perhaps, as Campbell and Corns suggest, Milton's "unwavering Protestantism"),[3] it also attests to an unchanging and perhaps unchangeable *animus*.[4] It was an *animus* that had by that date been molded in a number of ways: by the pedagogical methodology of St Paul's School, by Milton's experiences at Cambridge where by a strange paradox the confines of a university curriculum engendered the birth of a Latin voice, a vibrant linguistic means of communication and performance. In his averred immutability inscribed above, Milton may well be expressing a positive,[5] itself reflective perhaps of the "balanced biculturalism" that "often goes hand in hand with a balanced bilinguality."[6] Biculturalism is nowhere more

---

[1] The autograph book is now held in Houghton Library (Sumner 84).

[2] Horace, *Epistles* 1.11.27: *coelum non animum mutant qui trans mare currunt*.

[3] Campbell and Corns, *Life, Work and Thought*, 126.

[4] On Milton's unchanging *animus*, see E.S. Le Comte, *Milton's Unchanging Mind* (New York, 1973), which argues for a recurrent psychological patterning in his poetic corpus.

[5] Annabel Patterson, *Milton's Words* (Oxford, 2009), 165-195, illustrates ways in which Miltonic negatives frequently serve to present and reinforce positives.

[6] Hamers and Blanc, *Bilingualism and Bilinguality*, 11.

evident than in the Milton of the Italian journey, in an Englishman's proactive integration into and reception by the academic communities of Florence, Rome and Naples:

> But much latelier in the privat Academies of Italy, whither I was favor'd to resort, perceiving that some trifles which I had in memory, compos'd at under twenty or thereabout (for the manner is, that every one must give some proof of his wit and reading there), met with acceptance above what was lookt for, and other things which I had shifted in scarsity of books and conveniences to patch up amongst them, were receiv'd with written Encomiums, which the Italian is not forward to bestow on men of this side the Alps ...
> (*Reason of Church Government*)[7]

The passage strikes a contrast between the conventional and the unconventional: between the customary "manner" of displaying "wit and reading" before an Italian academy[8] and the unexpectedly favorable "acceptance" which his performance(s) received. It was a reception attested and reflected by a series of "written Encomiums" that, Milton implies, Italians would not normally bestow upon northerners ("men of this side the Alps"). Underlying the whole is an Englishman's sense of pride in being treated as a native Italian might have been, and in being acclaimed by Renaissance literati in encomiastic verse and prose.[9] These would later be prefixed to the *Poemata* "half" of the 1645 volume: *Poems of Mr John Milton Both English and Latin*,[10] introduced there as instances not of praise but of excessive praise (*non tam de se quam supra se esse dicta*). Excessive perhaps, but this is continental praise proffered, Milton is careful to tell us, by *praeclaro ingenio viri*, praise in which he takes pride, and of which he clearly wishes an English readership to be aware.[11]

Milton does not identify the language(s) in which these "trifles" and "patch[ed] up" works were composed, nor does he tell us whether

---

[7] *CM* 3, 235-236.

[8] See Estelle Haan, *From Academia to Amicitia: Milton's Latin Writings and the Italian Academies* (Transactions of the American Philosophical Society, 88.6: Philadelphia, 1998), passim.

[9] For fuller discussion of these encomia and of possible links with Milton's Latin poems, see Haan, *From Academia to Amicitia*, 38-52, 82-98, and 130-136.

[10] On the 1645 volume, see Chapter 5.

[11] Milton's prose preface to the encomia is characterized by its recourse to a mock modesty topos, which in itself is conveyed via litotes and a series of double negatives, e.g. *noluit tamen horum egregiam in se voluntatem non esse notam*. See note 5.

they constituted verse or prose.[12] Independent evidence, however, goes some way to solving this riddle. That it was his *Latin poetry* that he performed before the Florentine Accademia degli Svogliati[13] is attested by its minutes of 6/16 September 1638. These provide an interesting footnote to Milton's comments, and they do so in two ways: first, they single out "in particular" ("particolarmente") "il Giovanne Miltone Inglese," and second, they make a qualitative judgment about his performance: his reading of "a very erudite Latin poem of hexameter verses" ("una poesia Latina di versi esametri multo erudita").[14] Close scrutiny of the academy's minute book serves to indicate that this threefold highlighting of uniqueness, nationality and erudition in an individual performance is in fact quite unparalleled. Although the minutes of the meeting of the previous week (31 August/9 September)–an entry immediately preceding the current one–single out the performance of one academician, in this instance Francesco Rovai (albeit for an Italian sonnet rather than a Latin poem),[15] they fail to make any value judgment on the sonnet in question: "e *in particolar* un sonetto dal F. Rovai."[16] In fact the *absence* of qualitative judgments from the recorded minutes would seem to constitute the secretarial norm. Even in the rare instances in which judgments do occur, they typically consist of nothing more than such bland adjectives as "piacevole"[17] or "nobil."[18] More frequently

---

[12] For fuller discussion, see Haan, *From Academia to Amicitia*, 22-28.

[13] On the Accademia degli Svogliati, see Michele Maylender, *Storia dell'Accademie d'Italia* (Bologna, 1926-1930), V, 287; Haan, *From Academia to Amicitia*, 10-28.

[14] "Furono lett' alcune compositioni e particolarmente il Giovanni Miltone Inglese lesse una poesia Latina di versi esametri multo erudita" (Biblioteca Nazionale Centrale, Florence, MSS Magliabecchiana, MSS. Cl. IX, cod. 60, f. 48).

[15] That Rovai was well known to Milton is attested by Carlo Dati's comment in his letter to Milton (22 October/1 November 1647): "per quanto io credo da lei ben conosciuto" (*CM* 12, 296) and by his associated request that Milton compose a lament on the Italian academician's death, a request that seems to have remained unfulfilled. See Haan, *From Academia to Amicitia*, 61-71.

[16] Biblioteca Nazionale Centrale, Florence, MSS Magliabecchiana, MSS. Cl. IX, cod. 60, f. 48. Italics are mine.

[17] "e dal Signor Buonmattei un piacevole Prologo d'un suo Dramma" (15 July 1638) (Biblioteca Nazionale Centrale, Florence, MSS Magliabecchiana, MSS. Cl. IX, cod. 60, f. 47).

[18] "il signor Dati ha recitato un nobil e poetica sonetto" (4 May 1639) (Biblioteca Nazionale Centrale, Florence, MSS Magliabecchiana, MSS. Cl. IX, cod. 60, f. 54); "Furono recitati nobili Poesie Toscane dalli Signori Cavalcanti, Dati, Adimari" (14

performances are collectively minuted under umbrella terms such as "diverse poesie,"[19] "altre materie,"[20] or "alcune compositioni."[21] This indeed is true of the minutes of 7/17 March and 14/24 March 1639, which include Milton himself among those who read "alcuni nobili versi Latini"[22] and "diversi poesie Latine,"[23] respectively. All the more striking then is that earlier minute's recording of "particolarmente," "Inglese," and "molto erudita." The Latin hexameter poem in question, probably *Naturam Non Pati Senium*, but possibly *Ad Patrem*,[24] its performance, and no doubt its performer (an Englishman ["Inglese"] reciting Latin in Italy), seem to have made no slight an impression and impact upon a bilingual academic audience. Or as the speaker of *Epitaphium Damonis* would later put it:

> Ipse etiam tentare ausus sum, nec puto multum
> Displicui, nam sunt et apud me munera vestra
> Fiscellae; calathique et cerea vincla cicutae,
> Quin et nostra suas docuerunt nomina fagos
> Et Datis et Francinus, erant et vocibus ambo
> Et studiis noti, Lydorum sanguinis ambo. (*Ep. Dam*. 133-138)

Nov. 1641) (Biblioteca Nazionale Centrale, Florence, MSS Magliabecchiana, MSS. Cl. IX, cod. 60, f. 82).

[19] "diverse poesie Toscane delli Signori Bartolommei, Buommatei e Doni" (24 March 1639) (Biblioteca Nazionale Centrale, Florence, MSS Magliabecchiana, MSS. Cl. IX, cod. 60, f. 52^v); "recitarono diverse poesie ... il IX" (= Carlo Dati) (7 April 1639) (Biblioteca Nazionale Centrale, Florence, MSS Magliabecchiana, MSS. Cl. IX, cod. 60, f. 53^v).

[20] "sonetti in altre materie" (18 Feb. 1640) (Biblioteca Nazionale Centrale, Florence, MSS Magliabecchiana, MSS. Cl. IX, cod. 60, f. 71).

[21] "alcuni compositioni Latine, e volgari dall Signor Galilei" (25 April 1641) (Biblioteca Nazionale Centrale, Florence, MSS Magliabecchiana, MSS. Cl. IX, cod. 60, f. 74).

[22] "nell' Accademia si trovarono li signori ... Miltonio ... Furon ... letti alcuni nobili versi Latini" (Biblioteca Nazionale Centrale, Florence, MSS Magliabecchiana, MSS. Cl. IX, cod. 60, f. 52).

[23] "... e diversi poesie Latine del Signor Miltonio" (Biblioteca Nazionale Centrale, Florence, MSS Magliabecchiana, MSS. Cl. IX, cod. 60, f. 52-52^v). For a full discussion, see Haan, *From Academia to Amicitia*, 10-28.

[24] The only other eligible hexameter poem is *In Quintum Novembris*, which would have been singularly inappropriate for recitation in Catholic Italy. For discussion of the possible candidates, see Haan, *From Academia to Amicitia*, 25-28.

The element of audacity alluded to here (*ausus sum*) is self-referentially appropriate. In *Mansus* the Miltonic Muse *imprudens Italas ausa est volitare per urbes* (*Mansus* 29). And the motto of the Roman Accademia dei Fantastici, in which Milton was probably involved,[25] was none other than *quidlibet audendi*.[26] Audacity is in fact central to Milton's bicultural self-fashioning whereby the Englishman now in Italy "dares" to perform (quite literally) as an Italian academician would. And in the Italian academy, just as in Cambridge University, Latin is clearly his preferred linguistic medium. It is a performance that not only pleased (*nec puto multum/displicui* [*Ep. Dam* 133-134]) but was rewarded in the form of *munera*, allegorized as pastoral baskets and pipes, but constituting in effect those "written Encomiums" mentioned earlier. In these encomia, as in the academy's minutes, an Englishman's erudition is singled out, no more so than by the fellow-academicians (Antonio Francini[27] and Carlo Dati)[28] explicitly named by Milton in this passage from *Epitaphium Damonis*. Francini, writing in Italian, presents Milton as a traveler from an England that is set apart from the rest of the world ("Anglia …/Separata dal mondo" [14-15]); one who has turned his "peregrine piante" (39) to foreign parts; one who is a "fabro quasi divino" (43), daringly proactive in his attempts to penetrate a network that is essentially Tuscan: "Quanti nacquero in Floro/O in lei del parlar Tosco appreser l'arte … Volesti ricercar per tuo tesoro,/E parlasti con lor nell'opre loro" (49-53); one who is multilingual, possessing knowledge of Greek, Latin, Spanish, French, and Italian, in addition to his native language, English ("ch'ode oltr'all' Anglia il suo più degno Idioma/Spagna, Francia, Toscana, e Grecia e Roma" [59-60]). Carlo Dati, writing in Latin prose, presents Milton as a *novus Ulysses*, the perennial traveler availing of every opportunity to learn from his Italian experience, a polyglot who can make dead languages come to life again (*polyglotto, in cuius ore linguae iam deperditae sic reviviscunt …*).[29]

Revitalization of the classical *linguae … deperditae* is exemplified by Milton's academic performances and by the Latin poetry and prose that he composed in the course of his Italian sojourn. These works merit

---

[25] See Haan, *From Academia to Amicitia*, 81-98.

[26] An adaptation of Horace, *Ars Poetica* 9-10: *pictoribus atque poetis/quidlibet audendi semper fuit aequa potestas*. See Haan, *From Academia to Amicitia*, 82.

[27] On Antonio Francini, see Haan, *From Academia to Amicitia*, 38-43.

[28] On Carlo Dati, see *DBI* sv; Haan, *From Academia to Amicitia*, 29-31, 43-52, 53-80.

[29] See Haan, *From Academia to Amicitia*, 46-52.

close consideration in the context of the respective roles played by Latin and the vernacular in the academies themselves. The statutes of the Florentine Accademia degli Svogliati proclaim a refreshing sense of freedom in terms of a performer's choice of language, form and subject matter:

> ... s'esortano in virtù della virtù, à leggere, orare, disputare, mantener conclusioni, *in ogni lingua*, forma, e sopra ogni materia con ingenua Libertà.[30]

Examination of the academy's minutes for the months and years of Milton's attendance proves insightful in regard to the issue of language choice on the part of academic participants. It emerges in fact that performances in Latin seem to have been the exception rather than the rule. Thus for 1639 the only other meetings to include minuted performances in Latin are those of 1/10 March and 25 April/4 May.[31] In subsequent years Latin performances are recorded only for 8/18 February 1640,[32] 26 February/6 March 1640,[33] 6/16 May 1641,[34] and 3/13 July 1641.[35] By contrast, performances in Italian are widely attested in all of the extant minutes. These embrace sonnets (by far the most prevalent

---

[30] *Statuti Dell' Academia degli Svogliati Sotto I Principato dell' Illustrissime Signore Jacopo Gaddi, Suo Primo Principe, e Promotore Stabiliti* (Biblioteca Nazionale Centrale, Florence, MSS Magliabecchiana, MSS. Cl. VI, cod. 163, f. 2^v). Italics are mine.

[31] "tra quali recitarono nobile Poesie Toscane e Latine di Signori Adimari, Antinori, Bartolomei, Abb. D. Eusebio"; "Recitarono versi Latini D. Vitt. e'l V. Girolami"; (Biblioteca Nazionale Centrale, Florence, MSS Magliabecchiana, MSS. Cl. IX, cod. 60, ff. 51^v and 54).

[32] "Furono recitati dal Signor Girolami versi Latini in ode all Pindaria in lode di N.S. ... dal P. Bonin un elogio Latino in lode di Re d' Franci" (Biblioteca Nazionale Centrale, Florence, MSS Magliabecchiana, MSS. Cl. IX, cod. 60, f. 71).

[33] "Li Signori Accademici recitarono diverse poesie Latine e volgare" (Biblioteca Nazionale Centrale, Florence, MSS Magliabecchiana, MSS. Cl. IX, cod. 60, f. 60^v).

[34] "un elogio Latino dall' Abate Dr Eusebio ... un ode Latina dal P. de Rena" (Biblioteca Nazionale Centrale, Florence, MSS Magliabecchiana, MSS. Cl. IX, cod. 60, f. 75). The minutes of 5/15 August 1649 mention the delivery of epigrams, without naming the language. It is likely that these were Latin performances: "il Principe recito un Epigramma ... e'il signor Bartolommeo Gherardini un altro epigramma" (Biblioteca Nazionale Centrale, Florence, MSS Magliabecchiana, MSS. Cl. IX, cod. 60, f. 124).

[35] "versi Latini dall' Abat. Farrini" (Biblioteca Nazionale Centrale, Florence, MSS Magliabecchiana, MSS. Cl. IX, cod. 60, f. 75).

genre),³⁶ drama,³⁷ discourses on tragedy and comedy,³⁸ and epistles,³⁹ although performances of prose works are only very rarely attested.⁴⁰ One interesting minute (1 March 1640) refers to a performance of a translation (most likely in Italian) of an Ode of Horace.⁴¹

Linguistic versatility is much more readily apparent in a sister Florentine academy, the Accademia degli Apatisti, which we now know Milton to have attended in 1638.⁴² Although the academy's minutes do

---

³⁶ "Furon letti dal signor Adimari due nobili sonetti" (5/15 July 1638) (Biblioteca Nazionale Centrale, Florence, MSS Magliabecchiana, MSS. Cl. IX, cod. 60, f. 47); "e in particolar un sonetto dal F. Rovai" (31 October/9 September 1638) (Biblioteca Nazionale Centrale, Florence, MSS Magliabecchiana, MSS. Cl. IX, cod. 60, f. 48); "Il Signor Bart. lesse un sonetto sopra la narciso" (20/30 September 1638) (Biblioteca Nazionale Centrale, Florence, MSS Magliabecchiana, MSS. Cl. IX, cod. 60, f. 48ᵛ); "Adimari due sonetti; il Signor Cavancanti due sonetti; il Signor Bartolommei un sonetto" (20/30 Dec. 1638) (Biblioteca Nazionale Centrale, Florence, MSS Magliabecchiana, MSS. Cl. IX, cod. 60, f. 50ᵛ); "il Signor Dati ha recitato un nobil e poetica sonetto" (25 April/4 May 1639) (Biblioteca Nazionale Centrale, Florence, MSS Magliabecchiana, MSS. Cl. IX, cod. 60, f. 54).

³⁷ "e dal Signor Buonmattei un piacevole Prologo d'un suo Dramma" (5/15 July 1638) (Biblioteca Nazionale Centrale, Florence, MSS Magliabecchiana, MSS. Cl. IX, cod. 60, f. 47); "Giulio Pitti lesse alcuna scena della sua Tragicomedia" (27 July/5 August 1638) (Biblioteca Nazionale Centrale, Florence, MSS Magliabecchiana, MSS. Cl. IX, cod. 60, f. 47); "Doni, che lesse una scena da sua Tragedia" (24 March 1639) (Biblioteca Nazionale Centrale, Florence, MSS Magliabecchiana, MSS. Cl. IX, cod. 60, f. 52ᵛ).

³⁸ "del B. Buonmattei posso in Campo un discorso inguanio alla Tragedia e Comedia" (Biblioteca Nazionale Centrale, Florence, MSS Magliabecchiana, MSS. Cl. IX, cod. 60, f. 47ᵛ).

³⁹ "Signor Adimari lesse una lettera dedicasona" (23 July/1 August 1641) (Biblioteca Nazionale Centrale, Florence, MSS Magliabecchiana, MSS. Cl. IX, cod. 60, f. 77ᵛ).

⁴⁰ "Lesse il Signor Asserino una composizion in prosa" (20/30 December 1638) (Biblioteca Nazionale Centrale, Florence, MSS Magliabecchiana, MSS. Cl. IX, cod. 60, f. 50ᵛ).

⁴¹ "Furono recitate dal primo [= Cavalcanti] un traduzzione d'ode d'Hor" (1 March 1640) (Biblioteca Nazionale Centrale, Florence, MSS Magliabecchiana, MSS. Cl. IX, cod. 60, f. 60). For Milton's vernacular rendering of Horace (*Odes* 1.5), see page 17.

⁴² As first noted by Haan, *From Academia to Amicitia*, 36. Evidence for this is provided by a manuscript of Anton Francesco Gori (1692-1757). See Florence: Biblioteca Marucelliana MS A.36, ff. 11ʳ-142ᵛ, usefully transcribed by Allessandro Lazzeri, *Intellettuali e Consenso nella Toscana del Seicento: L'Accademia degli Apatisti* (Milan, 1983), 57-121. At f. 53ʳ there occurs under a list of the academy's membership in 1638 the name "Giovanni Milton inglese." On the Apatisti in general,

not survive, it is apparent from later testimony that among its membership in c. 1637 are to be found the names of many foreigners, in particular Poles, English, Germans, French and Flemish,[43] reflecting this academy's aspiration to embrace foreign *literati*.[44] Members were permitted moreover to deliver orations in their own language,[45] and multilingual participation was actively encouraged.[46] It is tempting to speculate that encomiastic depictions of Milton as a polyglot were inspired at least to some degree by multilingual performances on his part.

What is beyond question, however, is the fact that Milton's extant verse composed in the course of his Italian sojourn is cast exclusively in the medium of Latin. The same is also true of his letters (to Buonmattei and Holstenius) written while in Florence and Rome. Poems such as *Ad Salsillum*, *Mansus* and the Leonora epigrams constitute in all likelihood the verses "patch[ed] up" whilst in Italy and recited perhaps in the academies of Florence, Rome and Naples. That Milton performed several of his other Latin poems such as the *Naturam* (or *Ad Patrem*)[47] is, as noted previously, clearly evident from that minuted reference to "hexameter verses." It is also highly probable that he recited some of his Latin elegies. And here Gordon Campbell's suggestion that the reference to "Permessus" in Francini's encomium may be a subtle acknowledgment of Milton's accomplishment as an elegiac poet[48] merits further consideration. That allegorical passage in *Epitaphium Damonis*, describing in pastoral terms Milton's Florentine academic performance,

---

see Edoardo Benvenuti, *Agostino Coltellini e L'Accademia degli Apatisti a Firenze nel Secolo XVII* (Pistoia, 1910); Lazzeri, *Intellettuali*, passim; Meylender, *Storia* I, 219-222; Haan, *From Academia to Amicitia*, 29-37.

[43] Lazzeri, *Intellettuali*, 16: "Nel 1637 troviamo già molti stranieri, principalmente polacchi, inglesi, tedeschi, francesi, fiamminghi."

[44] Coltellini boasted: "L'Università da me fondata in casa mia più di 30 anni sono, ha per fine l'istituzione della gioventù nelle cose civili ... ed il servigio de' forestieri massime oltramontani" (Biblioteca Riccardiana Fiorentina Cod. Riccardiano 1949, f. 20^r). Cf. Lazzeri, *Intellettuali*, 17.

[45] Lazzeri, *Intellettuali*, 18.

[46] Cf. Maylender, *Storia*, I, 222. On the occasion of the funeral of Ferdinand II, for example, commemorative verses were recited before the academy in Latin, English, German and French (in addition to Italian). Cf. Lazzeri, *Intellettuali*, 18.

[47] See page 98.

[48] "Il Tamigi il dirà che gl'è concesso/Per te suo cigno pareggiar Permesso" (77-78). See Gordon Campbell, "Francini's Permesso," *MQ* 15 (1981), 122-133.

concludes with a rather enigmatic statement: *quin et nostra suas docuerunt nomina fagos/et Datis, et Francinus* (136-137). Bush comments that Dati and Francini "are imagined as shepherds singing *Milton's* praises among the trees;"[49] Hale speculates that the allusion is to poetic gifts from the two Florentines "recording his [Milton's] friendship with Damon."[50] Worthy of comment, however, is the occurrence of the plural *nostra* at this point. Although this may constitute a poetic plural for singular, it does seem to assume additional significance given the emphasis up until that point on first-person singular (*o ego quantus eram* [129], *potui* [132] *ipse etiam ... ausus sum* [133]; *apud me* [134]). How then have Dati and Francini taught their beech trees "our names" (the names of *both* Milton and Charles Diodati) as opposed to "my name" alone? Might this allude to their knowledge (via a Miltonic performance) of either or both of Milton's Latin elegies (*Elegia Prima; Elegia Sexta*)[51] addressed specifically to Diodati, or perhaps the fourth Italian sonnet of which he is likewise addressee? Finally, it is possible to read into Carlo Dati's Latin encomium knowledge of Milton's Latin prose *Prolusions*.[52] Thus Dati's assertion that "with astronomy as a guide [Milton] hears the harmonious sounds of the heavenly spheres" (*harmonicos caelestium sphaerarum sonitus astronomia duce audienti*) may refer to Milton's *De Sphaerarum Concentu*. This *Prolusion*, tracing its performative origins back to an essentially Anglo-academic world (that of Cambridge University), would certainly have found an ideal home in another academy, this time in Italy.

Weighing up the evidence, it would seem then that at least in regard to formal oral performance and poetic and epistolary composition Latin becomes the code selection, "the speaker's decision, in a given communication, interaction, situation, to use one code [language] rather than another"[53] for "il Giovanne Miltone Inglese" now upon Italian soil. This choice was probably informed by a number of factors: by the obvious fact that he was not a native Italian, by his greater competence in Latin than in Italian,[54] by the universality of Latin as linguistic medium in Renaissance Europe, by "the salient group identities of the participants

---

[49] Bush, *Variorum*, I, 312. Italics are mine.

[50] Hale, *Milton's Languages*, 58. See Haan, *From Academia to Amicitia*, 24.

[51] For discussion of *Elegia Prima* and *Elegia Sexta*, see pages 58-62 and 80-88.

[52] See Haan, *From Academia to Amicitia*, 50-51.

[53] Hamers and Blanc, *Bilingualism and Bilinguality*, 144.

[54] See page 106.

and other situational factors"[55] pertinent to the Italian academy, and no doubt by cultural context. As Meuter remarks, "language selection is determined by a number of factors, including relative proficiency, contextual cues, and monitoring ability."[56] Baker has noted that it is natural for an adult to assume different identities in different contexts,[57] and Hamers and Blanc assert that "the bilingual's language behaviour will vary according to whether he interacts with a monolingual or a bilingual interlocutor in a unilingual, bilingual or multilingual environment."[58] And this can be taken further. As a shared linguistic means of communication and articulation that could be understood in an intercultural context by a bilingual (Latin/Tuscan) audience, the *lingua Latina* becomes for the Milton of the Italian journey an exogenous language of sorts: "one used as an official, institutionalized language but has no speech community."[59] It also serves somewhat paradoxically as a means of both preserving, interrogating, and ultimately enhancing his cultural (and, as will be seen, his bicultural) self-fashioning.

3.1 Both Latin and Tuscan: Milton's Letter to Buonmattei

> Ego certe istis utrisque Linguis non extremis tantummodo labris madidus; sed siquis alius, quantum per annos licuit, poculis maioribus prolutus, possum tamen nonnunquam ad illum Dantem, et Petrarcham aliosque vestros complusculos libenter et cupide commessatum ire: nec me tam ipsae Athenae Atticae cum illo suo pellucido Ilisso, nec illa vetus Roma sua Tiberis ripa retinere valuerunt; quin saepe Arnum vestrum, et Faesulanos illos colles invisere amem.[60]

For the Milton of the Italian journey Latin becomes the key medium of interrogating things Italian. Moreover it is Dante and Petrarch who epitomize the Tuscan authors upon whom he is glad to "go for a feast"

---

[55] Hamers and Blanc, *Bilingualism and Bilinguality*, 146.

[56] Meuter, "Language Selection in Bilinguals," 365.

[57] Baker, *Parents and Teachers*, 88.

[58] Hamers and Blanc, *Bilingualism and Bilinguality*, 12.

[59] Hamers and Blanc, *Bilingualism and Bilinguality*, 11.

[60] *Ep. Fam.* 8 (*CM* 12, 34).

(*commessatum ire*)[61] and has willingly and eagerly done so in the past, not least, one would imagine, in the course of composing his Italian sonnets. That he has also consulted *aliosque vestros complusculos* is attested in a number of ways: by a letter from Milton to Charles Diodati datable to the autumn of 1637,[62] which indicates that he has undertaken quite a voracious reading program in Italian history;[63] by some of Milton's entries (tentatively datable to 1637)[64] in his *Commonplace Book*, embracing inter alios Dante, *Divina Comedia*,[65] Boccaccio, *Vita di Dante*, and Ariosto, *Orlando Furioso*. But the above statement about his reading of Italian literature is perhaps not without a degree of irony. For it is voiced in *Latin* in a letter composed in the course of an Italian sojourn—a letter addressed moreover to a Florentine academician (Benedetto Buonmattei) who was also a *Tuscan* grammarian and important linguistic theorist in his day.[66] Upon closer inspection, it emerges that despite that telling *possum tamen*, this Italian feast is in fact rendered all the more palatable and pleasing not despite but because of Milton's implementation of Latin as linguistic medium. After all, he has, as he proclaims, done much more than wet merely the tips of his lips in Latin and Greek. And as the Florentine Carlo Dati's "written encomium" proclaims, those are lips that possess an ability to bring dead languages back to life.[67] Dati's praise was probably elicited by hearing (and/or reading) Milton's Latin poetry, most likely in a formal academic setting, but it may also reflect the fact that for Milton in Italy it was Latin that consistently functioned as a vibrant exogenous language, and more specifically as the medium of his epistolary correspondence with Italian

---

[61] See A.M. Cinquemani, *Glad to Go For a Feast: Milton, Buonmattei, and the Florentine Accademici* (New York, 1998), passim.

[62] *Ep. Fam.* 7. Despite the date of 23 September 1637 attributed to the letter in the 1674 edition of the *Epistolae Familiares*, Campbell, *A Milton Chronology*, 57, convincingly argues from internal evidence in the letter for a November dating.

[63] *Italorum in obscura re diu versati sumus sub Longobardis* (CM 12, 28).

[64] By the occurrence of the Greek ε instead of the Italian *e*. Cf. Campbell, *A Milton Chronology*, 56-57.

[65] Milton also cites from Bernardino Daniello's commentary on Dante (Venice, 1568).

[66] On Buonmattei, see Michele Colombo, "Benedetto Buonmattei e La Questione della Lingua nel Primo Seicento," *Aevum*, 77 (2003), 615-634; Cinquemani, *Glad to Go For a Feast*, passim.

[67] *in cuius ore linguae iam deperditae sic reviviscunt*.

academicians. Still, at the end of the letter to Buonmattei Milton takes pains to offer a pseudo-apology for his epistolary code selection:

> De cetero, si forte cur in hoc argumento Latina potius quam vestra lingua utar miraris, id factum ea gratia est ut intelligas quam ego linguam abs te mihi praeceptis exornandam cupio, eius me plane meam imperitiam et inopiam Latine confiteri; et hac ipsa ratione plus me valiturum apud te speravi simul et illud si canam; et venerandam e Latio matrem in filiae causa suae mecum adiutricem adduxissem, credidi fore eius auctoritati et reverentiae augustaeque per tot saecula maiestati nihil ut denegares.[68]

The passage is colored by a metalinguistic awareness that is deeply self-conscious. Although emphasizing the somewhat ironic dichotomy between his use of Latin in order to advocate the adornment of Tuscan, Milton simultaneously reconciles the two by recourse to the image of a revered and somewhat magisterial mother (Latin) coming to the assistance of her daughter (Tuscan). It is a reconciliation that, as will be argued, likewise underlies his presentation of Buonmattei as "both Tuscan and Latin," and also mirrors his own bicultural self-fashioning while upon Italian soil. The *coelum* may indeed have changed, but the Miltonic *animus* is immutably rooted in *Latinitas*.

Dated Florence 31 August/10 September 1638, Milton's letter to Buonmattei was penned just six days prior to his delivery before the Svogliati of that most notably attested performance: his reading of "a very erudite *Latin* poem of hexameter verses."[69] It is possible moreover that Buonmattei witnessed the performance first hand.[70] That the two had already met probably several months earlier is highly likely. And there would have been several opportunities to do so. An Englishman of letters ("un letterato Inglese") seeking admission to the Academy ("che desiderava d'entrar nell'Accademia") on 28 June/8 July 1638[71] could be John Milton,[72] who may consequently have been proposed as a member

---

[68] *CM* 12, 38.

[69] See page 97.

[70] Cf. Parker, *Biography*, ed. Campbell, I, 171: "with Buonmattei probably present."

[71] Biblioteca Nazionale Centrale, Florence, Magliabecchiana MSS. Cl.IX, cod 60, f.46ᵛ. Cf. French, *Life Records*, V, 385; Haan, *From Academia to Amicitia*, 13.

[72] See Haan, *From Academia to Amicitia*, 13.

the following week.[73] If so, he could have witnessed a discussion of the academy's *impresa* (upon which Buonmattei had previously delivered two lectures)[74] and a recitation by the Florentine academician of "a pleasant Prologue from one of his dramas."[75] Buonmattei was also Regent of the Florentine Accademia degli Apatisti, in which role he had to approve in advance any prose or poetry that was to be read at its meetings.[76] Indeed it is not impossible that Milton's Latin letter was itself presented as one such candidate.[77] In addition, Buonmattei delivered regular lectures at the University of Florence (to which he had in 1637 been appointed lecturer in Tuscan language). According to his biographer Casotti, these lectures (especially those on Dante) enjoyed an unprecedented glory in that they were regularly attended by the entire Accademia degli Apatisti.[78]

For Milton: when in Florence, do as the Florentines do. The adoption of the cultural identity of the second-language group has been recognized as characteristic of bilingual experience.[79] That Tuscan was the medium of informal conversation between Milton and Buonmattei is clearly evident. Parker envisages Milton "talking to the elderly priest

---

[73] "furono proposti l'Abate D. Eusebio, e il Signor ... per Academia li quali vinsero nonostante una fava bianca" (Biblioteca Nazionale Centrale, Florence, Magliabecchiana MSS. Cl.IX, cod. 60, f.47). Neil Harris, "Galileo as Symbol: The 'Tuscan Artist' in *Paradise Lost*," *Annali dell' Istituto e Museo di Storio della Scienza di Firenze* 10 (1985), 3-29, at 6, discusses the blank space in this minute and proposes Milton as a possible candidate, suggesting that Jacopo Gaddi, the Academy's Secretary, had not yet been able to catch the newcomer's name, which he intended to fill in at a later date. See also Haan, *From Academia to Amicitia*, 14.

[74] Giovanni Battista Casotti, *Vita di Benedetto Buommattei* prefixed to *Della Lingua Toscana di Benedetto Buommattei Libri Due* (Milan, 1807), 50.

[75] "e dal Signor Buonmattei un piacevole Prologo d'un suo Dramma" (Minutes of Accademia degli Svogliati [5/15 July 1638]: Biblioteca Nazionale Centrale, Florence, Magliabecchiana MSS., Cl.IX, cod. 60, f. 47).

[76] Cf. Cinquemani, *Glad to Go For a Feast*, 26.

[77] For evidence of the recitation of epistles in Florentine academies, see note 39.

[78] Casotti, *Vita di Benedetto Buommattei*, 48: "Nè contenta di tutte queste significazioni di riconoscenza, e di stima, usò l'Accademia di andar sempre in corpo ad udir le sue publiche Lezioni sopra Dante allo Studio Fiorentino, onore, che io non trovo ne' Registri essere stato fatto ad altri giammai, nè che tutta l'Accademia interrompesse il corso de' suoi letterari esercizi, fuori che per questo fine."

[79] See Hamers and Blanc, *Bilinguality and Bilingualism*, 11.

[Buonmattei] in his *most careful Tuscan*."[80] Certainly what emerges from the letter is that both parties have already held conversations on several occasions (*quid ego tanto opere abs te contendere soleam ... quoties in istius rei mentionem incidimus*).[81] And it is worth noting that some sixteen years later Milton's recollection of his Italian sojourn would both single out and identify the city of Florence with the elegance of the Tuscan tongue (*illa in urbe quam prae ceteris propter elegantiam cum linguae tum ingeniorum semper colui*).[82] Such *elegantia*, however, both mirrors and transcends the conversational medium of a vibrant speech community. Hence it functions on a more formal level—that of grammatical and linguistic theory—epitomized perhaps by the *Vocabulario* (1612), the "founding document"[83] of the Tuscan cause produced by the Accademia della Crusca, of which Buonmattei was a member. Lewalski's suggestion that Milton may have attended sessions of this academy[84] is very plausible given his proactive and rapid integration into a Florentine academic network.

The speech community that was Tuscan is reflected in its most formal and literal sense in Milton's letter. This is achieved in a variety of ways: through the possibility of a series of veiled and hitherto unexplored allusions to Buonmattei's Tuscan oral performances; through possible points of contact between the letter itself and aspects of Buonmattei's grammatical and linguistic theory as articulated in his works in print or in manuscript, and, not least, through two specific recommendations on pronunciation and genre posited by Milton to the Florentine grammarian. Although the complex relationship between the letter and the Buonmattean corpus remains potentially insoluble, it may be possible nonetheless to unravel some of the complexities. And it is with Milton's first recommendation that the analysis will begin.

The first request made "with some temerity,"[85] is that Buonmattei include in his forthcoming work a little something for foreigners in regard to the correct pronunciation of Tuscan (*in nostram exterorum gratiam de*

---

[80] Parker, *Life*, ed. Campbell, I, 171. Italics are mine.

[81] *CM* 12, 36.

[82] *Defensio Secunda* (*CM* 8, 122). Cf. Cinquemani, *Glad to Go for a Feast*, 31: "The meaning Milton attaches to Florence is that familiarly imposed, in the context of the questione della lingua, by the Florentines themselves."

[83] Campbell and Corns, *Life, Work, and Thought*, 111.

[84] Lewalski, *Life*, 92.

[85] Campbell and Corns, *Life, Work, and Thought*, 111.

recta linguae pronuntiatione adhuc paululum quiddam adiicere). The request is contextualized within a rather daringly pejorative depiction of Italians as somewhat insular, as never looking beyond the confines of the Alps (*vos Itali intra Alpium duntaxat pomoeria sapere voluisse*)–almost a mirror-image of "Anglia.../Separata dal mondo," as Francini puts it. The forthcoming grammar in which the additions are to be inserted is clearly a "work in progress"[86] (*iam iam operi fastigium impositurus ... ordinem ... facile sis allaturus ... hanc operam ... ut pergas*). This suggests that Milton was aware of the fact that Buonmattei was busily engaged in the completion of the full-scale Tuscan grammar (*inchoatis, maiori etiam ex parte absolutis*) that would eventually see the light of day in 1643 as *Della Lingua Toscana Libre Due*. Still, even in 1638 the treatise was excitedly awaited by Buonmattei's fellow-academicians.[87] Earlier printed versions of the first part of the work in its original title *Delle Cagioni della Lingua Toscana* would have been accessible to Milton in either the first or second editions, which had appeared in Venice in 1623 and 1626, respectively. Cinquemani oversimplifies the issue by regarding Milton's request as an indication that he simply ignored the scattered and rather disparate discussion of pronunciation available to and likely accessed by him in either of these editions.[88] It is an oddly inverted argument. The solution may lie in its corollary–an approach adopted by Lewalski, who states that Buonmattei "did not incorporate these suggestions."[89] But even this viewpoint may reflect a misreading of the very nature of the Miltonic recommendation. All too frequently scholars have tended to regard *paululum quiddam adiicere* as a request for a specific "section"[90] or "appendix,"[91] or "chapter"[92] on pronunciation. Perhaps the indefinite nature of the Latin phraseology in which this request is couched may

---

[86] Lewalski, *Life*, 93.

[87] Cf. Masson, *Life*, I, 728: "already, in 1638, his friends were expecting it, and were urging its progress."

[88] "Though there is much discussion of pronunciation in the *Lingua Toscana*, Milton seems to ignore it" (Cinquemani, *Glad to Go For a Feast*, 55).

[89] Lewalski, *Life*, 93.

[90] Thus Cinquemani, *Glad to Go For a Feast*, 35: "Milton goes on to discuss two *sections* lacking from the grammar." Italics are mine.

[91] Thus Cinquemani, *Glad to Go For a Feast*, 63, freely translates the phrase as "some little appendix."

[92] Thus Campbell and Corns, *Life, Work, and Thought*, 111: "there is no chapter on pronunciation."

suggest the very opposite. Thus the absence of a formal "section" on pronunciation should not be read as precluding the possibility that at least *some* of the material on pronunciation intermittently scattered throughout the treatise of 1643[93] occurs therein partially in response to and in fulfillment of Milton's request. Campbell and Corns come close to the potential truth in their cautious observation that the absence of a manuscript draft of *Della Lingua Toscana* renders it difficult to gauge whether Buonmattei incorporated Milton's suggestion.[94]

A reading of the treatise reveals that comments on pronunciation are either technical or essentially provincial. Buonmattei draws attention to the correlation between "lingua" as language and "lingua" as tongue, the organ possessed by living creatures ("un membro della bocca dell'animale") whose function is to facilitate taste and vocal articulation ("formazion della voce").[95] Central to its latter role is "la qualità delle dizioni, e delle pronunzie."[96] "Lingua" also signifies dialect, and here the author takes pains to emphasize the linguistic mixing that ensued in Italy as a consequence of the Barbarian Invasions whereby "i Latini proffissero alcune parole barbare latinamente, ed all' incontro i Barbari ne pronunziassero altre latine barbaramente," the whole resulting in the generation of a rather new type of language: "e così tra lingue tanto diverse una nuova si generasse."[97] Such mixing also affected vocabulary, and here comments on pronunciation are confined to a debate as to whether words were pronounced "barbaramente"[98] or "latinamente,"[99] the

---

[93] This relevant point is also noted by Parker, *Biography*, ed. Campbell, II, 824: "pronunciation is treated in appropriate places," and by Campbell and Corns, *Life, Work, and Thought*, 111: "there are comments on pronunciation scattered throughout the volume."

[94] *Life, Work, and Thought*, 111.

[95] Benedetto Buonmattei, *Della Lingua Toscana Libri Due* (Florence, 1643), 1.

[96] *Della Lingua Toscana*, 2.

[97] *Della Lingua Toscana*, 5.

[98] "Se anno ricevuto la materia; ad unque la forma sarà barbara: perche e' saranno di quelli, che i barbari, barbaramente venivano a pronunziare" (*Della Lingua Toscana*, 8).

[99] "Quell'esser latini, e non esser pronunziati latinamente gli fa esser nostri volgari: che se, essendo naturalmente latini, fossero pronunziati latinamente" (*Della Lingua Toscana*, 8).

latter ultimately gaining the upper hand.[100] Although alert to such issues as linguistic hybridity, linguistic diversity, and the usefulness of language, Buonmattei's remarks on pronunciation are parochial for the most part. Thus it would seem that they do not fulfill or exemplify the Miltonic desideratum to discuss the issue with an eye toward foreigners (*in nostram exterorum gratiam*). That said, Milton's specific request may have been generated from his own acknowledgment of that essential parochialism and provincialism evident in Buonmattei's work (since these early sections were already in print since 1623).

There also exists the possibility that the manuscript of Buonmattei's *Trattato della Pronunzia*,[101] envisaged as book 3 of the *Della Lingua Toscana*[102] (and usefully edited by Fiorello),[103] is a late work partly inspired by Milton's recommendation. Cinquemani distorts the facts by overstating the case, assuming that Milton's recommendation means in turn that he had *not* read the treatise—"the Trattato Milton never saw."[104] Cinquemani dates the work to c. 1633 on the assumption that this is the already extant Buonmattean treatise on pronunciation alluded to in the preface to G.M. Ambrogi's *Modo di Pronunziare le Voci Toscane* (1634), while also conceding that Buonmattei may have begun two works on pronunciation, "the first lost, and the second (that published by Fiorello) incomplete."[105] Fiorello by contrast convincingly argues that the tract pertains to 1644-1647 largely on account of the fact that it is bound with works datable to 1645 and is written in a trembling hand closely resembling that of Buonmattei's failing years.[106]

The *Trattato* discusses the various meanings of "pronunzia" ("questa voce Pronunzia, e Pronunziare si truova in più, e vari significati").[107] Thus it can mean "declare" or "publish" ("Talora sta in

---

[100] "I quali non sono con regole barbare, ma con nostrali pronunziati" (*Della Lingua Toscana*, 8).

[101] Biblioteca Nazionale Centrale, Florence, MSS Magliabecchiana Cl. IV, cod. 61.

[102] Cf. Maurizio Vitale, *La Questione della Lingua* (Palermo, 1978), 175.

[103] Piero Fiorello, "Il *Trattato della Pronunzia* di Benedetto Buommatei," *Studi Linguistici Italiani* 1 (1960), 117-161.

[104] Cinquemani, *Glad to Go For a Feast*, 35.

[105] Cinquemani, *Glad to Go For a Feast*, 55.

[106] Fiorella, "Il Tratto della Pronunzia," 110.

[107] *Il Trattato della Pronunzia*, 118. All references are by pagination to Fiorelli's edition.

forza di Dichiarare, e Pubblicare") or "sentence" or "condemn" ("Talora si piglia per Sentenziare e Condennare"). It can also denote in a rhetorical context "a fitting moderation of voice, face and of gesture" ("I Maestri dell'eloquenza, che Rettorici sono appellati, dicono 'Pronunzia' esser' un' acconcia moderazion di voce, di viso, e di gesti"). Another meaning is to "narrate," "confess," or "name" ("Trovasi anche in significato di Narrare, di Confessare, di Nominare").[108] Buonmattei's own interpretation constitutes "un usitato modo di profferire il suono delle voci."[109] Interesting, however, is the rather self-conscious nature of the subsequent discussion of pronunciation as pertaining to "ciascun popolo" and an associated alertness to and discernment between differing nations: "Diro per tanto quel che ho osservato con molto studio della pronunzia del *nostro popolo*: non togliendo *ad alcun'altro* la faculta di parlar quanto vuole di quella del suo."[110] The approach is much broader than that exemplified by his other works, and the whole dovetails into a detailed discussion and exemplification of the pronunciation of vowels: closed and open e and o,[111] the pronunciation of o and e[112] and i and u;[113] the effects of accent[114] and of suffixes,[115] with specific emphasis upon the oddities of Italian regional pronunciation,[116] especially as manifested in consonants such as C, G, S.[117] Cinquemani, while summarizing such points,[118] fails to note that they are presented in a way that is far from parochial. In fact, it

---

[108] *Il Trattato della Pronunzia*, 118.

[109] *Il Trattato della Pronunzia*, 118.

[110] *Il Trattato della Pronunzia*, 119. Italics are mine.

[111] "Dell'E. e dell'O Larghi, e Stretti" (120-121).

[112] "Dov l'E. o l'O largo possa trovarsi" (121-124).

[113] "Dell'I. e dell'V" (134-136).

[114] "Se sotto l'accento sempre sia larga" (124-125); "Dell'E accentata in ultima sillaba" (128-130); "Dell'O accentato in ultima" (131-132).

[115] "Di alcuni Avverbi terminanti in Mente" (127-128).

[116] "Le voce accenate da questi due caratteri C. e G. si senton sonar nelle bocche di molti popoli Italiani" (136).

[117] "Dell C. e del G" (136-137); "De' due suoni dell'S" (137-140); "Dove so pronunzi l'S" (144-148).

[118] Cinquemani, *Glad to Go for a Feast*, 35.

might be remarked that this highly technical section, drawing attention to regional pronunciation ("si senton sonar nelle bocche di molti popoli Italiani"),[119] and citing useful examples from Italian literature, is accessible to any interested (and even foreign) reader. In short, if a late dating of the work is accepted, it is not impossible that at least some of Buonmattei's discussion of pronunciation was governed or even prompted by that Miltonic request: *de recta linguae pronuntiatione adhuc paululum quiddam adiicere*.

Among other Buonmattean works that might have been available to Milton was the *Delle Lodi della Lingua Toscana*. This oration, recited by Buonmattei before the Accademia Fiorentina in 1623,[120] is divided into two types of praise: "lodi commune, esterne" and "lodi particolari, interni."[121] It is not inconceivable that the "lodi commune" underlie Milton's description of Benedetto in the letter as entering upon a *commune ... iter ad laudem*, as the aptly Latinized Benedictus is perhaps punningly equated with good speech itself, and more generally with forms of praise that may be bestowed upon language. Here *laus* and *commune ... iter* may evoke the eponymous "lodi" that his work confers upon the Tuscan tongue, and may verbally echo the subdivision "lodi commune." Certainly Milton's concluding reconciliation between Tuscan and Latin, the latter of which is depicted as the mother coming to the rescue of her daughter, is in accordance with Buonmattei's constant emphasis in the *Delle Lodi* of the essential Latinity of Tuscan: "tutte [parole] riceveron il principio dalla Latina, o la materia, o la forma."[122] It is an emphasis that also shines through his *Della Lingua Toscana*, in such comments as: "la lingua nostra, quanto al corpo natural delle sue parole ricevè i suo' primi principi dalla latina."[123]

Milton's already noted allusion to Dante in the letter, signaled by an emphatically relevant demonstrative pronoun (*illum Dantem*), undoubtedly reflects his knowledge of the fact that Buonmattei was, in the words of Vitale, "studioso di Dante."[124] Buonmattei's Dantesque

---

[119] *Il Trattato della Pronunzia*, 136.

[120] Cinquemani, *Glad to Go for a Feast*, 13, regards this as "a work that Milton might have seen."

[121] Cf. Cinquemani, *Glad to Go For a Feast*, 13-15.

[122] Cinquemani, *Glad to Go For a Feast*, 15.

[123] *La Lingua Toscana*, 4.

[124] Vitale, *La Questione della Lingua*, 174. See in general, Cinquemani, *Glad to Go For a Feast*, 117-162.

interests, which were already apparent in his series of lectures to which the whole of the Apatisti had flocked,[125] had in fact reached something of a peak in 1638, the year of the publication of his *Division Morale dell'Inferno di Dante*. This in turn would be followed (in 1640) by the *Division Morale del Purgatorio di Dante*.[126] Finally, Milton's recourse to the metaphor of feasting (*commessatum ire*) and drinking (*madidus ... poculis maioribus prolutus*) to describe his literary and linguistic pursuits is particularly apt in view of the *Cicalate* or "idle talks" characteristic of the Accademia della Crusca (and published in 1635) on such topics as whether it is more exerting to eat or to drink ("Molti a Tavola e pochi in Coro").[127]

In short, Cinquemani's conclusions are at best understated and at worst misleading. Milton's letter, far from revealing "a rather cursory reading of Buonmattei's grammar," since "perhaps in 1638-39, Milton was preoccupied by travel,"[128] suggests that the opposite of this is probably the case; that he has familiarized himself with a wide range of Buonmattei's works, and has while upon Italian soil undertaken a reading program in Tuscan probably of an extent that matches if not surpasses that which he had already completed in advance of his Italian journey.[129] For Milton (and for the letter in question) Tuscan and Latin proceed hand in hand.

---

[125] See page 107.

[126] Cinquemani, *Glad to Go For a Feast*, 29, regards both works as "of significance, perhaps, because they reflect Buonmattei's interests, and therefore possibly his conversation, during the period of Milton's visits."

[127] *Le Tre Sirocchie di Benduccio Riboboli da Mattelica* (Pisa, 1635).

[128] Cinquemani, *Glad to Go For a Feast*, 36.

[129] See page 105.

3.2 *Novae Patriae Linguae Institutiones*: Buonmattei as Quintilian

> La Gramatica è il fondamento dell' Arte Oratoria, anzi di tutte le liberali Discipline, e molte, e sublimi sono le cognizioni necessarie a chi la professa da Quintiliano minutamente annoverate, e da Benedetto Buommattei possedute.[130]

That Buonmattei was regarded as a second Quintilian is hereby attested by Casotti, who saliently points out that what unites them both is a belief in grammar as the foundation of oratory. In his letter to the Florentine grammarian Milton's use of the term *Institutiones* as a means of characterizing Buonmattei's work is doing much more than "suggesting the analogy of Quintilian,"[131] as Cinquemani puts it. Rather, through a series of hitherto unnoticed points of contact between that letter and the Proemium to Quintilian's *Institutiones*, Milton presents the Tuscan grammarian as both succeeding and surpassing his Roman predecessor.

At the beginning of the letter Buonmattei's *Institutiones* are depicted as "new" (*novae*),[132] and as a work that is carefully situated in the context of its predecessors. The Florentine is envisaged as illuminating or polishing or ordering *ab aliis quae tradita iam sunt*.[133] This dual emphasis on novelty/newness and on the relationship between Buonmattei's work and that of his predecessors provides in effect a confident response to Quintilian's hesitant comments in the Proemium. There he articulates the reasons for his initial reluctance to undertake the task of composing something on the art of speaking,[134] and contextualizes his work alongside bilingual (here Greek and Latin) accomplishment on the topic. Thus he refers to *auctores utriusque linguae clarissimos*, who have left to posterity many writings that pertain to his work.[135] He

---

[130] Casotti, *Vita di Benedetto Buommattei*, xvii.

[131] Cinquemani, *Glad to Go For a Feast*, 31: "Milton characterizes the work as ... *patriae linguae Institutiones*, suggesting the analogy of Quintilian, and implies it is incomplete."

[132] *quod novas patriae linguae Institutiones adornas*. Cf. Milton's description of his own projected work: "the industry and art I could unite to the *adorning of my native tongue*" (*Reason of Church Government* [*CM* 3, 236-237]). Italics are mine.

[133] *ut qui ab aliis quae tradita iam sunt iis aut lucem aut copiam aut certe limam atque ordinem tuo marte facile sis allaturus* (*CM* 12, 30).

[134] *ut aliquid de ratione dicendi componerem* [1.pr.1]).

[135] *auctores utriusque linguae clarissimos non ignorabam multa quae ad hoc opus pertinerent diligentissime scripta posteris reliquisse* (1.pr.1).

proceeds to concede that even if he is not to invent any *new* precepts (*ut mihi si non inveniendi nova*) but can merely add a judgment concerning the old (*at certe iudicandi de veteribus*), the effort might be a just one.[136] Buonmattei by contrast *can* invent *novae institutiones*.

The opening of Milton's letter employs a metaphor of building.[137] Thus Buonmattei is about to place the keystone on the work (*iam iam operi fastigium impositurus*).[138] The language seems both to recall and to appropriate on a positive level Quintilian's reference to other writers who expect no credit for their ability to treat of subjects that, however necessary, are far removed from display. These he compares to the pinnacles of buildings (*operum fastigia*),[139] which are visible even though the foundations remain hidden.[140]

And it is in the context of Quintilian that some light may be shed upon Milton's seemingly ignored second recommendation: his suggestion that the Florentine grammarian include in his forthcoming work a list of exemplary Tuscan authors demonstrating, respectively, the genres of tragedy, comedy, epistolography, dialogue and historiography:

> Nec illa minus, si in tanta Scriptorum turba commonstrare separatim non gravabere, quis post illos decantatos Florentinae linguae auctores poterit secundas haud iniuria sibi asserere: quis Tragoedia insignis, quis in Comoedia festivus et lepidus, quis scriptis Epistologis aut Dialogis, argutus aut gravis, quis in Historia nobilis.

---

[136] *ut mihi si non inveniendi nova at certe iudicandi de veteribus iniungere laborem non inuste viderentur* (1.pr.2).

[137] Cf. Quintilian's use of the noun *materia* as a subject opening itself to him more widely (*latius se tamen aperiente materia* [1.pr.3]). He states that he voluntarily undertook a heavier burden than that imposed on him (*plus quam imponebatur oneris sponte suscepi*). Later he proclaims that those who strive to gain the summit will make higher advances than those who sink down at the foot of the ascent (*altius tamen ibunt qui ad summa nitentur quam qui praesumpta desperatione quo velint evadendi protinus circa ima substiterint* [1.pr.20]).

[138] *Fastigium* can also mean "the most important part; chief point" (*OLD*, sv 5). Cf. Quint., *Inst. Or.* 12.1.20: *stetisse ipsum in fastigio eloquentiae fateor*.

[139] Cf. *OLD*: *fastigium*, sv 4: "the roof or top of any erection."

[140] Quintilian, *Inst. Or.* 1.pr.4: *nullam ingenii sperantes gratiam circa res etiamsi necessarias, procul tamen ab ostentatione positas, ut operum fastigia spectantur, latent fundamenta.* Stating that there is no possibility of reaching the summit without previous efforts (*nec ad ullius rei summam nisi praecedentibus initiis perveniri*), he announces that he will not shrink from stooping to lesser matters, the neglect of which leaves no place for greater (*ad minora illa ... demittere me non recusabo* [1.pr.5]).

Cinquemani correctly observes that "no document answering Milton's second request seems to exist."[141] That Buonmattei did not incorporate this suggestion is likewise noted by Lewalski,[142] and Campbell and Corns.[143] But the potential inspiration for the request has remained unidentified and hence unstudied. Given Milton's presentation of Buonmattei as a second Quintilian, it is worth noting that such a list of exemplary authors is quite precisely articulated in *Institutiones Oratoriae* 10.1. 37ff. Here in answer to the *expectation* that he should recommend the authors who should be read and the peculiar virtue of each (*qui sint legendi, quae in auctore quoque praecipua virtus* [37]) Quintilian offers a subjective overview of Greek and Roman writers, prefacing his own comments with diverse opinions regarding each (44).[144] In all of this he stresses that reading these authors can only enhance linguistic attainment (44).[145] Beginning with Homer (46), he bestows extravagant praise upon his work. Hesiod by contrast he regards as rarely rising above the general level (52). Theocritus he considers admirable yet somewhat insular in his rustic and pastoral muse (55), whereas in terms of elegy Callimachus is *princeps* (58). Among the lyric poets Pindar is eminent in his nobility of speech, grandeur of thought, beauty of figure, and exuberance of matter and words (61). Interesting too is Quintilian's subsequent generic categorization of exemplary authors of comedy, tragedy, historiography, and oratory (an approach precisely advocated by Milton to Buonmattei). Thus he singles out Old Comedy as retaining the pure grace of Attic diction (65), highlighting Aeschylus as the first to introduce tragedy (66), and praising Sophocles and Euripides for shedding greater illumination (67). In regard to historiography, Thucydides and Herodotus assume pride of place (73); in terms of oratory, Demosthenes is the most eminent (76), and philosophy's greatest exemplar is Plato (81). Turning to Latin literature, he recommends the poetry of Virgil, which approximates that of Homer (85), and also discusses Macer and Lucretius (87), Ennius (88), and other writers closer to his own day (*propiores alii*) (88), Ovid (88), Cornelius Severus (89), Valerius Flaccus, Saleius Bassus and Lucan (90), Tibullus (93), the most terse and elegant of the elegists, Propertius, Ovid,

---

[141] Cinquemani, *Glad to Go For a Feast*, 36.

[142] Lewalski, *Life*, 93.

[143] Campbell and Corns, *Life, Work, and Thought*, 111.

[144] *de qua differentia disseram diligentius cum de genere dicendi quaerendum erit* (1.10.44).

[145] *a qua lectione petere possint qui confirmare facultatem dicendi volent attingam.* (1.10.44).

Gallus, Horace categorized here as a Roman lyric poet (96). In regard to historiography, he is not afraid to match Sallust against Thucydides or Livy against Herodotus (101). In oratory Cicero is presented as a match for Demosthenes (105-111).

It is tempting to suggest that this is precisely the sort of generic list that lies behind the request posited by Milton to Buonmattei—a request that asks the Florentine to single out instances of authorial pre-eminence as if in recognition of Quintilian's subjectivity. But there is of course one important difference: in this instance the list is to consist of *Tuscan* writers and genres. The recommendation can equally be viewed as presenting a rather flattering "written encomium" of its own whereby Buonmattei both here and elsewhere in the letter is seen as identifiable with, and a worthy successor to, a classical writer, whose own recently discovered *Institutiones* (by Poggio in 1416)[146] had already exerted a huge influence upon Renaissance pedagogical theory and practice. And if Milton's second recommendation was indeed ignored by the Florentine, it was taken on board and answered at least in part some four years later by the Englishman himself. In *Reason of Church Government* Milton presents an essentially generic categorization of epic, tragedy, the ode, and the hymn, along with a brief assessment of exemplary exponents of each:

> ... whether that epic form whereof the two poems of Homer and those other two of Virgil and Tasso are a diffuse, and the book of Job a brief, model ... or whether those dramatic constitutions, wherein Sophocles and Euripides reign, shall be found more doctrinal and exemplary to a nation ... Or if occasion shall lead, to imitate those magnific odes and hymns, wherein Pindarus and Callimachus are in most things worthy ...[147]

Here multicultural exemplars (Greek, Roman, biblical, Italian) are assessed in a Miltonic vernacular, a code selection informed perhaps by a context and associated readership that are essentially English.

---

[146] For the letter announcing the discovery, see William Shepherd, *The Life of Poggio Bracciolini* (Liverpool, 1802), 108.

[147] *CM* 3, 237-238.

Chapter 4

Italy, Bilingualism, and Biculturalism

Recent studies of bilingualism have emphasized that linguistic divergence frequently occurs when a speaker finds him or herself in an intercultural situation, for it is precisely in such circumstances that there arises a need to affirm cultural identity.[1] Viewed by his Italian encomiasts as the *Anglus* from a remote north,[2] Milton self-consciously transforms this concept into an imaginatively inventive defense of himself, his nation, and that nation's literary heritage. In the Latin poetry composed in the course of his Italian journey Milton's self-fashioning is frequently that of an English bird migrating from cold and blustery northern climes[3] to the sunny warmth of Italy. It emerges, however, that this is a bird that can readily acclimatize itself to its new environs, while simultaneously preserving and reinventing national and cultural identity. Apparently irreconcilable climates, diverse cultures, and different landscapes are united by shared imagery, by linguistic devices that are at times English, at times Italian, and ultimately by recourse to an ancient language that comes to function as a linguistic bridge joining the *Anglus* to his Italian addressee(s).

4.1 *Ad Salsillum*

Ad Salsillum, addressed to Giovanni Salzilli of Rome,[4] depicts "Milton, that nursling of London" (*alumnus ille Londini Milto* [9]) as leaving a "nest" (10) located in an essentially English climate. It is a

---

[1] For an overview, see Hamers and Blanc, *Bilinguality and Bilingualism*, 139.

[2] See page 99.

[3] See in general Z.S. Fink, "Milton and the Theory of Climatic Influence," *MLQ* 2 (1941), 67-80.

[4] On Salzilli, see J.A. Freeman, "Milton's Roman Connection: Giovanni Salzilli," *MS* 19 (1984), 87-104; Haan, *From Academia to Amicitia*, 81-98.

climate that is characterized by a personified wind, whose inability to control its heaving lungs and their panting blasts (11-13)[5] contrasts with the fertility of the Roman soil upon which that bird has now landed (14).[6] It also parallels the physical infection that perniciously breathes through (*spirat* [20]) the very being and body of the poem's Italian addressee.[7] The poem establishes a quasi-cultural mirror-imaging of sorts, and it does so through the theme of assuagement–of the physical, the climatic and the topographical. Milton's get-well wish to the sick (*aegrotantem*) academician is in effect a poetic token of assuagement in which the medium of Latin serves both to describe and to bridge a linguistic and cultural divide. The speaker invokes a Latin *Musa* (1-2), whose scazontic limping,[8] although in itself appropriately suggestive of Salzilli's ill health, is "less pleasing" than a dancing nymph (3-5).[9] Mock modesty serves here to camouflage a self-referential praise that is altogether fitting in a poem which is fashioned, after all, as a return compliment to an accomplished Italian poet, highly regarded among his contemporary academicians;[10] one "to whose heart" Milton's Latin poetry is "of such value,"[11] and "which he preferred undeservedly to the great gods."[12] This preference was articulated not in Italian, Salzilli's vernacular norm, but in

---

[5] *pessimus ubi ventorum,/insanientis impotensque pulmonis/pernix anhela sub Iove exercet flabra* (*Ad Sals*. 11-13).

[6] *venit feraces Itali soli ad glebas* (*Ad Sals*. 14).

[7] *cui nunc profunda bilis infestat renes,/praecordiisque fixa damnosum spirat* (*Ad Sals*. 19-20). That Salzilli recovered from the illness is attested by the existence of a letter dated 25 March/4 April 1644 addressed to him by Tomaso Stigliani. See Tomaso Stigliani, *Lettere* (Rome, 1664), 248-250.

[8] *O Musa gressum quae volens trahis claudum,/Vulcanioque tarda gaudes incessu* (*Ad Sals*. 1-2). On the poem's metrics, see S.M. Oberhelman and John Mulryan, "Milton's Use of Classical Meters in the *Sylvarum Liber*," *MP* 81 (1983), 131-145, at 137-138.

[9] *nec sentis illud in loco minus gratum,/quam cum decentes flava Dëiope suras/alternat aureum ante Iunonis lectum* (*Ad Sals*. 3-5). Cf. Virgil, *Aen*. 1.71-73.

[10] Salzilli contributed fifteen Italian poems (11 sonnets, 3 canzoni, 1 ottava) to the *Poesie de' Signori Accademici Fantastici* (Rome, 1637). As Freeman suggests ("Milton's Roman connection," 97), this quite substantial contribution (some 11% of the entire volume) indicates that he was highly esteemed by his fellow-academicians.

[11] *Comoena nostra cui tantum est cordi* (*Ad Sals*. 7). On *Camoena* as symbolizing Milton's Latin poetry, cf. Milton, *Elegia Sexta* 3-4, and Bush, *Variorum*, I, 115. See also page 83.

[12] *quamque ille magnis praetulit immerito divis* (*Ad Sals*. 8).

Latin—in one of those "written Encomiums" highlighted earlier.[13] And Milton's later plea draws an implicit equation between the envisaged assuaging (*levamen* [30]) of Salzilli's physical pain courtesy of an invoked Salus or the provision of medicinal herbs growing in an Italian landscape (27-30), and the soothing of that landscape by Salzilli's Italian verse (32).[14] This in turn will result in the calming of the swollen Tiber (*tumidus ... Tibris ... delinitus* [36]).[15]

But England and her poet are far from forgotten. The imagery expands upon the river motif central to Salzilli's *Latin* verses extolling Milton. There the rivers of Italy were said to be surpassed by an English river, the Thames. The Virgilian Mincius was enjoined to yield (1),[16] the Sebetus was to cease to babble constantly about Tasso (2).[17] The victorious Thames by contrast was to carry its waves higher than them all (*at Thamesis victor cunctis ferat altior undas* [3]). And that was something easily done because through Milton it alone was seen to be a match for all three taken together.[18] Milton's poetic response then is not without self-referential irony. The express wish that Salzilli's Tiber rein in its surging waves is potentially double-edged. On the one hand, it praises the poetic prowess of an Italian addressee, whose vernacular sonnets and canzoni (some of which seem to be echoed in Milton's poem),[19] captivate and soothe a Roman readership, and will continue to do so. On the other, the lines confer upon the Tiber a role not dissimilar to that of the rivers depicted in Salzilli's encomium as yielding to, silenced, and ultimately upstaged by the Thames—by Milton himself.[20]

---

[13] See page 96.

[14] *vicina dulci prata mulcebit cantu* (*Ad Sals.* 32).

[15] On Milton's inversion in these lines of Horace, *Odes* 1.2.13-20, see Haan, *From Academia to Amicitia*, 89-90.

[16] *cedat depressa Mincius urna* (1).

[17] *Sebetus Tassum desinat usque loqui* (2).

[18] *nam per te, Milto, par tribus unus erit* (4).

[19] See Haan, *From Academia to Amicitia*, 88-98, especially the discussion (94-97) of Salzilli's sonnet "Ricco Mercante ucciso in duello, per volersi vendicar d'una parola ingiuriosa" (*Poesie de' Signori Accademici Fantastici*, 155), in which a merchant, assisted by a tranquil wind, reaches a longed-for shore, a "native nest" ("patrio nido" [7]), only to find himself begging for death.

[20] On *Ad Salsillum* as praising itself, see also Freeman, "Milton's Roman Connection," 96.

Linguistically too the poem's *Latinitas* surprisingly transports things English to an Italian shore. It does this by virtue of a series of puns on the name *Salsillus* and *sal* ("salt"). In so doing it seems to appropriate to Italy (and to Latin verse) aspects of the Latin prose "salting," an event pertaining to an essentially English world, that of Cambridge University. In fact, as noted previously, wordplay on "salt" lay at the heart of these witty performances. Milton's sixth *Prolusion* is thus riddled with puns on salt.[21] Likewise *Ad Salsillum* (or implicitly perhaps "To the Little Salted One") punningly alludes to "the salty kingdoms" (*salsa regna* [41]) of Portumnus, Roman god of harbors. And here, as in *Prolusion* 6, Milton plays on other words beginning with *sal*, such as *Salus* (23) and *salubre* (29).[22] Implicit also is a cooking metaphor, discernible perhaps in the use of the culinary verb *condere* to describe Salzilli's poetic practices (*tam cultus ore Lesbium condis melos* [22]).[23] Metaphors of food and drink and "meals of a dinner" are characteristic of the salting,[24] notably attested by the imagery of feasting permeating Milton's *Prolusion*,[25] and reworked in the associated *At a Vacation Exercise*.[26] But the poem may also evince

---

[21] See page 89.

[22] A not dissimilar practice may underlie the predominance of "dis"- words in *Paradise Lost* 9. 6-9: " ... foul *dis*trust, and breach/*Dis*loyal on the part of man, revolt,/And *dis*obedience: on the part of heaven/Now alienated, *di*stance and *di*staste." Italics are mine. See Christopher Ricks, *Milton's Grand Style* (Oxford, 1963), 69-72; Neil Forsyth, "Of Man's First Dis," in *Milton in Italy: Contexts, Images, Contradictions*, ed. M.A. Di Cesare (Binghamton, 1991), 345-369, neither of whom, however, relate the passage to academic practice either at Cambridge or in Italy.

[23] If so, then Milton's possible pun finds a parallel in a later work: the volume celebrating members of the Venetian academy of the Incogniti: *Le Glorie degli Incogniti O vero Gli Huomini Illustri dell' Accademia de' Signori Incogniti di Venetia* (Venice, 1647), 66, sv Anton Giulio Brignole Sale Genovese: SAL *erit insulsum, salibus nisi* condiat *illud/hic Ligur, ex ipso qui* SALE *nomen habet*. Cf. Milton's letter to Charles Diodati: *Nae ipsum te nuper Salutis condum promum esse factum oportet, ita totum Salubritatis penum dilapidas* (CM 12, 22).

[24] Hale, *Milton's Cambridge Latin*, 200.

[25] Cf. *ecce convivium vobis apparatum! Ecce mensas ad luxum Persicum exstructas* (*Prol.* 8); *iam vero libere et genialiter epulamini* (*Prol.* 10); *quaeso vos, quibus palato sunt, comissamini. Verum hariolor dicturos vos, epulas hasce (veluti nocturnae illae dapes quae a Daemone veneficis apparantur) nullo condiri sale* (*Prol.* 14).

[26] Hence "The daintiest dishes shall be served up last" (*At a Vacation Exercise*, 14). Hale, *Milton's Cambridge Latin*, 215, notes that "this continues the metaphor of 'dishes' of a long banquet, but applies it no longer to members of the audience but to his own offering."

bilingual visual word recognition. Dijstra has wondered "whether [for the bilingual] lexical candidates from different languages that share their script are activated when a letter string is present," citing as an example: "is the Dutch word VORK activated on presentation of the English word PORK?").[27] Lines 4-5 may contain a possible word wrap: suraS/ALTernat, resulting if so in an ingeniously concealed macaronic pun on the English word "salt" and the Latin word *sal*, the first syllable of the addressee's name (41). Milton may also play on the letter string exemplified by the final two syllables of *SalSILLE* in such phrases as *sentiS ILLud* (3), *ILLE* (8), *alumnuS ILLe* (9) and *sic ILLE* (31). The latter example may constitute a very apt macaronic pun on *SIC* and "SICK." In all of this it could be argued that Milton hereby exemplifies interlingual flexibility, "the bilingual's ability to manipulate the two languages [Latin and English] simultaneously."[28] It is tempting to suggest that Milton during one or both of his sojourns in Rome had already familiarized Salzilli with the *Prolusion* itself either informally or in a more formal academic context. It is not inconceivable moreover that the river metaphor permeating the final lines of *Ad Salsillum* reworks in an inverted form the conclusion (91-100) of "At a Vacation Exercise," in which a whole catalogue of rivers (probably a punning allusion to a Cambridge academic named Rivers)[29] is enjoined to "arise."[30] In short *Ad Salsillum* uniquely transposes a Cambridge academic setting to Italy, to Rome, and possibly to an Italian academy itself: the *Accademia dei Fantastici* of which Salzilli was a member. By the end that self-consciously limping Latin *Musa* (1) has served paradoxically both to differentiate between and to unite two countries (England and Italy), two academic communities (Cambridge and Rome), two languages (Latin and the vernacular), and the two "Johns" of the piece, aptly juxtaposed in the heading of Salzilli's tribute: *Ad Ioannem Miltonem Anglum ... Epigramma Ioannis Salsilli Romani*.

---

[27] Dijkstra, "Bilingual Visual Word Recognition and Lexical Access," 180.

[28] Hamers and Blanc, *Bilinguality and Bilingualism*, 19.

[29] Cf. Hale, *Milton's Cambridge Latin*, 218.

[30] "Rivers arise; whether thou be the son,/Of utmost Tweed, or Ouse, or gulphy Dun,/Or Trent, who like some earth-born giant spreads/His thirty arms along the indented meads,/Or sullen Mole that runneth underneath,/Or Severn swift, guilty of maiden's death,/Or rocky Avon, or of sedgy Lee,/Or coaly Tyne, or ancient hollowed Dee,/Or Humber loud that keeps the Scythian's name,/Or Medway smooth, or royal towered Thame" (*At a Vacation Exercise*, 91-100).

4.2 *Mansus*

Something of a similar paradox underlies *Mansus* addressed to the Neapolitan poet and patron Giovanni Battista Manso, founder of the Accademia degli Oziosi.[31] Here Milton's avian self-fashioning is couched in language of alterity. He is the "young foreigner sent from the Hyperborean skies" (26);[32] his poetry constitutes a *longinqua ... musa* (27), which despite being nurtured with some difficulty beneath the frozen Bear, has ventured to wing its way (*volitare*) through the cities of Italy (27-29).[33] The imagery is suggestive of a young fledgling, improperly nourished in an icy climate, leaving its snug nest before it has reached maturity, and undertaking a flight that is motivated by a quasi-Pegasean daring (and perhaps even an Icarian rashness?).[34] But if this bird will ultimately find cultural and intellectual nourishment in Italy, it has in fact left behind a flock of already nourished birds. In lines characterized by a sense of national pride the speaker proclaims what is in effect a defense of English poetry: he too has heard swans/poets[35] singing upon the Thames (30-33).[36] The analogy with the swan is significant, as is that culturally self-conscious *nos etiam* governing *cygnos/credimus ... sensisse* (30-31). Discussion of the swan was among topics debated by the

---

[31] On the Accademia degli Oziosi, see Haan, *From Academia to Amicitia*, 118-129.

[32] *missus Hyperboreo iuvenis peregrinus ab axe* (*Mansus* 26).

[33] *nec tu longinquam bonus aspernabere musam,/quae nuper gelida vix enutrita sub Arcto/imprudens Italas ausa est volitare per urbes* (*Mansus* 27-29).

[34] Cf. Milton, *Epistolae Familiares* 7 (addressed to Charles Diodati and datable to the autumn of 1637) in which his assertive proclamation *volare meditor* is qualified by *sed tenellis admodum adhuc pennis evehit se noster Pegasus* (*CM* 12, 26). See Haan, *From Academia to Amicitia*, 1-2.

[35] On the analogy between the poet and the swan in classical and neo-Latin poetry, cf., for example, Horace, *Odes* 2.20; John Leland, *Synchrisis Cygnorum et Poetarum* and *Cygnea Cantio*. See in general Estelle Haan, "John Milton Among The Neo-Latinists: Three Notes on *Mansus*," *N&Q* 22.2 (June, 1997), 172-176, at 173-174; Haan, *From Academia to Amicitia*, 165-178.

[36] *nos etiam in nostro modulantes flumine cygnos/credimus obscuras noctis sensisse per umbras,/qua Thamesis late puris argenteus urnis/oceani glaucos perfundit gurgite crines* (*Mansus* 30-33). On poets as swans on the Thames, cf. Spenser, *Prothalamion* 11: "Along the shoare of silver streaming Themmes"; 37-38: "with that I saw two Swannes of goodly hewe/Come softly swimming downe the Lee." Cf. Ben Jonson, viii. 392 (of Shakespeare): "Sweet Swan of Avon! What a sight it were/To see thee in our waters yet appeare,/And make those flights upon the bankes of Thames,/That did so take Eliza, and our James!"

Accademia degli Oziosi during Manso's lifetime,[37] while its members were frequently depicted as swans. The latter point is attested by a series of Italian encomia addressed to Manso and appended to the latter's *Poesie Nomiche* (Venice, 1635), a volume that Manso in all likelihood gifted to Milton himself.[38] Here Neapolitan academicians are described as "a band of swans unique and rare in song,"[39] while one aspiring member longs to "sing as a swan upon the waves."[40] But England has swans of her own. Milton proceeds to state that even Tityrus once visited Italy (34),[41] almost certainly an allusion to Chaucer (via Spenser).[42] Indeed by the end of *Mansus*, it could be argued, one of the speaker's multiple stances is pseudo-Chaucerian: he will ascend, not unlike Troilus,[43] to a Christian Heaven (95-98), from which he will both applaud himself and smile upon the world he has relinquished in death (98-100).[44] The poem's pagan *Latinitas* is subverted by its concluding engagement with a vernacular intertext.

---

[37] Thus the academy considered such intellectually challenging questions as: "Why does the dying swan sing?" (Giuseppe Battista, *Le Giornate Accademiche* [Venice, 1673], pt 3, 170); "Why does Horace call swans *purpurei*?" (*Le Giornate*, 182). Indeed Horace in *Odes* 2.20 had created an analogy between the poet and the swan, and had linked both to the theme of immortality.

[38] See Michele De Filippis, "Milton and Manso: Cups or Books?" *PMLA* 51 (1936), 745-756; D.C. Dorian, "Milton's *Epitaphium Damonis*, lines 181-197," *PMLA* 54 (1939), 612-613. Haan, *From Academia to Amicitia*, 119-120.

[39] "schiera di Cigni al canto unica e rara" (Ferrante Rovitto, "Poesie Diversi a Gio. Battista Manso," appended to Manso, *Poesie Nomiche* [Venice, 1635], 288).

[40] "potrò cantar anch'io Cigno su l'onde" (Gio. Camillo Cacace, *Poesie Nomiche*, 274). The Accademia degli Oziosi was even symbolized by a bird: its *impresa* consisting of an eagle sitting upon a hill with its gaze focused directly upon the sun, accompanied by the motto: *non pigra quies*. See Maylender, *Storia*, IV, 183.

[41] *quin et in has quondam pervenit Tityrus oras* (*Mansus* 34).

[42] Spenser uses the name Tityrus for Chaucer at *The Shepheardes Calender*, *Februarie* 92, *June* 81 and *December* 4. On Milton and Chaucer, see pages 71-75.

[43] Cf. Chaucer, *Troilus and Criseyde* 5.1807-1827, especially 1821-1822: "And in hymself he lough right at the wo/Of hem that wepten for his deth so faste."

[44] *et tota mente serenum/ridens purpureo suffundar lumine vultus/et simul aethereo plaudam mihi laetus Olympo* (*Mansus* 98-100).

4.2.1 Balanced Biculturalism in *Mansus*: Milton and Marino

The poem's conclusion is also couched in an irony that is quasi-Italian in essence. The Miltonic smile from heaven (*ridens* [99]) finds a parallel in an earlier smile in *Mansus*—that of Giambattista Marino (the "poet of the marvelous")[45]—a smile (*arridentem* [16]) from a Neapolitan bronze statue,[46] which Manso in his *pietas* (15) had erected posthumously in the Italian poet's honor. And the parallel is particularly pertinent in a piece that, it could be argued, is strikingly marinesque at times. On the one hand the speaker seems to acknowledge certain characteristic features of Marinism[47] (hence Marino is both *dulciloquus* [9] and *mollis* [12]) and of Marino's *L'Adone* (1623) (*dum canit Assyrios divum prolixus amores* [11]), a lengthy (hence *prolixus* [11]) rendering (over 5,000 octavos in ottava rima) of the Venus and Adonis myth. On the other hand, at certain points *Mansus* itself may be seen to replicate in Latin some of the excessive conceits inherent in Marinism—its keen wit and acuity ("arguzia"), its recourse to pungent statement ("concetto"), the associated element of wonder and surprise ("meraviglia"),[48] its rhetorical tropes, its abundant use of word play—all evocative of a vernacular movement inaugurated by a poet who could "manipulate words as though they were bits of mosaic or musical notes."[49] Something rather similar is evident in Milton's poem: in, for example, a series of possible anagrams (*Manse tuae* [1]/*mansueti* [60]; *Manse* [1]/*manes* [15]); quasi-baroque word play[50] (*mansueti* [60]/Manso;[51] *habitasse* [54]/Tasso); the frequent

---

[45] See J.V. Mirollo, *The Poet of the Marvelous: Giambattista Marino* (New York, 1963).

[46] *vidimus arridentem operoso ex aere poetam* (*Mansus* 16).

[47] On Marinism, see, among others, Guglielmo Damiani, *Sopra La Poesia del Cavalier Marino* (Turin, 1899); Henrico Canevari, *Lo Stile del Marino nell'Adone* (Pavia, 1901); Francesco Croce, "Nuovi Compiti della Critica del Marino e del Marinismo," *Rassegna della Letteratura Italiana* 61 (1957), 459-473; Mirollo, *The Poet of the Marvelous*, especially 115-120.

[48] See Mirollo, *The Poet of the Marvelous*, 116-118.

[49] Mirollo, *The Poet of the Marvelous*, 132.

[50] Cf. Mirollo, *The Poet of the Marvelous*, 137.

[51] This marinesque inclination toward word play on Manso's name (and formal title) also underlies some of the Italian tributes in his honor. This is most clearly illustrated by a poem entitled "Lodi espresse nel nome" by Gennaro Grossi: "La *MAN SO*vrana, onde'l Monarca Hispano/Debellò più d'un campo, e più d'un mostro,/Voli' hai,

employment of the alliterative initial M (*Manse* [1 and 2]; *Mecaenatis* [4]; *mox ... Musa Marinum* [9]; *mollis* [12]; *manes* [15]; *Minervae* [21] *Mycalen* [22]);[52] keen wit in, for example, the potential allusion to Manso's wig (*nondum deciduos servans tibi frontis honores* [76]);[53] the evocation of the stupefying effect (*stupefecit* [12]) of the marinesque upon its audience.[54] As Mirollo states, "Meraviglia is most often discussed in terms of a response aroused in the reader by a *concetto*, a poem, a painting, a statue etc."[55] This element of wonder combined with the essentially sonorous power of the marinesque (*sentit solitas ... silvas* [67]) give birth to an associated "newness" ("novità"),[56] which is reflected in the Orphic power of "new poetry/song" *mulcenturque novo maculosi carmine lynces* [69]), in a surprisingly jingling and somewhat jarring juxtaposition (*ergo ego* [24]) or even perhaps in the virtual assimilation of an Italian vernacular "totalmente" in the Latin ablative phrase *tota mente* (98).

Signor, da ogni tenzon lontano/Solitaria à trattar penna, ed inchiostro" (1-4); "Di tue glorie il gran *MAR, CHE SE*mpre nove/Piaggie, e Reggie circonda, adduce al Mondo/Te *DI VILLA*, e Cittade, hor Pane, hor Giove" (12-14) (*Poesie Nomiche*, 277). The same device is used by Margherita Sarrocchi, who proclaims: "Già mira in te risorti il secol nostro/Gli antichi honori, e'l tuo gran nome adita/Di Virtù *MAN SO*vrana altero mostro" (12-14) (*Poesie Nomiche*, 303). See Haan, *From Academia to Amicitia*, 145-146.

[52] For marinesque alliteration, cf. Marino, *Lira* I: "Un vago vezzo di vermiglie rose."

[53] Masson, *Poetical Works*, III, 535, cites evidence from the *Pinacotheca* of a certain Janus Nicius Erythraeus that Manso wore a wig, which he would good-humoredly remove upon request: " ... and, as is the fashion in the club-meetings of the Blessed Virgin, in which he was ranked as one of the members (*ut mos est in sodalitiis B. Virginis, in quibus ille numerabatur*), he would good-humoredly bear to have his defects publicly exposed. If bid lick the ground with his mouth, or kiss the feet of his club-fellows, he would not refuse, or escape the authority of the master of the revels; nor was he less obedient if he were ordered to snatch from his head the periwig with which he concealed his baldness (*caliendrum e capite quo calvitiem occultabat*), but immediately did as he was ordered, and made no scruple about exhibiting, amid the great laughter of the beholders, his perfectly bald head (*neque dubitabat, magno intuentium cum risu, caput pilis nudum ostendere*)."

[54] *mollis et Ausonias stupefecit carmine nymphas* (*Mansus* 12).

[55] Mirollo, *The Poet of the Marvelous*, 117.

[56] Cf. Mirollo, *The Poet of the Marvelous*, 119: "NOVITÀ: freshness, newness, novelty, innovation; and since nuovo also connotes the extraordinary and the surprising, novità is usually very close to meraviglia."

Mansus moreover presents a speaker whose aspirations, both poetic and autobiographical, mirror and surpass the realities of iconographical and literary commemoration enjoyed by Marino thanks to his patron and biographer, Manso himself. Thus just as the dying Marino[57] entrusted his bones and final wishes to Manso alone (*ille itidem moriens tibi soli debita vates/ossa tibi soli, supremaque vota reliquit* [13-14]), a bequeath fulfilled by the erection of the statue in question, so Milton expresses the wish for such a friend (*o mihi si mea sors talem concedat amicum* [78]) who knows so well how to adorn poets, for one who might tearfully stand at his deathbed, take his body into his care, place his ashes in an urn, and perhaps even fashion his image in marble:

> Tandem ubi non tacitae permensus tempora vitae,
> Annorumque satur cineri sua iura relinquam,
> Ille mihi lecto madidis adstaret ocellis
> Adstanti sat erit si dicam "sim tibi curae";
> Ille meos artus liventi morte solutos
> Curaret parva componi molliter urna.
> Forsitan et nostros ducat de marmore vultus,
> Nectens aut Paphia myrti aut Parnasside lauri
> Fronde comas, at ego secura pace quiescam. (*Mansus* 85-93)

Here, as if in a transposition of the Oziosi's motto *non pigra quies*, the speaker seals, as it were, his own RIP. In imagining his life's end, he describes that *vita* retrospectively as *non tacita* (85). The envisaged absence of silence here is quite telling, suggestive perhaps of a Miltonic quest for a biographer, for a second Manso, who, as stated earlier in the poem (20-21), had written lives of both Tasso and Marino,[58] thereby rivaling Herodotus (22-23). And might the phrase punningly allude to Tacitus, the Roman historian and biographer, author of annals, histories and among others the *De Vita et Moribus Iulii Agricolae*? Is Milton's special request necessary because he fears that his life will *not* be immortalized in a quasi-Tacitean biography? Whether or not this is the case, the imagined iconographical commemoration of his deceased self is conveyed in language reminiscent of Anchises's jubilant prediction of the

---

[57] Marino was appointed president of the Accademia degli Oziosi in 1624 (the appointment was not without controversy. See Meylender, *Storia* IV, 187), a post to which Manso succeeded upon Marino's death in 1625.

[58] *amborum genus et varia sub sorte peractam/describis vitam, moresque, et dona Minervae* (20-21). Manso's biography of Tasso (*Vita di Torquato Tasso*) was published in Venice in 1621; his MS biography of Marino is not extant. See Michele Manfredi, *Giovanni Battista Manso nella Vita e nelle Opere* (Naples, 1919), 259. Manso also assisted Francesco Loredano in his *Vita del Cavalier Marino* (Venice, 1633).

advancement and development of Roman craftsmanship and art (*excudent alii spirantia mollius aera/(credo equidem), vivos ducent de marmore vultus* [*Aen.* 6.846-847]). But there is one notable difference. In Milton's case bronze is discarded in favor of marble alone in a stunningly grandiose poetic self-fashioning evocative perhaps of the Horatian "monument" that can outlive bronze (*exegi monumentum aere perennius* [*Odes* 3.30.1]). As in Horace, the Miltonic monument, the Miltonic moment is ultimately the poetic creation. Its bard is now garlanded with a wreath—either a myrtle-wreath evocative of Venus[59] or a laurel-wreath representative of Apollo, god of poetry, or perhaps the mighty Tasso himself.

4.2.2 Bicultural Assimilation in *Mansus*: Milton and Tasso

> Ad quem Torquati Tassi dialogus extat de amicitia scriptus;[60] erat enim Tassi amicissimus; ab quo etiam inter Campaniae principes celebratur, in illo poemate cui titulus *Gerusalemme conquistata*, lib 20.
>
> Fra cavalier magnanimi, e cortesi
> Risplende il Manso — [61]

At the heart of *Mansus* lies a bicultural assimilation achieved via a series of potential equations between the speaker and Tasso who, like Marino, had enjoyed Manso's friendship, patronage and the fruits attendant upon biographical legacy. As I have argued elsewhere, Milton appropriates to his autobiographical self-fashioning scenes and language reminiscent of Tasso's life (perhaps as depicted in Manso's *Vita di Torquato Tasso* [Venice, 1621]),[62] by confident articulation of a projected epic subject, and by recourse to mythological allegory.

---

[59] Venus and Paphos are likewise associated in *Elegia Prima* 84. On the myrtle's links with Venus, cf. Virgil, *Ecl.* 7.62 and further examples cited at Bush, *Variorum*, I, 281.

[60] The full title of Tasso's Dialogue is *Il Manso, overe Dell' Amicitia Dialogo del Sig. Torquato Tasso al Molte Illustre Sig. Giovanni Battista Manso* (Naples, 1596). Prefixed to the work are a dedication and five sonnets from Tasso to Manso.

[61] Headnote to *Mansus*. Milton cites only the relevant lines. The entire canto (20: 142) is as follows: "e di Circello e d' Ansa altri marchesi,/e'l figlio, indegno di fortuna avversa,/gli animi avranno al vero onore accesi,/e'l conte di Loreto, e quel d'Anversa./Fra' cavalier magnanimi e cortesi/risplende il Manso, e doni e raggi ei versa./Ma cieco oblio giá non asconde e copre/del buon duca di Sora il nome e l'opre." Text is that of Tasso, *Gerusalemme Conquistata* (Rome, 1593).

[62] See Haan, *From Academia to Amicitia*, 179-184.

The prose *argumentum* to *Mansus* signals the relationship between Manso and Tasso by highlighting three facts: that Tasso addressed his *Dialogue on Friendship* to Manso; that Manso was a great friend of Tasso, and that in the *Gerusalemme Conquistata*[63] Tasso actually praised Manso by name.[64] These are precisely the points singled out in the opening pages of Manso's *Vita*. There Manso is described as "a close friend of Tasso, as is attested by his verse and prose in many passages and especially the *Gerusalemme* and the *Dialogue on Friendship* which he entitled *Il Manso*...."[65] Elsewhere in the work Manso describes the nature of a friendship,[66] whose sacred laws Tasso observed[67] and exemplified by his deeds, and also by his *Dialogue* on the subject. He was in short a "fidelissimo amico."[68] The theme of *amicitia* is central to *Mansus*, with the noun *amicus* occurring on no fewer than three specific occasions and in the context of three different friendships: line 15 (Manso and Marino), line 63 (Chiron and Apollo), and finally line 78. The context of this last occurrence is that of a projected national epic, an *Arthuriad*:[69]

> O mihi si mea sors talem concedat amicum
> Phoebaeos decorasse viros qui tam bene norit,
> Si quando indigenas revocabo in carmina reges,

---

[63] Cf. Angelita Scaramuzza, "Il Loda nelle lodi del Tasso, e del Marino," *Poesie Nomiche*, 300: "Voi protettor de l'alta, che Buglione/Tromba cantò con celebrato grido," an allusion to the *Gerusalemme Liberata*, the hero of which was Godfrey of Bouillon (hence "Buglione" [9]). For parallels between Scaramuzza's poem and *Mansus*, see Haan, *From Academia to Amicitia*, 141-143.

[64] The latter point is highlighted in the poem proper (*et aeternis inscripsit nomina chartis* [8]). The theme also occurs in one of Tasso's tributes to Manso, in which he states that Manso's name is inscribed by the gods not only in one thousand pages, but also in beautiful metal or in stone ("E'l il nome vostro in bel metallo, o in pietra/Scriver si dee, non solo in mille carte." [*Poesie Nomiche*, 257]).

[65] "stretto amico del Tasso, come i suoi versi, e le prose in molti luoghi, e spetialmente la *Gerusalemme*, e'l *Dialogo dell' Amicitia*, ch' egli intitolò *il Manso*, feciono fede ..." (Manso, *Vita di Torquato Tasso*, 4).

[66] Thus the very title of Tasso's *Dialogue*: *Il Manso overe Dell' Amicitia Dialogo* is seen to reflect "quasi per forma della vera amicitia, ch'haveva in lui per molti anni e per molte pruove fedelissima sperimentata" (Manso, *Vita di Torquato Tasso*, 210).

[67] Manso, *Vita di Torquato Tasso*, 243: "Quindi è ch'egli fù così leale osservatore delle sacre leggi dell' Amicitia."

[68] Manso, *Vita di Torquato Tasso*, 243.

[69] Cf. *Epitaphium Damonis* 162-171.

> Arturumque etiam sub terris bella moventem;
> Aut dicam invictae sociali foedere mensae,
> Magnanimos heroas, et (O modo spiritus adsit)
> Frangam Saxonicas Britonum sub Marte phalanges. (*Mansus* 78-84)

Friendship, patronage and epic are interrelated here. The *amicus* is unnamed because this is an imaginary friend. The Miltonic quest for *amicitia* is inextricably linked to a quasi-Italian quest for patronage, for a prototype of Manso who knows how to adorn poets (*Phoebaeos decorasse viros* [79]) or, more specifically, how to "decorate" and immortalize a future epic bard. *Decorasse* recalls the etymologically related noun *decus* attributed earlier in the poem to Tasso himself (*Torquati decus, et nomen* 50]).[70] And it is hardly without significance that the ensuing lines should combine the bellicose and the chivalric in a Tasso-like way. The projected epic's theme (epitomized here by *indigenas ... reges* [80], the Knights of the Round Table, and the military exploits of King Arthur leading British resistance to Germanic invaders) conforms, as Bush has noted,[71] to the principle established by Renaissance epic theory and practice that the heroic poet (of which Tasso and Ariosto were acclaimed the prime exemplars) should deal with the early history or legends of one's country. *Mansus* thus articulates a confident aspiration, which highlights the element of daring possessed by the speaker,[72] and proclaims itself in forcefully consonantal Latin.[73] It is an advertisement for a projected epic voiced by an English poet to his Italian addressee; by a *Miltonus Anglus* in Italy both asserting and interrogating poetic, national and cultural identities, viewing them through an Italian lens, and assimilating aspects of Tasso's biography to his own poetic autobiography.

Just three years later in *Reason of Church Government* Milton would discuss "that Epick form whereof the two poems of Homer, and

---

[70] Both the *Vita* and *Mansus* emphasize the immortality that poetry may confer upon its subject. Thus Milton had confidently predicted an *iter immortale* (53) for Manso himself wherever the glory and mighty name of Tasso are celebrated throughout the world: *quacumque per orbem/Torquati decus et nomen celebrabitur ingens* (*Mansus* 49-50). A similar point was made in the introduction of the *Vita*: Tasso's fame is not confined to Italy, but is celebrated through "tutto' il mondo" (Manso, *Vita di Torquato Tasso*, 1-2).

[71] Bush, *Variorum*, I, 279.

[72] Cf. [*musa*] ... *quae ... Italas ausa est volitare per urbes* (*Mansus* 27-29).

[73] E.M.W. Tillyard, *Milton* (New York, 1966), 91, states: "There is great power in the crash of *frangam* after the hushed parenthesis of *O modo spiritus adsit*."

those other two of Virgil and Tasso are a diffuse, and the book of Job a brief model,"[74] proceeding to declare:

> And as Tasso gave to a Prince of Italy his chois whether he would command him to write of Godfreys expedition against the infidels, or Belisarius against the Gothes, or Charlemain against the Lombards; if to the instinct of nature and the imboldning of art ought may be trusted, and that there be nothing advers in our climat, or the fate of this age, it haply would be no rashnesse from an equal diligence and inclination to present the like offer in our own ancient stories (*Reason of Church Government*).[75]

Bicultural assimilation is once again envisaged as an artistic possibility. The Italian poet, his methodology, his subject matter can be mirrored in an English world.

4.3   *Thuscus Tu Quoque*: Bicultural Identities in *Epitaphium Damonis*

If Milton's Italian experience facilitated a twofold assimilation and interrogation of culture (both Italian and English) and language (both Tuscan and Latin) it was an experience that was not confined to 1638-9. Although it was in the course of his Grand Tour that he received news of the death of Charles Diodati, his closest friend since boyhood,[76] *Epitaphium Damonis*, his poignant pastoral lament on that death, was composed only upon his return to England, or, as the headnote puts it: *domum postea reversus et rem ita esse comperto, se, suamque solitudinem hoc carmine deplorat*. But despite or maybe because of the "domesticity" surrounding its composition, the piece is deeply rooted in things Italian. This manifests itself in a variety of ways not least through the juxtaposition of both speaker and lamented subject as if in a mirror-image of the Anglo-Italian identity of the London Diodati clan[77] and indeed of John Milton

---

[74] *CM* 3, 237. See page 118.

[75] *CM* 3, 237.

[76] Charles Diodati died in London and was buried on 27 August 1638. For critical interrogation as to when and where Milton may have been informed of Diodati's death, see J.T. Shawcross, "*Epitaphium Damonis*: lines 9-13 and the Date of Composition," *MLN* 71 (1956), 322-324; W.R. Parker, "Milton and the News of Charles Diodati's Death," *MLN* 72 (1957), 486-488; Rose Clavering and J.T. Shawcross, "Milton's European Itinerary and His Return Home," *SEL* 5 (1965), 49-59; Sergio Baldi, "The Date of Composition of *Epitaphium Damonis*," *N&Q* 25 (1978), 508-509.

[77] See Dorian, *The English Diodatis*, passim.

while upon Italian soil. For, as the headnote states, Charles was descended on his father's side from the Tuscan city of Lucca, but was in every other respect an Englishman: *Carolus Deodatus ex urbe Hetruriae Luca paterno genere oriundus, caetera Anglus.* The poem thus constitutes the commemoration of an *Anglus* who was also a Tuscan (*Thuscus tu quoque Damon/antiqua genus unde petis Lucumonis ab urbe* [127-128])—a commemoration by a speaker for whom "Italy and Diodati are indissolubly linked together."[78] One might add moreover that Milton's self-fashioning in the poem is similarly twofold: at times he is the *Anglus*, an Englishman proclaiming a national identity, cherishing memories of an English landscape, announcing a projected national epic on King Arthur, and heralding his assumption of the vernacular henceforth; at others, he is, as it were, *Thuscus ... quoque*: quasi-Italian in his re-creation in verse of his travels to Rome and Florence, in his re-enactment via pastoral allegory of his Florentine academic experiences and the associated acclaim which he received there, and in his ekphrastic description of two "cups" or books (of Italian verse and prose) gifted to him by the Neapolitan Manso.[79] As ever the choice of linguistic medium (Latin) serves as a crucial means of communication between, and unification of, two cultures.

Communication works on another level also. That Milton had the poem printed separately probably for the purpose of sending to his erstwhile fellow-academicians in Florence is attested by Bradner's discovery in the British Museum of an anonymous separately printed edition (c. 1640).[80] Milton's letter to Carlo Dati (1647) indicates that he had sent this to the Florentine academy. Composed in response to a now lost communication from the Florentine, the letter reveals that the poem did reach Italy (*siquidem ad vos carmen illud pervenit, quod ex te nunc primum audio*),[81] and draws attention to the piece's "emblematic" section on the academies themselves (*amoris autem adversum vos mei ... testimonium haudquaquam obscurum vel illis paucis versiculis, emblematis ad morem inclusis*).[82]

That sense of interconnectedness, of communication, between two countries and two cultures serves to unite the piece in several ways. The

---

[78] Bush, *Variorum*, I, 291.

[79] See page 125.

[80] BL C.57.d.48. See Leicester Bradner, "Milton's *Epitaphium Damonis*," *TLS* 18 August 1932, 581; H.F. Fletcher, "The Seventeenth-Century Separate Printing of Milton's *Epitaphium Damonis*," *JEGP* 61 (1962), 788-796.

[81] *CM* 12, 48.

[82] *CM* 12, 48.

opening lines urge that a Sicilian song be sung through London, described here as the "city of the Thames" (*dicite Sicelicum Thamesina per oppida carmen* [3]), a river later heralded as *Thamesis meus* (177). The description is fittingly evocative of *Elegia Prima* where, addressing Diodati, the speaker had rejoiced in his presence in a city washed by the flowing Thames (*me tenet urbs reflua quam Thamesis alluit unda* [*El.* 1.9]). But the allusion is not without irony. For now Miltonic presence is replaced by Miltonic absence. At the time of Diodati's death he was *not* present in London (*nec dum aderat Thyrsis* [12]), detained instead by love of the sweet muse in a very different city, Florence (*Thusca ... in urbe* [13]) as if in a bicultural appropriation and reinvention of that cross-comparison at the heart of *Elegia Prima* itself.[83] The river Thames has been replaced by the Arno and its environs, which are depicted as the speaker's essentially Tuscan *locus amoenus* (*O ego quantus eram, gelidi cum stratus ad Arni/murmura* [129-130]). Absent from the burial of his closest friend yet promising him sepulchral honors (*indeplorato non comminuere sepulchro* [28]), he questions the human cost of a self-imposed exile, a *vagus error* (113), that drove him to witness a city (Rome) itself buried (*Romam ... sepultam* [115]), an abstractly metropolitan substitute for the human burial in London that he missed.

Biculturalism is thus central to a poem about identity and the quest for, and acknowledgment of, identity—a poem about recognition and the lack of recognition, about things and people known and unknown, named and unnamed. Thus the *sine nomine virtus* (21) of a Diodati initially envisaged as bereft of celestial reward is countered by the acclaimed *nomina* (of Milton and perhaps of Diodati too)[84] that the Florentine Carlo Dati and Antonio Francini have taught their beech trees (*quin et nostra suas docuerunt nomina fagos* [136]). That name will be transformed into the *divinum nomen* (210) punningly possessed by the "god-given" *Deodatus*, envisaged in the poem's climactic lines as receiving a celestial reward. The speaker too is associated with things known and unknown: he has traveled to the unknown shores of Italy (*ignotas ... in oras* [113]); his proposed recourse to the vernacular henceforth may perhaps render him *ignotus in aevum* (173) and *inglorius* (174) as though plunged into a linguistic obscurity matching the *obscurae umbrae* (22) into which Damon is initially imagined to descend. But the poem ultimately serves to subvert these fears through imagery of resurrection and metamorphosis, through linguistic as well as celestial apotheosis, and through a marriage of things English and Italian, pagan and Christian, classical and biblical.

---

[83] See pages 58-62.

[84] See page 103.

4.3.1 A Phoenix Reborn: *Epitaphium Damonis* and "La Questione della Lingua"

> Has inter Phoenix divina avis, unica terris
> Caeruleum fulgens diversicoloribus alis
> Auroram vitreis surgentem respicit undis.
> (*Ep. Dam.* 187-189)

Damon's apotheosis is mirrored in the ekphrastic representation of the Phoenix watching the rising dawn (187-189). The phoenix as a resurrection symbol would later form the subject of one of Carlo Dati's letters (dated 19 August 1670). Dati waxes eloquently on ways in which the bird epitomizes the "risurrezione della carne."[85] Given the late date, it is hardly surprising that Dati makes no mention of *Epitaphium Damonis*, even if it is not impossible that the Miltonic passage was somewhere in the back of the Florentine's mind. Milton's lines allude in all likelihood to Manso's "La Fenice," a vernacular rendering of Claudian's *Phoenix*, placed virtually in the middle (*in medio* [185]) of the *Poesie Nomiche*.[86] But this is a bird whose resurrection is also equated with a rising vernacular.

In *Epitaphium Damonis* the change from Latin to English and from pastoral to epic is achieved through the symbol of the *fistula* or reedpipe, that will either be hung up for good or, having undergone an important metamorphosis, will utter a British theme in the English language:

> ... O mihi tum si vita supersit,
> Tu procul annosa pendebis fistula pinu
> Multum oblita mihi, aut patriis mutata camoenis[87]
> Brittonicum strides, quid enim? omnia non licet uni,
> Non sperasse uni licet omnia; mi satis ampla
> Merces, et mihi grande decus (sim ignotus in aevum
> Tum licet, externo penitusque inglorius orbi)
> Si me flava comas legat Usa, et potor Alauni,
> Vorticibusque frequens Abra, et nemus omne Treantae,
> Et Thamesis meus ante omnes, et fusca metallis
> Tamara, et extremis me discant Orcades undis. (168-178)

---

[85] See *Lettere di Carlo Roberto Dati* (Florence, 1825), 105-109, at 106.

[86] "La Fenice" occurs on pages 242-250 of a volume consisting of 333 pages in total.

[87] Lines 170-171 have received various interpretations. Mac Kellar, *The Latin Poems of John Milton*, 169, translates *patriis mutata camoenis* as "forsaking your [the pipe's] native songs," and explains in a note (347) "its paternal Muses, i.e. Latin." It is much more likely, however, that the phrase means Milton's native Muses, the English language, by which the Latin *fistula* will be transformed.

These lines seem at first glance to constitute a farewell-speech to the Latin language. Hence it might be argued that just as the poem has to break through its pagan, pastoral genre to describe the apotheosis of Diodati in a Christian Heaven, so Milton, in aiming to be an essentially national poet, must move outside the Latin world of the poem and assume the vernacular. The passage, however, ought to be read in conjunction with the following statement from *The Reason of Church Government*, in which Milton proceeds to announce that in choosing the vernacular he is following in the footsteps of Ariosto:

> These thoughts at once possess me, and these other. That if I were certain to write as men buy Leases, for three lives and downward, there ought no regard be sooner had, then to Gods glory by the honour and instruction of my country. For which cause, and not only for that I knew it would be hard to arrive at the second rank among the Latines, I apply'd my selfe to that resolution which Ariosto follow'd against the perswasions of Bembo, to fix all the industry and art I could unite to the adorning of my native tongue; not to make verbal curiosities the end, that were a toylsom vanity, but to be an interpreter and relater of the best and sagest things among mine own Citizens throughout this Iland in the mother dialect. That what the geatest and choycest wits of Athens, Rome, or modern Italy, and those Hebrews of old did for their country, I in my proportion with this over and above of being a Christian, might doe for mine: not caring to be once nam'd abroad, though perhaps I could attaine to that, but content with these British Ilands as my world ... [88]

In both passages Milton is aware that his code selection (English) will automatically mean a reduction in the extent of his audience. Where the Latin lines assume that he will remain totally unknown to readers on the continent (... *externo penitusque inglorius orbi* [174]), the English passage, although certainly aware of this possibility, articulates a slightly more optimistic aspiration "... though perhaps I could attaine to that." Both emphasize the British nature of the poet's reading public, yet where the English goes no further than mentioning "these British Ilands," the Latin lines allude to certain regions to which Milton's fame will spread (175-178). The English passage in mentioning Ariosto moves beyond the Latin poem. Indeed the reference works on both an explicit and implicit level: Milton explicitly states that he is following the precedent of this Italian poet, who ignored the dissuasions of Bembo and wrote his epic in the vernacular. Implicitly, however, he echoes features from a *Life* of Ariosto and applies them to his own personal experience. The *Life* in question is by Sir John Harington: *The Life of Ariosto briefly and Compendiously gathered out of Sundrie Italian Writers*, and was appended to Harington's translation of the *Orlando Furioso* (London,

---

[88] *CM* 3, 236-237.

1591). There is conclusive evidence that Milton was familiar with this edition.[89] The *Life* describes Ariosto's decision as follows:

> [Ariosto] determined, as it should seeme, to make some Poem, finding his strength to serve him to it, and though he could have accomplished it very wel in Latine, yet he chose rather his native tongue, either because he thought he could not attaine to the highest place of praise, the same being before occupied by diverse, and specially Virgill and Ovid, or because he found it best agreed with his matter and with the time, or because he had a desire (as most men have) to enrich their owne language with such writings, as may make it in more account with other nations: but the first of these was the true cause indeed, for when Bembo would have disswaded him from writing Italian, alledging that he should winne more praise by writing Latine: his answere was, that he had rather be one of the principal and chiefe Thuscan writers, then scarce the second or third among the Latines.[90]

Harington speaks of Ariosto's desire to "enrich [his] owne language"; Milton applies this to himself in his explicit wish for "the adorning of my native tongue." Both convey the difficulty of arriving at even second rank among "the Latines."[91] Finally, both extracts mention the Ariosto/Bembo incident, which now serves as the acknowledged model governing a Miltonic code selection.

In announcing his decision to write his magnum opus in the vernacular Milton significantly compares himself to an Italian poet. The

---

[89] In *Of Reformation* (1641) Milton offers a translation of *Orlando Furioso* 34. 72: "And to be short at last his guid him brings/Into a goodly valley, where he sees/A mighty masse of things strangely confus'd,/Things that on earth were lost, or were abus'd" (*CM* 3, 27). This is virtually identical to Harington's version: "But to be short, at last his guide him brings/Unto a goodlie vallie, where he sees,/A mightie masse of things straungely confused,/Things that on earth were lost, or were abused" (*Orlando Furioso* [London 1591], 286). For a convincing dismissal of the spurious tradition that the marginal comment "questo libro duo volte ho letto, Sept. 21, 1642" (referring to book 46) inscribed in a copy of this edition is in Milton's hand, see Roy Flannagan, "Reflections on Milton and Ariosto," *EMLS* 2.3 (1996), 4, 1-6.

[90] *Orlando Furioso*, 416-417.

[91] There is some doubt as to what period of Latin literature is represented by "the Latines." M.Y. Hughes, *John Milton: Paradise Regained, The Minor Poems and Samson Agonistes* (New York, 1937), xix-xx, suggests that Milton is referring to Renaissance Latin poets. It is equally possible, however, that he is alluding to Latin poets of the classical period. Cf. his use of the phrase in the *History of Britain*: " ... I might also produce example, as Diodorus among the Greeks, Livie and others of the Latines ... " (*CM* 10, 3).

comparison is tellingly insightful. For "la questione della lingua,"[92] itself not unconnected to the contemporary bilingualism of Italian humanists,[93] had been and continued to be the subject of endless debate in Italy for some two centuries. Literati wondered whether Renaissance Rome was in itself possessed of two languages, and if so, which was preferable. On the one hand were those who admired the polished eloquence of Cicero[94] and argued for the usefulness of Latin in all spheres of life; on the other were those whose aim it was to defend the vernacular as a sufficiently eloquent language in itself. The use of Latin was promoted by Uberto Foglietta in his *De Linguae Latinae Usu Retinendo*. On the other hand, the case for the vernacular had been expounded in such an early work as Leon Battista Alberti's *Della Famiglia* (1434). The *Proemio* to Book 3 acknowledges the fact that Latin is a very ornate language, but proceeds to remark that the same could easily be applied to Tuscan if scholars would only take pains to refine it.[95] The vernacular was further defended by Valeriano in his *Dialogo della Volgar Lingua* (1524) and by Bembo who, having been "converted," as it were, to the cause of Tuscan, and thereby contrasting with his earlier stance, published in 1525 his *Prose della Volgar Lingua*, the first book of which argues the respective cases for and against the use of Latin and Tuscan.[96] Tuscan was upheld by Sperone Speroni in his *Dialogo delle Lingue* (1543) and by Alessandro Citolini in a *Lettera in difesa della Lingua Volgare* (1540).

It was a debate that continued to flourish in seicento Italy. Milton's active participation in Italian academies such as the Florentine Svogliati

---

[92] See, among others, Thérèse Labende-Jeanroy, *La Question de la langue en Italie* (Strassburg, 1925); Vincenzo Vivaldi, *Storia della Controversie Linguistiche in Italia de Dante ai Nostri Giorni* (Catanzaro, 1925); R.A. Hall, *The Italian Questione della Lingua, An Interpretative Essay* (Chapel Hill, 1942); A.C. Baugh, *A History of the English Language* (London, 1951), 240-305; Cecil Grayson, *A Renaissance Controversy: Latin or Italian?* (Oxford, 1960); Giacomo Devoto, *The Languages of Italy* (Chicago and London, 1978), 236-257; Vitale, *La Questione della Lingua*.

[93] See Grayson, *A Renaissance Controversy*, 11.

[94] Among the main representatives of Ciceronianism were Gasparino Barzizza (1370?-1431), Poggio Bracciolini (1386-1459), Lorenzo Valla (1407?-57), and Paolo Cortesi (1465-1510).

[95] "E sia quanto dicono quella antica apresso di tutte le genti piena d'auctorità, solo perché in essa molti docti scrissero, simile certo sarà la nostra s'e docti la voranno molto con suo studio et vigilie essere elimata e polita." Text is that of *Opere Volgari di Leon Batt. Alberti* (Florence, 1843-9), II, 222.

[96] It is striking that of the four speakers, only one (Ercole Strozzi) supports Latin, whereas the other three support the vernacular.

and Apatisti would have afforded him countless opportunities to witness and participate in discussion of the relative merits of Latin and the vernacular. As Grayson remarks, "Florence was heir in a unique way to both the classical and vernacular traditions; and it was her especial function to unite and reconcile these two earlier and with greater felicity than anywhere else in Italy."[97] Likewise the importance of Milton's association with such an ardent champion of the vernacular as the Florentine Benedetto Buonmattei or potentially with the Accademia della Crusca, vociferous promoters of the Tuscan cause,[98] can hardly be emphasized enough. One question, however, remains to be asked. Do the lines in *Epitaphium Damonis* actually present an unequivocal vote in favor of the vernacular? Is that *fistula* of Latin poetry to be hung up in quasi-linguistic retirement to suffer lifelong oblivion? Or perhaps the speaker is contemplating something rather different: not an abandonment of one language, but a linguistic apotheosis that will ultimately be realized in the vernacular *Latinitas* of *Paradise Lost*.[99] Hale perceptively asks: "Is he giving up pastoral, or Latin, or both, or what? Does he really know yet? My view is that he does not, and that *that* is the point."[100] It is hardly coincidental that the Milton who publishes his collected poetry in 1645 presents himself as an essentially bilingual poet.

---

[97] Grayson, *A Renaissance Controversy*, 15.

[98] See page 108.

[99] See Chapter 6.

[100] Hale, *Milton's Languages*, 59.

Chapter 5

"Both English and Latin": The 1645 Volume

Gemelle cultu simplici gaudens liber,
    Fronde licet gemina ...   (*Ad Ioannem Rousium*, 1-2)

5.1   *Gemellus Liber*

Milton's 1645 volume of poetry[1] is a *gemellus ... liber*, a twin book. Thus is it described by its author in the opening lines of *Ad Ioannem Rousium*,[2] a neo-Latin Ode composed in 1647 and sent (along with a replacement of a lost copy of the volume) to John Rouse,[3] the Bodleian Librarian.[4] The lines are marked by their literary self-consciousness and by an interesting alertness to the material text. *Gemellus* seems to operate on two levels: this "small" book (an octavo, whose size is encapsulated in the diminutive adjective and later in the address *parve liber* [13] and *libelle* [37])[5] is bipartite, divided into two

---

[1] On the 1645 volume, see L.L. Martz, *Poet of Exile: A Study of Milton's Poetry* (New Haven, 1980), 31-59; G. H. Carrithers Jr, "*Poems* (1645): On Growing Up," *MS* 15 (1981), 161-179; C.W.R.D. Moseley, *The Poetic Birth: Milton's Poems of 1645* (Aldershot, 1991), 79-85; J.K. Hale, "Milton's Self-Presentation in Poems ... 1645," *MQ* 25.2 (1991), 37-48; S.P. Revard, *Milton and The Tangles of Neaera's Hair: The Making of the 1645 Poems* (Columbia, 1997).

[2] See S.P. Revard, "*Ad Ioannem Rousium*: Elegiac Wit and Pindaric Mode," *MS* 19 (1984), 205-226, reworked in her *Milton and the Tangles of Neaera's Hair*, 237-263; Estelle Haan, "Milton's *Ad Ioannem Rousium* and the 1645 Volume," *N&Q* 51 (2004), 356-360.

[3] On Rouse, see Ian Philip, *The Bodleian Library in the Seventeenth and Eighteenth Centuries* (Oxford, 1983), 42-44.

[4] There exists in the Bodleian Library a manuscript of the Ode (Bodleian MS Lat. Misc. d.ff but kept at Arch.F.D.38) that was pasted to the verso of the Latin title page of a copy of the 1645 volume. (8^0M.168.Art. kept at Arch.G.f.17). This may be the substitute volume sent to Rouse.

[5] T. N. Corns, "Ideology in the *Poemata* (1645)," *MS* 19 (1984), 195-203, at 195, remarks that "it is a curious volume in its context, totally distinct from all that Milton had recently committed to the press. ... It is a smallish octavo: all other Miltonic items of the period are quartos."

fairly equally balanced halves. But also, as its title page clearly advertises, this is a bilingual work: "Poems of Mr John Milton *Both English and Latin*."[6] Milton's twin book is thus a *gemellus ... liber* both structurally and linguistically.

The first half of the volume (denoted by the collective appellation "English") contains 28 poems;[7] the second half (denoted by the collective appellation "Latin") consists of *Poemata* (26 poems).[8] Each half possesses a distinctly separate title page[9] and separate pagination,[10] and the whole is bound by a single cover—the latter reflected perhaps in the phrase *cultu simplici ... liber* (*Rous*. 1). Hale regards this Miltonic *liber* as "in fact two books."[11] Indeed there is evidence that the two halves (or "two books") also appeared separately though probably in a very small print run. Copies survive of the vernacular poems only,[12] and of the *Poemata* divorced from the English.[13] It is possible that Milton was influenced to some degree by the structure and the linguistic differentiation evident in the Cambridge volume of laments for the drowned Edward King, *Iusta Edovardo King* (1638), to which he famously contributed *Lycidas*. This had appeared as a bipartite collection

---

[6] Italics are mine. It should be noted, however, that despite Milton's signaling only two languages on the title page, the volume also includes poems in Italian and Greek as well as those "both English and Latin." This apparent discrepancy may be reconciled perhaps if Milton's phrase is read as an umbrella term for the respective sections: the "English" half (including poems in Italian); the "Latin" half (including poems in Greek).

[7] Of these 22 are in English; 6 are in Italian.

[8] Of these 24 are in Latin; 2 are in Greek.

[9] Thus "Poems of Mr John Milton Both English and Latin" and *Poemata* respectively.

[10] The "English" half runs to 120 pages; the "Latin" to 87 pages.

[11] Hale, "Milton's Self-representation," 39.

[12] See, for example, British Library G18844.

[13] Harvard 92-661-664 has the *Poemata* only bound with other Latin works by other writers. In a letter to Carlo Dati (dated 21 April 1647) Milton, announcing (inter alia) the publication of the volume, promises to send the Florentine academician the Latin part only: *sermone patrio haud pauca in lucem dedimus ... poematum quidem quae pars Latina est, quoniam expetis, brevi mittam* (*CM* 12, 50). He proceeds to state that he would have done so already were it not for his concern that some of its anti-papal content might not be too pleasing to the ears of Dati (and no doubt fellow-academicians). See Haan, *From Academia to Amicitia*, 59.

with separate title pages[14] for each of the classical and English halves,[15] and in this instance too it is possible that its two parts were bound and distributed separately.[16] However, Milton's volume differs from the *Iusta* in at least three important respects: first, it inverts the linguistic sequencing by placing the English before the classical half;[17] second, it includes a much wider variety of poems, encompassing many genres and topics, as opposed to the monothematic *Iusta* consisting entirely of *epicedia* on the death of Edward King; third, this is a single- rather than a multi-authored volume. The significance of this last point should not be underplayed for, as Hale notes, "volumes of verse composed by a single author and assembled into a book by the author remained rare in the England of 1645."[18] In fact Milton's organizational hand seems at work throughout. Far from constituting the product of a *manus iuvenilis ... haud nimii poetae* (*Rous*. 4-6), as Milton self-deprecatingly puts it,[19] this self-consciously bipartite volume of poetry is a quite stunning testament not only to a seventeenth-century author's bilingual self-fashioning, but also to that author's careful assembling and ordering of his verse. The result is an unprecedentedly imaginative structuring of a collection, reflecting both an alertness to the nature and efficacy of the material text and a keen metalinguistic awareness. Further insight may be gained upon closer examination of that Latin Ode to Rouse, and an assessment of its description of, and interaction with, the 1645 volume.

Unpublished until the second edition of his poems in 1673, Milton's Ode assumes therein the final place among the *Poemata* as a concluding "valedictory piece,"[20] which also serves to summarize aspects of the volume as a whole. As a description of a collection gleaming in its elegance (*munditieque nitens non operosa* [3]) it is colored by a self-

---

[14] Thus *Iusta Edouardo King* and "Obsequies to the Memorie of Mr Edward King."

[15] Part 1 contains 19 Latin and 3 Greek poems. Part 2 contains 22 English poems (*Lycidas* being the last and longest).

[16] Hale, *Milton's Languages*, 21, remarks: "we might guess he drew thence [i.e. from the *Iusta*] the idea for his own bilingual volume."

[17] This point is also noted by Revard, *The Tangles of Neaera's Hair*, 3.

[18] Hale, *Milton's Languages*, 21.

[19] Cf. Catullus's self-deprecating description of his *libellus* as *meas ... nugas* (1.4) and *quidquid hoc libelli/qualecumque* (1.8-9).

[20] Cf. Revard, "*Ad Ioannem Rousium*," 205: "he regarded it as a kind of valedictory piece, fitting to conclude the section of Latin poems and to sum up the contents of his first and earliest poetic output."

referential mock modesty that is Catullian in essence.[21] The bipartite structure of the *liber* with its individual title pages is conveyed in the phrase *fronde ... gemina* (2) or "twin leaf"—a possible pun on the classical expression *geminae frontes* or "twin brows," the latter noun (*frons-frontis*) signifying "the top or bottom end of a papyrus roll"[22] that was smoothed with pumice stone.[23] As Bush suggests, "Milton shift[s] to *fronde* ('leaf') in a sort of punning metaphor suited to the form of a modern book."[24] But the phrase's reworking of classical precedent operates in several hitherto unexplored ways. Closer scrutiny of this engagement may shed further light on Milton's defiantly self-deprecatory description of "Poems ... Both English and Latin."

The topos of a poet addressing his book of verse and bidding it a fortunate journey (a *propemptikon* of sorts) is attested in the works of Horace, Ovid, Martial inter alios. And it is with Martial that the discussion will begin. *Epigrams* 3.2, addressed to the *libellus*, commences with the speaker asking to whom would it wish to be given as a present.[25] This is followed by a warning that it may end up in some sooty kitchen, wrapping fish in its sodden papyrus or else serving as a paper cornet for incense or pepper.[26] This degrading fate, depicted in overtly hyperbolic language, can be avoided if the book seeks refuge in the bosom of Faustinus (*Faustini fugis in sinum?* [6]), who will afford it protection in Rome. The reference is to Julius Faustinus, dedicatee and recipient of several of Martial's epigrams,[27] and wealthy owner of a chain

---

[21] On links between the poem and Catullus, 1, see Haan, "Milton's *Ad Ioannem Rousium*," passim.

[22] *OLD* sv 8b. The phrase occurs in Martial, Ovid, Tibullus, among others, on which see pages 144-146.

[23] Cf. Catullus 1.1-2: *cui dono lepidum novum libellum/arida modo pumice expolitum?* Revard, *The Tangles of Neaera's Hair*, 241, pertinently remarks that Milton's Ode presents the volume "almost as though it were a Roman scroll whose ends were to be polished with pumice."

[24] Bush, *Variorum*, I, 327.

[25] *cuius vis fieri, libelle, munus?* (1). All quotations are from *M. Valerii Martialis Epigrammaton Libri*, ed. Jacobus Borovskij (Leipzig, 1976).

[26] *ne nigram cito raptus in culinam/cordylas madida tegas papyro/vel turis piperisve sis cucullus* (3-5).

[27] Faustinus is the prime dedicatee of *Epigrams*, Books 3 and 4, and is the recipient of some nineteen epigrams in total.

of impressive villas (at Tivoli, Terracina, Trebula and Baiae).[28] Under his protection the book may proudly strut abroad (*licet ambules* [7]) anointed with cedar-oil, and spruce in the twin honor of its "brow" (*et frontis gemino decens honore/pictis luxurieris umbilicis* [8-9])—an allusion to the papyrus edges and, more specifically, the ornamental edges of the cylinder on which the papyrus roll was wound. With such a protector the book need not fear criticism.[29] The epigram, although exemplifying, in the words of Sullivan, "polished jocularity"[30] and encapsulating, as White suggests, an "informal mode of presentation,"[31] is nonetheless quite formally self-referential in its concluding alertness to the material text's visual beauty.

In a sense what constitutes the conclusion to the classical poem becomes a Miltonic opening. Martial's *decens* sandwiched between *frontis gemino* and *honore* may lie behind the Miltonic *gaudens*: (*cultu simplici gaudens liber,/fronde licet gemina* [1-2]) and *nitens* (*munditieque nitens non operosa* [3]). But the speaker of *Ad Ioannem Rousium* posits a very different question, asking his book not to whom should it be gifted, but by whom has it been stolen.[32] As in Martial, the book is personified, and that proud strutting movement (*licet ambules* [7]) is mirrored to some degree in the initial illustrious journey (*illustre tendebas iter* [17]) to Oxford—a journey in the course of which, however, the *liber* wandered astray (*erraveris* [39]). The potentially negative and essentially demeaning fate of a book's pages ending up as fish-wrapping in a kitchen[33] or as a cornet for incense or pepper finds a parallel in an envisaged horror that may befall the Miltonic *liber*: its leaves suffering the vile thumbing of a stupid shopkeeper (*vili/callo tereris institoris insulsi* [41-42]).[34] The lower-class kitchen is both mirrored and displaced by the domain of the seventeenth-century *institor* (a small retailer,

---

[28] See J.P. Sullivan, *Martial: The Unexpected Classic: A Literary and Historical Study* (Cambridge, 1991), 18, 31.

[29] *illo vindice ne Probum timeto* (12). Probus was a celebrated critic. See Suetonius, *De Gram.* 24.

[30] Sullivan, *Martial: The Unexpected Classic*, 30.

[31] Peter White, "The Presentation and Dedication of the *Silvae* and the *Epigrams*," *JRS* 64 (1974), 40-61, at 56.

[32] *quis te, parve liber, quis te fratribus/subduxit reliquis dolo?* (*Rous.* 13-14).

[33] Contrast the Miltonic *munditieque nitens non operosa* (*Rous.* 3).

[34] Contrast in Martial the envisaged ornamental *cocco rubeat superbus index* (11).

shopkeeper, peddler).³⁵ Like Martial's *libellus*, Milton's *liber* is in urgent need of a protector. And that he will find in an Oxford Librarian, who, like Faustinus, is in possession of riches. Rouse is appropriately Romanized as a *quaestor* (55) (here perhaps in its sense as "a financial officer employed by a local authority under Roman rule")³⁶ in charge of a treasure. But this *gaza* (55) is literary in essence and richer than the treasuries of Apollo's sanctuary (55-60). The *sinus* of the affluent Faustinus is matched by that of the book's anticipated readership (*adhibebit integro sinu* [84]) and by the sanctuary afforded by Rouse. Crucially, however, the physical beauty of Martial's preserved and embellished *libellus* is in Milton ultimately transformed into a predicted aesthetic glory (*ibis honestus* [67]), an eternal place in the "sacred shrine" (*adytis ... sacris* [52]) of the Bodleian Library, Oxford, where the book will (and does) sit forever in the company of Greek and Latin authors. This may also be true of the poem itself and its *auctor*.

5.2 Geminus Auctor

Underlying Milton's Ode is the potential equation of *liber* and *auctor*. Indeed, it could be argued, the volume becomes its author not only in the sense that it befits him, but also because it vibrantly embodies and epitomizes on a literary and material level frequently conflicting aspects of its "twin poet"—its *poeta gemellus*. For, as Ainsworth remarks, "a book, as the living embodiment of a process of thought and composition, preserves the life of its creator in multiple senses."³⁷ Milton had confidently declared in *Areopagitica* (1644):

> Books are not absolutely dead things, but doe contain a potencie of life in them to be as active as that soule was whose progeny they are; nay they do preserve as in a violl the purest efficacie and extraction of that living intellect that bred them. I know they are as lively, and as vigorously productive, as those fabulous Dragon's teeth; and being sown up and down, may chance to spring up armed men.³⁸

---

³⁵ See *OLD* sv.

³⁶ See *OLD* sv 2d.

³⁷ David Ainsworth, *Milton and the Spiritual Reader: Reading and Religion in Seventeenth-Century England* (Routledge, 2008), 32.

³⁸ *CM*, 4, 297-298.

That "potencie of life" is evident in the proactively performative role accorded Milton's personified *liber*. And once again classical precedent is not lacking. Horace, *Epistles* 1.20, depicts his *liber* in terms that not only align it with slave[39] and child, but also present it as a virtual surrogate of the poet himself.[40] This "surrogacy" theme is developed to greater effect by Ovid (not without a backward glance at Horace)[41] in *Tristia* 1.1, which is in turn answered by *Tristia* 3.1.

Ovid introduces *Tristia* Book 1 with a poem in which the exiled speaker addresses his book and proceeds to send it on a journey from Tomis to Rome, a journey that is however forbidden to the poet. His *liber* becomes in effect a surrogate Ovid,[42] traveling on a journey that he is unable to undertake,[43] speaking words that he cannot speak,[44] and in short going to Rome in place of a poet (*tu, tamen, i pro me* [57]) who can only wish that he *were* his book (*Di facerent possem nunc meus esse liber* [58]).

Initially the *liber* is described as *incultus*, an adjective equally applicable to an exile (*vade, sed incultus, qualem decet exulis esse* [3]); it is unpolished, lacking in pumice stone, the color of which is unsuited to its grief (*nec te purpureo uelent uaccinia fuco/non est conueniens luctibus ille color* [5-6]). Nagle notes the "concrete and colorful expression of the relation of the book's contents to its author's misfortune."[45] In a series of negatives[46] the speaker bewails what is absent from his material text (*nec*

---

[39] On the potential intratextual tensions inherent in these identifications, especially in regard to other Horatian passages indicating conflict between Horace and his slaves, see M.J. McGann, *Studies in Horace's First Book of Epistles* (Latomus: Brussels, 1969), 85-86. On Ovidian patterns of addressing his elegies or books as children or slaves, see Nagle, *The Poetics of Exile*, 82-98.

[40] See Nagle, *The Poetics of Exile*, 83.

[41] Nagle, *The Poetics of Exile*, 83, regards Horace, *Epistles* 1.20 as "the immediate predecessor and direct model for *Tristia* 1.1."

[42] See G.D. Williams, "Representations of the Book-Roll in Latin Poetry: Ovid, *Tr.*1,1, 3-14 and Related Texts," *Mnemosyne* 45.2 (1992), 178-189.

[43] *Parve (nec invideo) sine me, liber, ibis in urbem/ei mihi, quod domino non licet ire tuo* (*Tr.* 1.1.1-2).

[44] *Vade, liber, verbisque meis loca grata saluta/contingam certe quo licet illa pede* (*Tr.* 1.1.15-16).

[45] Nagle, *The Poetics of Exile*, 84.

[46] As Williams, "Representations of the Book-Roll in Latin Poetry," 181, notes: "[Ovid] sets up a negative correlation between his book's shabby appearance, his own

cedro charta notetur [7]).⁴⁷ Its *frons* is black (8), unable to wear the white *cornua* (the ends of the stick [*umbilicus*] round which rolls of papyrus were wound).⁴⁸ Yet despite this, the *liber* is charged with the task of defending its author as the speaker imagines it entering Augustus's palace.⁴⁹ The exiled, displaced poet ironically promises his book a home (*domus*) in his own study at Rome where it will find a place among its *fratres* or fellow-books (105-108).⁵⁰ And the tone is mockingly self-deprecatory: for whereas his other authored works on his bookshelves openly display their titles, the infamous *Ars Amatoria*, very likely the poem that was at least partly responsible for its author's banishment,⁵¹ is so ashamed that its three volumes try to conceal themselves in a dark corner (109-112).⁵²

Aspects of Ovid's description recur in *Ad Ioannem Rousium*: the address to the *libellus*, the personification of the book as traveler, and perhaps most notably the depiction of its fellow-books as *fratres*. But not without a twist. For Milton's volume has been stealthily abducted from the rest of its brethren (*quis te, parve liber, quis te fratribus/subduxit reliquis dolo?* [*Rous*. 13-14]). More striking perhaps is Milton's possible appropriation and reworking of aspects of *Tristia* 3.1 (itself a rejoinder to *Tr*. 1.1). Here the book in an attempt to fulfill Ovid's instructions had gone searching for its *fratres* (*quaerebam fratres* [65]). It had done so in three different public libraries, from each of which it was ejected in turn. The first of these is particularly relevant, for here the book is refused admission by the *custos* of a library depicted as a virtual sanctuary (*quaerentem frustra custos e sedibus illis/praepositus sancto iussit abire*

---

miserable experiences in Tomis and the mournful nature of the verse he composes there."

⁴⁷ Contrast Martial, *Epig*. 3.2.7: *cedro nunc licet ambules perunctus*.

⁴⁸ See *OLD* sv 7d.

⁴⁹ *an in alta Palatia missum/scandere te iubeam Caesareamque domum* (*Tr*. 1.1.69-70).

⁵⁰ *cum tamen in nostrum fueris penetrale receptus,/contigerisque tuam, scrinia curva, domum,/aspicies illic positos ex ordine fratres,/quos studium cunctos evigilavit idem* (*Tr*. 1.1.105-108).

⁵¹ See page 59.

⁵² *cetera turba palam titulos ostendet apertos,/et sua detecta nomina fronte geret;/tres procul obscura latitantes parte videbis:/hi quia, quod nemo nescit, amare docent* (*Tr*. 1.1.109-112)

loco [67-68]). The opposite of this is the case of Milton's *liber*. It will ultimately find a home in a library that is likewise described as though it were a sacred shrine (*teque adytis etiam sacris/voluit reponi quibus et ipse praesidet* [52-53])[53] under the protection of a seventeenth-century Oxonian *custos* (*aeternorum operum custos fidelis* [*Rous.* 54]).[54] In Ovid, the *libellus* eventually comes to realize that its banishment (*fuga*) is in effect that of its *auctor* (*is genus auctoris miseri fortuna redundat,/et patimur nati, quam tulit ipse, fugam* [73-74]).[55] The banned book becomes to some degree the banished poet. In Milton, the fate of exile (*fuga*) endured by both the Ovidian book (and potentially its author? — a question to which this discussion will return)[56] is displaced by the sanctuary afforded the 1645 volume. Indeed the poem concludes in a very different form of epiphanic revelation — in the optimistic anticipation of a *cordatior aetas* (82) and *iudicia rebus aequiora* (83), and in the speaker's express hope that his poems will win the acclaim of posterity (85-87).[57] Strikingly absent from the Miltonic lines is any sense of the potential apology implicit in Ovid's humorous depiction of the *Ars Amatoria* seeking concealment in *Tr.* 1.1, or in the book's wry comment that it went looking for all its brethren apart from those *quos suus optaret non genuisse pater* (*Tr.* 3.1.66). Is this because the 1645 volume is unapologetically representative of Milton the youthful poet as opposed to Milton, the controversial polemicist of the mid-1640s? It is in this context that *Ad Ioannem Rousium* may operate on a further self-referential level.

---

[53] Cf. Milton's inscription in a volume of tracts presented to Rouse for the Bodleian Library in 1646: *Joannes Miltonius opuscula haec sua in Bibliothecam antiquissimam atque celeberrimam adsciscenda libens tradit, tanquam in memoriae perpetuae fanum* (*CM* 18, 269).

[54] The promise of a favorable home afforded by a library occurs in a neo-Latin poem (*Ad Leonem Baptistam Albertum*) by the Italian humanist Cristoforo Landino. There, Pope Leo will welcome the poet's *libellus* and place it in the Vatican Library: *hinc te, parve liber, sinu benigno/laetus suscipiet, suisque ponet/libris hospitulum* (Text is that of *Carmina Illustrium Poetarum Italorum*, ed. G.G. Bottari [Florence, 1719-1726], VI, 25-27). For further parallels between Landino and Milton, see Haan, "Milton's *Ad Ioannem Rousium*," passim.

[55] See Nagle, *The Poetics of Exile*, 85-86.

[56] See pages 152-157.

[57] *tum livore sepulto,/si quid meremur sana posteritas sciet/Rousio favente* (*Rous.* 85-87). Similarly Catullus wishes that his *libellus* will survive the test of time (*plus uno maneat perenne saeclo* [1.10]).

5.3 Geminae Frontes

Although *frons-frondis* (leaf) is almost certainly a pun on *frons-frontis* as applied to the edge of the papyrus roll, this latter noun possesses another meaning ("the forehead, brow ... [as the place where garlands or crowns are worn]")[58] — a meaning that may be latent in Milton's punning appropriation in *Ad Ioannem Rousium*. It may not be insignificant that the title page to the 1645 volume includes as its epigraph a Virgilian injunction to crown with foxglove the *frons* (brow) of the poet:

> —Baccare frontem
> Cingite, ne vati noceat mala lingua futuro (Virgil, *Ecl.* 7.27-28)[59]

The Latin half of the volume is prefaced by a series of "written encomiums" from Italian literati, heralding Milton as worthy of a laurel-wreath (or indeed wreaths) in reward for his multilingualism. For example, the encomium by Giovanni Salzilli of Rome describes him as one who deserves to be garlanded with a triple laurel-wreath of poetry: Greek, Latin and Tuscan.[60] He is moreover heralded as a neo-Latin poet on a par with the poets of classical Greece and Rome. For the academician Matteo Selvaggi (alias David Codner)[61] England boasts of Milton just as Greece does of Homer, and Rome does of Virgil.[62] But the whole is not without irony. In Virgil, Thyrsis, the speaker of those lines printed on the Miltonic volume's titlepage, eventually *loses* the competition in question (*victum frustra contendere Thyrsin* [*Ecl.* 7. 69]). Be this as it may, Thyrsis will recur as the speaker of the final poem (*Epitaphium Damonis*) of Milton's 1645 *Poemata*, where he functions as the Miltonic voice of a piece deeply concerned with the artist and his subject matter—a piece that, despite its debt to classical pastoral (indeed

---

[58] *OLD* sv 1. Cf. *doctarum hederae praemia frontium* (Horace, *Odes* 1.1.29); *turba frontibus laurum gerens* (Seneca, *Herc. Fur.* 828). Martz, *Poet of Exile*, 32, perceptively remarks that Milton's allusion to the double leaf "may suggest the double wreath of laurel that the poet has won for his performance in two languages."

[59] Cf. *tibi .../errantis hederas passim cum baccare tellus/...fundet* (Virgil, *Ecl.* 4.18-20).

[60] *Ad Ioannem Miltonem Anglum triplici poeseos laurea coronandum Graeca nimirum, Latina, atque Hetrusca.*

[61] See Edward Chaney, *The Grand Tour and the Great Rebellion* (Geneva, 1985), 244-248.

[62] *Graecia Maeonidem, iactet sibi Roma Maronem,/Anglia Miltonum iactat utrique parem.*

to *Eclogue* 7 in particular),[63] ultimately renounces the pastoral pipe in favor of epic. How (if at all) can this poet's seeming self-alignment with failed song be reconciled with the self-proclaimed future epicist announced in *Epitaphium Damonis*? The answer may lie at least in part in the Virgilian context from which the epigraph has been abstracted.

Thyrsis in the immediately preceding lines had asked: *Pastores, hedera crescentem ornate poetam,/Arcades, invidia rumpantur ut ilia Codro* (*Ecl.* 7.25-26). There is something of a tension here between the *crescens ... poeta* and the *vates futurus*. Is the Ode's concluding proud prophecy (*ibis honestus* [67]) with its express longing for the absence of a *lingua procax* (79) evocative of the aspiration articulated by the Virgilian Thyrsis: *ne vati noceat mala lingua futuro* (*Ecl.* 7.28)? For perhaps it is not only the author's *libellus* that requires sanctuary. The Ode's final lines seem to explode outward in their confidently daring anticipation of the volume's favorable reception. The speaker looks forward to a *cordatior aetas* (82) characterized by *iudicia rebus aequiora* (83), as he expresses the hope that posterity will bury all malice (*tum livore sepulto* [85]) and come to acknowledge the merits of both the poet and his work (*si quid meremur sana posteritas sciet* [86]). The language takes the discerning reader right back to the beginning of the *Poemata*, to Milton's prose *apologia* introducing those "written Encomiums" prefixed to the "Latin" half of the volume:

> ... Dum enim nimiae laudis *invidiam* totis ab se viribus amolitur, sibique quod plus aequo est non attributum esse mavult, *iudicium* interim hominum *cordatorum* atque illustrium quin summo sibi honori ducat, negare non potest.[64]

The whole has come full circle. The end of *Ad Ioannem Rousium* ("end" in the dual sense perhaps of both conclusion and purpose) is to some degree the *Poemata*'s beginning. The Ode is in effect making an implicit appeal: that England will accord the *liber* the favorable reception that its *auctor* (and his Latin poetry) had met with in Italy. It is an appeal couched in linguistic irony given Milton's statements in *Epitaphium Damonis* and *Reason of Church Government*, respectively, in regard to code selection. On the one hand, it is in a Latin poem that the *auctor geminus*, the poet "both English and Latin" first articulates his seeming

---

[63] For example, the refrain of Milton's poem: *ite domum impasti, domino iam non vacat, agni* is modeled on Virgil, *Eclogue* 7.44: *ite domum pasti, si quis pudor, ite iuvenci*. Cf. *Eclogue* 10. 77: *ite domum saturae, venit Hesperus, ite capellae*. *Epitaphium Damonis* 169: *tu procul annosa pendebis fistula pinu* seems to echo *Eclogue* 7. 24: *hic arguta sacra pendebit fistula pinu*.

[64] Italics are mine.

renunciation of Latin; on the other, the vernacular prose work in which he voices his assumption of English henceforth aligns him in so doing with the linguistic choice of the poets of classical Greece and Rome, who, after all, composed their great epics in their own vernacular:

> That what the greatest and choycest wits of Athens, Rome, or modern Italy, and those Hebrews of old did for their country, I in my proportion with this over and above of being a Christian, might doe for mine.[65]

Here, in his purported renunciation of Latin, Milton's self-fashioning is as a poet who in a sense will thereby become *more* Roman. Despite or perhaps because of this code selection the author will remain a "twin poet" in a uniquely complex way. It is a complexity that moves beyond the linguistic and the literary to embrace the iconographical.

5.4 Geminus Miltonus?

The title page and frontispiece to the 1645 volume present incongruities that continue to puzzle scholars. How can these be explained? To begin to answer this question it is necessary to turn from the classical to the early modern; from Martial the epigrammatist to Marshall the engraver. The frontispiece, when juxtaposed and viewed in conjunction with its title page is, in the words of Annabel Patterson, "difficult to accommodate."[66] Both seem to suggest something of a divided Milton. Divided indeed he is, and, as will be argued,[67] in ways that seem to move beyond the purely iconographical incongruities noted by scholars. The volume's engraving by William Marshall depicts what might in effect be described as a *geminus Miltonus*—a Milton whose age seems much closer to fifty-one than to twenty-one, the age cited in the Latin inscription on the oval.[68] Milton was later to state in the *Pro Se Defensio* (1655), that he allowed himself to be depicted by an unskillful engraver because there was no other artist available in a time of war.[69] But since Marshall was clearly a

---

[65] *CM*, 3, 236.

[66] Annabel Patterson, *Pastoral and Ideology: Virgil to Valery* (Berkeley, 1987), 157.

[67] See pages 153-155.

[68] *Ioannis Miltoni Angli Effigies Anno Aetatis Undevigesimo.*

[69] *Tu effigiem mei dissimilem praefixam poematibus vidisti. Ego vero si impulsu et ambitione Librarii me imperito Scalptori propterea quod in urbe alius eo belli*

very talented engraver,[70] it would seem odd that he should have failed to achieve an accurate likeness. The answer may lie in Leo Miller's argument that Marshall, who was also a cartoonist, deliberately engraved the Milton of the present day, the "heretic divorcer,"[71] not the youthful man of twenty-one as presumably commissioned. But the argument can be taken further.

Although the poet's gaze seems focused upon us as readers, our gaze is directed (or diverted) to a background scene. The drawing back of a curtain[72] reveals a rural landscape of shepherds dancing and making music. The image is very much in accordance with scenes from Milton's early vernacular poetry.[73] It is as if the mature Milton is inviting or even challenging the reader to look beyond and behind his portrait: to focus perhaps upon his earliest attempts at composition and to see therein the *crescens ... poeta*, who one day will become a bard (*vates ... futurus*). This possibility is strengthened by the fact that in the volume itself he takes pains to indicate the date or his precise age at the time of his early compositions.[74] The divided Milton is a Milton who is perhaps *both* the contemporary darkened prose controversialist and the erstwhile youthful carefree poet.

And the contrast may go further than this. For when Marshall's engraving is viewed alongside Milton's description of the *libellus* in *Ad Ioannem Rousium*, it emerges that what we have before us (in perhaps a punningly iconographical sense) are the *gemini ... frontes* ("twin ... brows") of its depicted subject. The outer oval of the engraving is mirrored by the inner oval of its subject's face, which, as Richard Johnson has perceptively noted, is almost divided in the middle.[75] It is as

---

tempore non erat, infabre scalpendum permisi, id me neglexisse potius eam rem arguebat, cuius tu mihi nimium cultum obiicis (*CM* 9, 124).

[70] See A.M. Hind, *Engraving in England in the Sixteenth and Seventeenth Centuries* (Cambridge, 1964), III, plates 52-93.

[71] Leo Miller, "Milton's Portraits," 16.

[72] This detail also occurs in Marshall's engravings of Edmund Gregory and Bathsua Makin. See Hind, *Engraving in England*, ad loc.

[73] See, for example, *L'Allegro* 93-98: "When the merry bells ring round,/And the jocund rebecks sound/To many a youth, and many a maid,/Dancing in the chequered shade;/And young and old come forth to play/On a sunshine holiday."

[74] See page 18.

[75] R.M. Johnson, "The Politics of Publication: Misrepresentation in Milton's 1645 'Poems,'" *Criticism* 36.1 (1994), 45-71 at 47-50.

though one side pertains to the youthful poet; the other to the crabbed controversialist. The folds in the darkened curtain on the left seem to be mirrored in the darkened folds in the sleeve of the author's doublet.[76] That whole side presents a continuum of black: curtain, hair, sleeve. By contrast the right side of the image is characterized by brightness, the unveiling of a pastoral scene of dancing, and the illuminated side of the author's visage. Johnson states: "The way in which the cloak is folded under the right arm suggests that the arm is in a sling."[77] And yet the left arm is more subtly depicted, almost hidden, hinting perhaps at some half-concealed deformity. Johnson rather vaguely suggests that this seeming concealment may denote something sinister.[78] Not necessarily. Perhaps the attempted concealment of a "deformed" left hand has some deeper significance than has hitherto been acknowledged. In *Reason of Church Government* (1642) Milton had used the term "left hand" as a virtual metonym for his composition of prose. His albeit self-deprecatory statement in that instance[79] reveals something of a divided self:

> ... wherein knowing my self inferior to my self, led by the genial power of nature to another task, I have the use, as I may account it, but of my left hand.[80]

Marshall's "caricature" seems to take the volume's linguistically divided Milton one stage further, as *gemellus ... liber* is mirrored by a *geminus ... Miltonus*, a twin author. The young poet, whose current volume of poetry is the product of a hand pertaining to his light, youthfully immature days (*quam manus attulit/iuvenis olim,/sedula tamen haud nimii poetae* [*Rous.* 4-6]), is perhaps trying to conceal the more recent, more mature, even "deformed" prose controversialist. That the portrait's iconographical discrepancies did not go unnoticed by Milton is attested by the Greek

---

[76] Cf. Johnson, "The Politics of Publication," 50: "... the folds and disposition of the cloak help draw our attention to the heavy folds of the curtain over the figure's right shoulder."

[77] Johnson, "The Politics of Publication," 50.

[78] Johnson, "The Politics of Publication," 50.

[79] On the unquestionable merits of Milton's prose writings, see, among others, *Achievements of the Left Hand: Essays on the Prose of John Milton*, eds. Michael Lieb and J.T. Shawcross (Massachusetts, 1974); *Politics, Poetics, and Hermeneutics of Milton's Prose*, eds. David Loewenstein and J.G. Turner (Cambridge, 1990).

[80] *CM* 3, 235.

epigram, which he composed and which Marshall, presumably ignorant of Greek, unwittingly inscribed beneath the engraving itself:

In Effigiei Eius Sculptorem

Ἀμαθεῖ γεγράφθαι χειρὶ τήνδε μὲν εἰκόνα
ἁμῶ τάχ' ῥ νϕπρὸθ εἶδοθ αδτοϕὲ ἐθ ἰ κόπων·
ὸν δ' κτὲπωτὸν οδκ πιγνόντεθϕϕμκοιϕ
εκατε ϕαύκοὲ δὲ ι μμηνμα τωγράϕοὲ.

Against the Engraver of his Portrait

Looking at its model in nature, you would say perhaps that this likeness has been drawn by an unskilled hand. If, friends, you fail to recognize the subject of this print, laugh at a poor artist's bad representation.[81]

This is a clever form of revenge as with terse epigrammatic irony Milton, in the words of Hale, "converts the displeasing portrait into another act of multilingual wit."[82] It is fitting that the revenge should be articulated in Greek since Milton now assumes the stance of the epigrammatists of the *Greek Anthology*, who had likewise rebuked artists for failing to paint the requested subject or for creating an inaccurate likeness.[83] But *Ad Ioannem Rousium* may itself allude to and ironically mirror aspects of Milton's Greek epigram. Marshall's unskilled hand Ἀμαθεῖ ... χειρὶ) and the poor artist's bad representation ϕαύκοὲ δὲ ι μμηνμα τωγράϕοὲ find a parallel of sorts in the poet's mock modest self-description: his hand, his poetic powers (or lack of them): *manus ... / iuvenilis olim,/sedula tamen haud nimii poetae* (*Rous.* 4-6). That *olim* of carefree youthfulness denotes a wistful contrast between then and now, a contrast evident in the engraving itself where conversely the twenty-one year old Milton, the growing poet, has been misrepresented as a middle-aged man.

But if the volume's titlepage and frontispiece present a *geminus Miltonus*, an author who is "twin" on an iconographical, linguistic and

---

[81] Translation is mine.

[82] Hale, *Milton's Languages*, 22. Contrast Moseley's rather banal and even blinkered viewpoint, *The Poetic Birth*, 83: "Milton must have seen and agreed to put up with it, for he wrote some very sarcastic Greek verses which were included on it."

[83] The artist Diodorus, for example, is criticized by Lucilius for failing to paint a pretty child as requested (*The Greek Anthology* [Loeb Classical Library: London, 1916-18], IV, 172) and by Leonidas of Alexandria for creating a portrait that does not resemble the subject in the slightest (*The Greek Anthology*, IV, 172).

methodological level, *Ad Ioannem Rousium* constitutes in itself a "twin" poem of sorts. This is achieved not only linguistically and syntactically through repetition (*gemelle* [1] *gemina* [2]; *nunc ... nunc* [7-8]; *parve liber* [13] *libelle* [37]; *seu quis te* [40] *seu qua te* [41]; *ibis* [62, 63, 67]), but also structurally: three Strophes answered by three corresponding Antistrophes, the whole concluding in an Epode. Or as Milton explicitly puts it in the *apologia* appended to the poem: *Ode tribus constat Strophis, totidemque Antistrophis una demum epodo clausis*. This structural self-consciousness is not without significance especially when Milton proceeds to draw attention to the fact that the strophes and antistrophes do not exactly correspond in terms of the number of lines or in the distribution of their metrical units. The reader is invited perhaps to look much more closely for other types of correspondence. What emerges is a series of thematic and frequently ironic twinnings, epitomizing the inspiration derived from twin-peaked Parnassus (*bifidoque Parnassi iugo* [66]).

Strophe 1 alludes to the travels of a Milton who sported (*lusit* 8]) and who was *insons populi* (9). These are literal and literary travels among things both Italian (*Ausonias ... per umbras* [7]) and British (*Britannica per vireta* [8]), doubtlessly symbolizing the Latin, Italian and English poetry of the volume and especially the verse associated with the Italian journey. These travels are mirrored in the corresponding Antistrophe by the *illustre ... iter* (17) undertaken by the *liber* as it made its way *Thamesis ad incunabula* (18). Likewise Strophe 2's depiction of the claws of the filthy Harpies threatening England at a time of Civil War (*immundasque volucres/unguibus imminentes* [33-34]) may find a parallel of sorts in the threat of the vile thumbing of the volume's pages by a stupid shopkeeper (*vili/callo tereris institoris insulsi* [41-42]). At the same time, this is an Ode of both light and shade: the carefree sporting of Strophe 1 with a vibrantly youthful poet at work countered by the gloomy affairs of the English Civil War, a period of poetic inactivity for Milton. Hence the plea that some divine power may recall *alma ... studia* (30) and reinstate the exiled Muses (*relegatas sine sede Musas* [31]) may have implications that are personal and artistic as well as national and geographical. Is there a veiled allusion here to the Milton of the 1640s who had abandoned verse for prose (his right hand for his left, so to speak), to the erstwhile poet who had by now become the all too contemporary and controversial prose pamphleteer.[84] One wonders too if the depiction of the lost 1645 volume as wandering astray from the

---

[84] Hence *Of Reformation, Of Prel. Episc., Animadversions* (all 1641); *Reason of Church Government* and *Smectymnuus* (both 1642); *Doctrine and Discipline of Divorce* and *Of Education* (both 1644).

company of its brethren (*quis te fratribus/subduxit reliquis dolo?* [13-14]; *erraveris agmine fratrum* [39]) may reflect a Miltonic appropriation of a quasi-Ovidian autobiographical alterity.

In a Latin letter to the Florentine Carlo Dati (written in the same year [1647] as this Latin Ode) Milton reflects on the deep sorrow he felt (*gravis ... discessus ille ... meo animo aculeos infixit, qui etiam nunc altius inhaerent*) upon bidding his farewells to a now lost fraternity of Italian academicians (*tot simul sodales atque amicos tam bonos tamque commodos*). His departure from the coterie of Italian friendship and scholarship is depicted as a virtually enforced exile (*invitum me et plane divulsum reliquisse*),[85] a wandering from his literary *fratres*, as it were. He proceeds to convey something of his sense of alterity on a literary, domestic and civic level, complaining that the most turbulent state of England has forced him to turn from study to the realities of everyday life:

> Turbulentissimus iste ... Britanniae nostrae status, qui animum meum paulo post ab studiis excolendis ad vitam et fortunas quoque modo tuendas necessario convertit.[86]

His account of the recurring recollection of a painful departure from everything that is dear, all couched in imagery of exile, is almost Ovidian:

> Cum subit illius tristissima noctis imago,
>   quae mihi supremum tempus in urbe fuit,
> cum repeto noctem, qua tot mihi cara reliqui,
>   labitur ex oculis nunc quoque gutta meis. (Ovid, *Tristia* 1.3.1-4)

Milton's letter, like *Ad Ioannem Rousium*, like the author engraved on the frontispiece to the 1645 volume, is a letter divided against itself, striking a contrast between past and present: between the joys of a buoyantly vibrant youthfulness sporting in an idealized pastoral Arcadia and the all too real horrors of a civil war in England; between light and darkness, between a paradise lost and an unwelcome paradise regained.

---

[85] *CM* 12, 48.

[86] *CM* 12, 50.

5.5 Geminae ... Linguae

The volume's "twinning" operates most conspicuously on a linguistic level. In terms of its linguistic differentiation it is carefully balanced with 28 poems in the "English" and 26 poems in the "Latin" halves, respectively. Hence, as Moseley notes, it "divides almost exactly in half between the modern and the ancient languages."[87] Balance is also visible in terms of (individual and separate) pagination, with the English part running to 120 and the Latin to 87 pages.

Although it is not the purpose of the present discussion to offer a summary of the content and themes of each of the two halves, it might be pertinent to draw attention to some general structural features. First, it seems reasonable to state that both halves, though not always adhering to strict chronological ordering, do so for the most part[88] or are at the very least arranged in a way that suggests the growth of the poet. There exists then perhaps a quasi-autobiographical subtext to the volume's organization, a wish to convey a "portrait of the artist" not just "as a young man" but as a growing young man and poet, a *crescens ... poeta* destined to become a *vates futurus*, as the volume's Virgilian epigraph implies. Second, as Revard has argued,[89] there is evidence throughout of generic alertness and subsequent grouping. In the English half, for example, occasional poems are collectively grouped into odes dealing with religious or funerary themes, respectively. The same can be said of the sonnets and of poems either formally pastoral or concerned with pastoral material, the latter constituting the climax of the English half. Similarly, the Latin half is generically organized, here under an *Elegiarum Liber Primus* and a *Sylvarum Liber*, an organization largely informed by meter. Thus the seven Latin Elegies are collectively grouped. The same is true of the anti-papal poems on the Gunpowder Plot and the Latin epigrams on Leonora Baroni. Occasional epicedia are grouped together as are the Latin poems addressed to Italian academicians. And this Latin half likewise has recourse to pastoral for its climactic conclusion. Such observations can only serve to reaffirm the reader's

---

[87] Moseley, *The Poetic Birth*, 85-86.

[88] Cf. Revard, *The Tangles of Neaera's Hair*, 1-2: "Both English and Latin sections follow a roughly chronological order of presentation." Contrast Moseley, *The Poetic Birth*, 85: "The order ... is not that of composition"—an overstatement, which rather distorts the issue.

[89] Revard, *The Tangles of Neaera's Hair*, 2.

sense of authorial control[90] over the sequencing and organization of the poems in both halves of the volume. And perhaps more than that.

Of relevance to the present argument is the likelihood that the poems are arranged in such a way as to invite the reader to read across the linguistic divide, to read the English and the Latin halves not separately but side by side. Here Revard's comment is particularly pertinent:

> Understanding how the second volume relates to the first—reading the Latin poems in tandem with the English—considerably enhances our understanding both of the English poems and their Latin counterparts.[91]

However, Revard's essentially thematic study does not investigate the structural and linguistic mirror-imaging between the two halves of the volume, nor does it address the consequential ironies and tensions that ensue from reading across the material and linguistic division of the whole into "both English and Latin." Read in this way, the volume's elaborately twin structures seem to become one (*cultu ... simplici* [*Rous.* 1]) by means of intersections between its two main languages and by ways in which the "Latin" half may mirror or invite comparison with aspects of its "English" equivalent.

---

[90] Martz, *Poet of Exile*, 31, tends to overstate the issue: "Milton's original arrangement creates the growing awareness of a guiding, central purpose ..."

[91] Revard, *The Tangles of Neaera's Hair*, 2.

Poems of Mr John Milton: Both English and Latin (1645)

PART 1: ENGLISH

1. On the Morning of Christ's Nativity (1629)
2. A paraphrase on Psalm 114
3. Psalm 136
4. The Passion (1630)
5. On Time (1633)
6. Upon the Circumcision (1632/33)
7. At a Solemn Music (1633)

---

8. Epitaph on the Marchioness of Winchester
9. Song: On May Morning (1629-30)
10. On Shakespeare
11. On the University Carrier
12. Another on the Same

---

13. L'Allegro
14. Il Penseroso

---

15. Sonnet 1: "O Nightingale" (1630)
16. Sonnet 2: "Donna Leggiadra" (1630)
17. Sonnet 3: "Qual in colle aspro" (1630)
18. Canzone: "Ridonsi donne ..."
19. Sonnet 4: "Diodati, e te'l dirò" (1630)
20. Sonnet 5: "Per certo I bei vostr' occhi" (1630)
21. Sonnet 6: "Giovane piano" (1630)
22. Sonnet 7: "How soon hath Time" (1632)
23. Sonnet 8: "Captain, or Colonel" (1642)
24. Sonnet 9: "Lady that in the prime" (1645)
25. Sonnet 10: "Daughter to that ... Earl" (1645)

---

26. Arcades (1632)
27. Lycidas (1637)
28. Comus (1634)

PART 2: LATIN

Elegiarum Liber Primus

1. Elegia Prima (1626)
2. Elegia Secunda (1626)
3. Elegia Tertia (1626)
4. Elegia Quarta (1627)
5. Elegia Quinta (1629)
6. Elegia Sexta (1629)
7. Elegia Septima (1630)

---

8. In Prod. Bomb. (1626)
9. In Eandem (1626)
10. In Eandem (1626)
11. In Eandem (1626)
12. In Invent. Bomb. (1626)

---

13. Ad Leonoram (1639)
14. Ad Eandem (1639)
15. Ad Eandem (1639)

Sylvarum Liber

16. In Obit. Proc. Med. (1626)
17. In Quintum Nov. (1626)
18. In Obit. Praes. El. (1627)
19. Naturam (1628)
20. De Idea Platonica (1628)
21. Ad Patrem (1637)
22. Psalm 114 (in Greek)
23. Philosophus (in Greek)
24. Ad Salsillum
25. Mansus

---

26. Epitaphium Damonis (1639)

The first seven English poems, as Moseley suggests, "are all in some sense devotional or religious."[92] The first seven Latin poems form "a book within a book"[93] an *Elegiarum Liber Primus*, a Miltonic *monobiblos*, so to speak. In both halves these seven are followed by occasional poems. It can also be stated that poems with Italian headings (*L'Allegro* and *Il Penseroso*) or those composed in the Italian language (the six Italian sonnets) seem to balance those pieces in the Latin half associated with Milton's Italian journey (the Leonora epigrams, *Ad Salsillum*, *Mansus*–composed in honor of Italian poets, academicians and an Italian soprano). Such parallelism is afforded greater efficacy if credence is given to the possibility that the fluency of the published Italian sonnets reflects the polishing hand of Milton's Florentine friend and fellow-academician, Valerio Chimentelli, a possibility certainly not dismissed by recent Milton scholarship.[94] Noteworthy too is the fact that both the English and Latin halves culminate in pastoral works. Thus *Lycidas* and the pastoral masque *Comus*, the latter featuring the attendant spirit as the shepherd Thyrsis (with possible allusions to Milton's friend Charles Diodati, the "shepherd lad" and his knowledge of medicine), are balanced by Milton's Latin pastoral lament on the death of Charles Diodati. Here the grieving speaker assumes that pastoral name Thyrsis and praises Diodati's medical expertise. As will be argued, the structural positioning of *Epitaphium Damonis* invites a cautious cross-reading not only with *Lycidas* (which likewise draws a parallel between the speaker's reinvention of his poetic role and the envisaged apotheosis of the deceased in a Christian heaven) but also (and crucially) with Milton's vernacular masque which closes the English half of the volume.

But links are more than merely structural. And they operate from English to Latin and from Latin to English. It may not be accidental that the Milton who introduces himself to his readership in the first Elegy of the Latin *Poemata* is a Milton in exile, an outcast, a refugee from the ordered and stiflingly barren intellectual world of Cambridge University.[95] It has long been acknowledged moreover that his self-presentation in *Elegia Prima* is that of an inverted Ovid. By means of a series of cross-comparisons with Ovid's exile and the language in which

---

[92] Moseley, *The Poetic Birth*, 87.

[93] Moseley, *The Poetic* Birth, 89.

[94] Campbell and Corns, *Life, Work, and Thought*, 114, suggest: "perhaps Chimentelli was the friend who helped to bring the Italian of Milton's sonnets to native-speaking proficiency."

[95] See pages 58-62.

that exile was depicted in the *Tristia* and *Epistulae ex Ponto*, Milton turns an enforced seventeenth-century exile (his own purported "rustication" from Cambridge to London) into a voluntary one. Hence the forbidden hearth (*vetiti .. laris* [12]) of the University and the ensuing exile (*exilium* [17]) become an actual blessing whereby the speaker may rejoice in visiting his *patrios ... penates* (17) and can embrace the very fate and indeed name of exile (*profugi nomen* [19])—a fortunate fall of sorts. But self-presentation here is essentially pagan throughout: not only in the speaker's alignment with Ovid, but also in his enjoyment of metropolitan life (London as a second Rome)—its theaters, its pretty girls—all depicted in terms reminiscent of the *Ars Amatoria*. Milton dares to assume the role of the other, the banished figure of alterity, who is temporarily redeemed by London itself.

When the reader looks across to the opening poem of the English half (*On the Morning of Christ's Nativity*) he or she may be struck by, in the words of one critic, its "new creation of self in orientation toward the divine child."[96] This poem likewise contains a contrast between two different exiles: a voluntary exile whereby the incarnate Christ laid aside his heavenly glory and "forsook the courts of everlasting day" (13), and an enforced exile effected by Christ's nativity whereby pagan deities were displaced and routed from their shrines and temples in a fate antithetical to the Miltonic return to his *patrios ... penates* (17). Thus Apollo leaves Delphos (178) while Peor and Baalim "forsake their Temples dim" (198) and "sullen Moloch fled" (205). The Latin poem with its depiction of speaker as pagan exile converting an enforced exile into a voluntary one provides an ironic contrast to the English poem in which all that represents the pagan world is forced to flee by the Christian godhead's voluntary exile from heaven to earth.

The positioning of *Epitaphium Damonis* at the end of the *Poemata* reflects much more than chronological ordering. Here the speaker laments the death of the addressee of the very first Latin Elegy, Charles Diodati, whose vibrant personality colors not only the *Elegiarum Liber*, but also the Italian sonnets of the "English" half. In this concluding Latin poem, however, the Ovidian is displaced by the Virgilian as *elegia* yields to pastoral. In terms of bilingual mirror-imaging, the poem invites comparison not only with *Lycidas*, which has recourse to many of the shared pastoral motifs, but also with *Comus*, the pastoral masque with which the "English" volume concludes. A reading of the Latin poem alongside both English works is insightful for a number of reasons—not least for the fact that the speaker of the *Epitaphium* assumes the very name of the masque's attendant spirit.

---

[96] Carrithers, "Poems (1645): On Growing Up," 161.

Milton scholars have drawn attention to the many differences between *Lycidas* and *Epitaphium Damonis*.[97] Although this is entirely appropriate, it has resulted perhaps in two extreme viewpoints. On the one hand are those who argue that any similarities between the two poems constitute nothing more than a reflection of the fact that both draw upon a shared pastoral elegiac tradition. On the other hand, general parallels cited by Dust (the fact that both poems idealize the theme of friendship, both use river imagery to symbolize immortality, both contain Biblical allusion to the faithful as sheep and the devil's agents as wolves, and conclude in the apotheosis of the dead in a Christian heaven)[98] fail to convince. The dangers of the latter approach are perfectly epitomized in Dust's misguided statement that "*Lycidas* is very much an English source for the neo-Latin *Epitaphium Damonis*."[99] But a comparison can begin to prove fruitful when both poems are viewed as affording the reader an example of Milton's engagement in "both English and Latin" with shared classical intertexts, and of ways in which code selection may impact upon methodology, tone and envisaged audience. For example, recourse to the vernacular in *Lycidas* not only facilitates the Anglicizing of classical landscape, but also highlights perhaps the "Englishness" of a poem that criticizes the Anglican church ("foretells the ruin of our corrupted clergy then in their height") and an English university. By contrast, the use of Latin in *Epitaphium Damonis* is tellingly suited to a piece that looks to an Italian world, a highly personal poem significantly cast, as its title suggests, in the linguistic medium of the classical epitaph.

Aspects of the volume's structure invite a parallel reading of *Epitaphium Damonis* and *Comus*. Both constitute the culminatory pieces of the respective halves; both present a character named Thyrsis recalling a certain "shepherd friend" who was highly skilled in medicine; in both this is set in contrast to the shepherd who is skilled in music; both works are concerned with the concept of virtue and chastity and the associated rewards for such. It can also be stated that both move beyond the confines of an English nationalism to embrace things Italian. It should not pass unremarked that the *Comus* of the 1645 volume is significantly prefaced by a letter from Sir Henry Wooton, giving advice to Milton in regard to

---

[97] A.S.P. Woodhouse, "Milton's Pastoral Monodies," in *Studies in Honour of Gilbert Norwood*, ed. M.E. White (Toronto, 1952), 266-277; W.R. Parker, *Biography*, ed. Campbell, I, 187-190; R.W. Condee, "The Structure of Milton's *Epitaphium Damonis*," *SP* 62 (1965), 577-594; Bush, *Variorum*, I, 288-297.

[98] Philip Dust, "Milton's *Epitaphium Damonis* and *Lycidas*," *HL* 32 (1983), 342-346.

[99] Dust, "Milton's *Epitaphium Damonis* and *Lycidas*," 346.

his imminent Italian journey[100] — a journey central to the depiction of both the lamented and the mourner in *Epitaphium Damonis*.

The much debated "shepherd lad" recollected by the Thyrsis of *Comus* is a memory "brought to my mind" (618); in *Epitaphium* it is an idle dream in which Thyrsis imagines future events as actually occurring at the present moment (*praesentia finxi* [146]). The Latin poem inverts the order in the English masque. There it was the singer who was the first to display his skill. Then in turn ("And in requital" [625]) the shepherd friend showed him a wide variety of medicinal herbs. In the Latin lines, on the other hand, Damon's skill in medicine *precedes* Thyrsis's song. And now the emphasis is upon a deceased friend. In *Comus*, moreover, the friend begged Thyrsis to sing as he himself sat on the grass and listened (622-624). In *Epitaphium* the roles are reversed as it is Thyrsis who invites Damon to recline with him in the shade by the riverside (147-149). In both instances a shepherd describes many different herbs (625-629)/(150-152). Some of the "simples of a thousand names" (626) are mentioned in the Latin lines: hellebore, crocus, hyacinth (151-152). An element of poignancy is attached to Thyrsis's statement that even such plants were unable to save Damon's life (153-154) when it is remembered that the Thyrsis of *Comus* did in fact possess "a small unsightly root,/But of divine effect" (628-629) which the shepherd friend "culled me out" (629). And it is only after the account of Damon's medical skill that Thyrsis in turn (*ipse etiam* [155]) mentions his own singing. There is a telling difference, however. Unlike the Thyrsis of Comus "whose artful strains have oft delayed/The huddling brook to hear his madrigal,/And sweetened every musk-rose of the dale" (493-495) and whose singing caused the shepherd friend "to hearken even to ecstasy" (624), the Thyrsis of the Latin poem self-consciously asserts that his reedpipe fell apart under the weight of his song (158-159). Juxtaposing the two may help to resolve the debate as to whether the "shepherd lad" in *Comus* is perhaps Diodati,[101] but it may also do much more than that.

Diodati as Damon shares with the Lady of *Comus* the quality of virginity and the safeguarding protection afforded by chastity. Thus "through the sacred rays of chastity,/No savage fierce, bandit or mountaineer/Will dare to soyl her Virgin purity" (424-426). Damon will receive heavenly rewards mirroring his virginal chastity upon earth (*quod tibi purpureus pudor, et sine labe iuventus/grata fuit, quod nulla tori libata voluptas,/en iterum tibi virginei servantur honores* [212-214]).

---

[100] See *Poems of Mr John Milton Both English and Latin* (1645), 72-73, especially 72: "Now Sir, concerning your travels ... the shaping of your farther journey into Italy ... the passage into Tuscany ... I hasten as you do to Florence, or Siena."

[101] See, for example, Bush, *Variorum*, I, 313.

These rewards answer at last the speaker's fear that Damon's *virtus* would remain in obscurity (*siccine nos linquis, tua sic sine nomine virtus/ibit, et obscuris numero sociabitur umbris?* [21-22])—a fear intensified perhaps when read alongside the confident allusion by the masque's Thyrsis to "the crown that virtue gives/After this mortal change, to her true servants/Amongst the enthron'd gods on sainted seats" (9-11).[102] Or, as proclaimed in that autograph inscribed by the Miltonic Thyrsis abroad:

> —if Vertue feeble were
> Heaven it selfe would stoope to her
> *Coelum non animum muto, dum trans mare curro*

---

[102] On virtue receiving its due reward in heaven, cf. *Mansus* 95-96, here appropriated on a self-referential level: *ipse ego caelicolum semotus in aethera divum,/quo labor, et mens pura vehunt, atque ignea virtus.*

Chapter 6

After "Word"
Surprised by Syntax: The *Vox Bilinguis* of *Paradise Lost*

Milton's Latin poetry, as argued in this study, is both the product and the manifestation of an inherent bilingualism whereby "both English and Latin" co-exist not only in terms of the organization of the 1645 volume, but also in some of the individual *Poemata* contained therein. This co-existence has been seen to be closely associated with an author's bicultural self-fashioning. What, if any, might have been the linguistic repercussions of this for the mature poet of *Paradise Lost*? What in effect were the consequences of that metamorphosis envisaged and first articulated in *Epitaphum Damonis*: of a reedpipe (*fistula*) transformed by native muses (*patriis mutata camoenis*). A Latinate vernacular perhaps? A vernacular *Latinitas*? How in turn might this affect a twenty-first-century reading of Milton's epic? How might it lend itself to a variety of post-modern readings informed by such issues as hybridity, intertextuality—issues that are surely facilitated by bilingualism itself?

Scholars have debated at length the cases for and against the Latinity of the language of *Paradise Lost*. To summarize this debate: there have been three camps. First, the anti-Miltonists, a trend inaugurated in many ways by Samuel Johnson's professed animosity toward Milton's language as un-English: "both in prose and verse he had found his style by a perverse and pedantic principle. He was desirous to use English words with a foreign idiom."[1] For F.R. Leavis "Milton has forgotten the English language" with the result that his style has "barred Milton from the essential expressive resources of English."[2] T.S. Eliot criticized the alteration of ordinary language and use of foreign idiom as "a particular act of violence which Milton has been the first to commit,"[3] and Ezra Pound proclaimed that Milton did "wrong to his mother

---

[1] Samuel Johnson, *Lives of the Poets*, ed. G.B. Hill (Oxford, 1905), I, 190.

[2] See in general F.R. Leavis, *Revaluation* (Harmondsworth, 1967), 49-56.

[3] T.S. Eliot, "Milton," *PBA* 33 (1947), 61-79, at 69.

tongue."⁴ But one might question the applicability of these somewhat blinkered value judgments to an epic governed by a syntax that, as Christopher Ricks usefully demonstrated, is very successfully controlled.⁵

There followed the school of linguistic denial: supposedly pro-Miltonists, such as Boone⁶ and Emma,⁷ who offered in the poet's so-called defense a refutation of the charge of his Latinisms. Similarly Fowler's otherwise excellent Longman edition of *Paradise Lost* tried in its introduction and notes to de-Latinize Milton's vocabulary.⁸ This hardly does justice to a writer molded by an inherent bilingualism or to an epic, whose language, like its author, can in many respects be viewed as "both English and Latin."

The end of the twentieth century saw some progress in this regard in what might be termed the "Milton language school." This was inaugurated by Thomas Corns's scientific approach to the language of *Paradise Lost*,⁹ and was developed more recently by John Hale, who exemplified just how Latinate Milton's English is. Hale defined a Miltonic Latinism as "the felt presence of Latin diction and usage within the English, interacting with it."¹⁰ He proposed that rather than trying to de-Latinize Milton's English, the reader should be proactive in searching out Latinism of thought, of diction, of sound, of syntax and (equally important) of allusion. This proposal provides a useful point of departure for future work in Milton studies. The present discussion will both demonstrate and develop Hale's argument, but it will also take it in a rather different (and admittedly somewhat radical) direction. It will do so by suggesting that diction, sound, allusion in Milton's epic may operate in an imaginatively new way whereby the vernacular serves at times to recreate and appropriate the *Latinitas* of a classical intertext or, more specifically, of a particular passage with which the epic is engaging. And it does so both syntactically and verbally. Here it is possible to move beyond a Saussurian reading of classical texts which argues that Virgil's

---

[4] Ezra Pound, *ABC of Reading* (New York, 1934), 51.

[5] Christopher Ricks, *Milton's Grand Style* (Oxford, 1963), passim.

[6] L.P. Boone, "The Language of Book VI, *Paradise Lost*," *SAMLA Studies in Milton*, ed. J. Max Patrick (Gainesville, 1953), 114-127.

[7] R.D. Emma, *Milton's Grammar* (London, 1964).

[8] See Fowler, ed. *Paradise Lost*, 419-455.

[9] T.N. Corns, *Milton's Language* (Oxford, 1990).

[10] Hale, *Milton's Languages*, 105.

Aeneid and Lucretius's *De Rerum Natura* construct themselves upon a "theme-word" ("mot-thème"), which "at the same time opens and limits the field of possibility of the developed verse."[11] Rather the Saussurian "theme-word" becomes for Milton what might be termed a "bilingual signifier." This, it will be argued, operates in a variety of interrelated ways: the use of a particular English word in a Latin sense; the phonological replication in the vernacular of a particular Latin word; the recourse to Latinate syntax, all of which not only exemplify the intersection of both languages in the poem, but may also function at certain points to signal linguistically the classical intertext (and indeed a moment in that intertext) with which Milton's epic engages. The results of such a reading are frequently surprising.

Stanley Fish in his monumental study argued that the reader of *Paradise Lost* is "surprised by sin" as he or she in the course of engaging with the text falls, like Adam and Eve, into sin and error and is brought up short. Through a "programme of reader harassment"[12] the experience of the fall is re-enacted in the process of reading, wherein lies the poem's meaning. And reader response criticism was born. But if for Fish the twentieth-century reader is "surprised by sin," might not the twenty-first-century reader, an all too frequently Latinless reader, be surprised by syntax, a syntax that despite of (or maybe because of) its inherent Latinity and associated linguistic alterity functions as a seductively attractive other. The reader, like Eve, is indeed surprised: enchanted, bemused, seduced by the abundant classicism, by the formal Latinate rhetoric achieved by a Miltonic unison of "Voice and Verse"[13] and also by the language of a Satanic tempter who is — in the pejorative sense of the Latin adjective *bilinguis*—"double-tongued, deceitful, treacherous."[14] It is hardly an accident that this adjective (with which Milton qualifies hellish betrayal in his Latin gunpowder epic)[15] was typically applied to the forked tongue of a serpent.[16] As will be noted, key to the success of the

---

[11] See Jean Starobinski, *Les Mots Sous Les Mots: Les Anagrammes de Ferdinand de Saussure* (Paris, 1971), especially 64-65.

[12] Fish, *Surprised by Sin*, 4.

[13] "Sphere-born harmonious sisters, Voice and Verse" (*At a Solemn Music*, 2).

[14] Cf. *OLD sv bilinguis*.

[15] *nunc torvi spelunca Phoni, Prodotaeque bilinguis/effera quos uno peperit Discordia partu* (*In Quintum Novembris*, 141-142).

[16] Thus in Plautus's *Persa* a deceitful youth is compared to a *serpens bilinguis*: *ut istunc di deaeque perdant./Tamquam proserpens bestiast bilinguis et scelestus* (*Persa*

double-tongued Miltonic *serpens bilinguis*, is his use and abuse of Latinate language and rhetoric.[17] Might this be mirrored in the linguistic methodology of the *poeta bilinguis*, the *geminus Miltonus*? For if, like Eve, the twenty-first-century reader of *Paradise Lost* is surprised by syntax, by the Miltonic use and the Satanic abuse of a Latinate voice, might not he or she also be surprised by the text's bilingual speaking voice? It is a voice that is sounded in the poem's opening lines.

6.1 Epic Openings: "Of Man's First"/*Arma Vir*

> A beginning immediately establishes relationships with works already existing, relationships of either continuity or antagonism or some mixture of both.[18]

That bilinguals draw upon both their lexicons in monolingual processing has, as noted previously, been attested by a whole series of recent studies.[19] This in turn may give rise to syntactical and interlingual ambiguity in that "... the more balanced a subject is, the less he will decode these words as belonging to one language to the exclusion of the other."[20] As Stubbs remarks, "languages are not incompatible. We can translate between them."[21]

> Of man's first disobedience, and the fruit
> Of that forbidden tree, whose mortal taste
> Brought death into the world, and all our woe,
> With loss of Eden, till one greater man
> Restore us, and regain the blissful seat,   5
> Sing heavenly Muse, that on the secret top
> Of Oreb, or of Sinai, didst inspire

298-299). Text is that of *T. Maccius Plautus: Persa*, ed. Erich Woytek (Wien, 1982). An English-Latin teaching manual by the Renaissance grammarian John Withal defines a serpent by stating *Bilinguis dicitur, that hath two tunges as serpents have.* (*A Short Dictionarie for Young Begynners* [London, 1553], under "A serpent, *serpens, tis*").

[17] See pages 180-184.

[18] E.W. Said, *Beginnings: Intention and Method* (New York, 1975), 3.

[19] See page 88. For an overview, see Hamers and Blanc, *Bilinguality and Bilingualism*, 91.

[20] Hamers and Blanc, *Bilinguality and Bilingualism*, 91.

[21] Stubbs, "Language and the Mediation of Experience," 359.

> That shepherd, who first taught the chosen seed,
> In the beginning how the heavens and earth
> Rose out of chaos: or if Sion hill   10
> Delight thee more, and Siloa's brook that flowed
> Fast by the oracle of God, I thence
> Invoke thy aid to my advent'rous song,
> That with no middle flight intends to soar
> Above the Aonian mount, while it pursues   15
> Things unattempted yet in prose or rhyme.

The opening lines of *Paradise Lost* are characterized by a linguistic and syntactical complexity not dissimilar to the opening of Virgil's *Aeneid*:

> Arma virumque cano, Troiae qui primus ab oris
> Italiam, fato profugus, Laviniaque venit
> litora, multum ille et terris iactatus et alto
> vi superum saevae memorem Iunonis ob iram;
> multa quoque et bello passus, dum conderet urbem,   5
> inferretque deos Latio, genus unde Latinum,
> Albanique patres, atque altae moenia Romae.

Virgil's poem commences with a single sentence, which runs over no fewer than seven lines of hexameter verse. It consists of a main clause proclaiming two objects "arms" and "man" (*arma virumque* [1]), a relative (*qui* [1]) clause qualifying the *vir* in question and describing his exile from Troy and the fact that he was the first to come (*venit* [2]) to Italy and the Lavinian shore. Two participles (*iactatus* [3] and *passus* [5]), conveying that this is a storm-tossed hero who has suffered, give way to a climactic "until" (*dum* [5]) clause, which moves the whole forward from loss to recovery, from the negative to the positive, from exile to the finding and the founding of a city, to the installation of the Trojan gods in Latium and to the rising walls of Rome to which this settlement will give birth. The whole is governed by the forceful *cano* as the customary Homeric imperative is displaced by the first-person proclamation.[22]

Milton's epic opening is characterized syntactically by "two enormous sentences."[23] The first, both sweeping and seemingly endless, was described thus by Matthew Arnold: "So chary of a sentence is he, so

---

[22] Cf. A.D. Nuttall, *Openings: Narrative Beginnings From the Epic to the Novel* (Oxford, 1992), 3: "The grand sequence of the poem, arms and the man, the long sufferings of the journey from Troy to Latium, the Latin wars, the building of Rome's high walls, and the founding of the race—all these are governed grammatically by 'I sing.'" Nuttall suggests that this displacement of the Homeric imperative is perhaps "the first visible mark of a developed literacy" (*Openings*, 3).

[23] Nuttall, *Openings*, 74-75.

resolute not to let it escape him till he has crowded into it all he can, that it is not till the thirty-ninth word in the sentence that he will give us the key to it, the word of action, the verb."[24] Ricks notes that "the word-order quite literally encompasses the huge themes,"[25] and Nuttall regards the sentence as "superhuman."[26] Central to the syntactical sweep of the lines is the fact that this, like Virgil's Latin hexameters, constitutes unrhymed verse. Indeed as T.S. Eliot states: "The peculiar feeling, almost a physical sensation of a breathless leap, communicated by Milton's long periods, and by his alone, is impossible to procure from rhymed verse."[27]

Milton, like Virgil, proclaims two object nouns as the content of the epic song: in this instance "disobedience" (1) and "fruit" (1). The second object noun ("fruit") is qualified by a relative clause "whose mortal taste" (2), thus corresponding syntactically to Virgil's *qui* clause. But the passivity of heroic and essentially human victimhood in Virgil, a passivity conveyed in those participles *iactatus* and *passus*, is displaced by agency—in this case the agency of an apple that "brought" two things into the world: "death" (3) and "woe" (3). However, as in Virgil, this gives way to a climactic "until" clause "till one greater man" (4) likewise predicting an important progression from loss to recovery, and a movement away from the negative to the positive. If the loss of Troy finds a parallel in "loss of Eden" (4), so the predicted rising of Rome is mirrored in "restore us, and regain the blissful seat" (5). But Milton's English, although seeming to mirror the Latinate syntax of Virgil, is marked by ambiguities, puns, and false starts which surprise the reader. The Virgilian first-person *cano* ("I sing"), denoted as a *verbum heroicum* by the seventeenth-century Virgilian commentator De la Cerda,[28] becomes a Homeric imperative "Sing heavenly Muse" (6),[29] which in turn

---

[24] Matthew Arnold, *On Translating Homer* (London, 1861), 72.

[25] Ricks, *Milton's Grand Style*, 28.

[26] Nuttall, *Openings*, 75: "In the 'superhuman' sentence structure employed by Milton we are instead made to breathe hard, to feel intensely the need of a main verb, so that when at last it is given, it comes with a saving force."

[27] T.S. Eliot, *On Poetry and Poets* (London, 1957), 158.

[28] Juan Luis De la Cerda, *P. Virgilii Maronis Aeneidos Libri Sex Priores* (Cologne, 1628), 3.

[29] Nuttall, *Openings*, 75, states that this "prayer-ful imperative ... binds the English poet to Homer, divides him from Virgil." Later, however, as the Miltonic voice intrudes, "the opening Homeric prayer-imperative is after all overtaken in the end by a colossal assertion of self" (83).

governs the epic's opening word "Of." That same word "Of" is repeated at the beginning of line 2 but on this occasion it denotes possession "[fruit] Of that forbidden tree." And "fruit" itself assumes a punning significance—as both literal apple, and consequence.[30] The Virgilian *vir* becomes Miltonic *viri*, so to speak: Adam, the "man" (1) and Christ, the "one greater man" (4); the *deos* or *penates*, inanimate symbols of a lost city but soon to be imported to Latium, are humanized in a stunningly daring shift: "Restore us" (5). Christ's agency facilitates the regaining of a sense of godhead in "us," in humankind. This Miltonic shift may owe some debt to Servius's suggestion that the Virgilian *deos* may also embrace Aeneas himself, Ascanius and their descendants addressed as begotten and future begetters of gods.[31] *Primus* qualifying the *vir*, a point that had caused some controversy,[32] now qualifies the initial instance of human transgression as the "first man" is proleptically displaced by his sin: "first disobedience." This is just one of the "beginnings strangely nested in beginnings"[33] characterizing these opening lines.

Miltonic syntax both matches and moves beyond its Virgilian equivalent. The opening words of Virgil's epic are, as Nuttall aptly notes, "strangely abrupt,"[34] so much so in fact that their sudden loudness seems to have disconcerted contemporaries. In Virgil moreover *arma* precedes *virumque*, a word-order that seems to run counter to the epic's structural content and division. Servius notes this seeming disparity, but remarks that similar inversion is also to be found in prose.[35] De la Cerda defends

---

[30] On Milton's macaronic puns on "apple," "malice" and *malus/malum*, see pages 48-49, 53.

[31] *"deos" vero utrum penates, ut talibus attonitus visis et voce deorum, an se et Ascanium et posteros suos, de quibus dictum est dis genite et geniture deos?* (Servius, *In Vergilii Carmina Commentarii*, eds. George Thilo and Hermann Hagen (Leipzig, 1878-1902], ad loc).

[32] On *primus*, see De la Cerda, *P. Virgilii Maronis Aeneidos Libri Sex Priores*, 3: *non video cur Servius reiiciatur, ut vel primus sit princeps: nam tametsi alii ante illum venerint in Italiam, sed nemo, neque Antenor ipse conferendus est cum Aenea dignitate, et rebus gestis; vel, ut loquatur Poeta ex antiquo Italiae limite, qui cum ad illam Aeneas appulit, tunc erat ad Rubicon.*

[33] The phrase is that of Nuttall, *Openings*, 79, who also remarks: "Except for the one forward reference to the end of time ... the hammer descends, over and over again, this way and that, on the idea of inception."

[34] Nuttall, *Openings*, 1.

[35] *Figura usitata est ut non eo ordine respondeamus quo proposuimus; nam prius de erroribus Aeneae dicit, post de bello. Hac autem figura in prosa utimur* (Servius, ed.

Virgil rather more specifically by pointing out precedent in both oratory and historiography,[36] and by reading the militaristic aspects of book 2 as akin to the initial positioning of *arma*. He also remarks that these two opening words have become the virtually synonymous signifier of the epic itself.[37]

If Milton's vernacular syntactically mirrors this famous epic opening, might it also do so on a linguistic and phonological level? "Where couldst thou words of such a compass find?"[38] The answer to Andrew Marvell's pertinent question may lie in *Latinitas* itself and in vernacular appropriation. For example, the opening three syllables of Virgil's poem *Ar-ma-vir*[39] may be echoed phonologically in the vernacular monosyllabic "Of man's first" (the *vir*/"first" linguistic replication is rendered possible since Milton favored the Italian pronunciation of Latin):

>   Ar **ma**   **vir**umque cano   (1)
>   Of **man's**   **fir**st disobedience   (1)

The alliteration of f, m, t (*fato profugus* [2], *multum ille et terris iactatus et alto* [3]) is matched by "first," "fruit," "forbidden tree," "mortal taste," and the line-ending of 3 *et alto* is mirrored perhaps by its equivalent line-ending in Milton:

>   .... **et   alto**   (3)
>   ....**and all** our woe   (3)

Juxtaposed and read together, syntactical and linguistic mirroring is quite evident as the vernacular begins to "sound" at times like Virgil's Latin.

Thilo, I, 6). Nuttall, however, perceptively notes how "The *Odyssey* was deemed from the first to be subsequent to the *Iliad*" (*Openings*, 3).

[36] De la Cerda, *P. Virgilii Maronis Aeneidos Libri Sex Priores*, 3: *arma virumque:] sunt qui Poetam reprehendant, quod virum postposuerit, ad quem pertinent sex priores libri: arma praeposuerit, ad quae sex posteriores. Sed sciant hi, non constringi oratores aut historicos hac lege, adeo nec Poetas.*

[37] *ceterum initium hoc Arma virumque adeo auspicatum est, ut qui velint Aeneidem Maronis signare, signent illam per duo haec verba* (De la Cerda, *P. Virgilii Maronis Aeneidos Libri Sex Priores*, 3).

[38] Andrew Marvell, "On Paradise Lost," 41.

[39] De la Cerda, *P. Virgilii Maronis Aeneidos Libri Sex Priores*, 2, describes the phrase *arma virumque cano*: *altiora haec sunt, grandiora, consonantiora.*

> Ar**ma vir**um**que** <u>cano</u>, Troiae <u>qui primus</u> ab oris
> Italiam fato profugus Laviniaque venit
> Litora, **multum** ille et terri**s** iac**tatus** <u>et</u> **alto**
> Vi superum, saevae memorem Iononis ob iram,
> Multa quoque et bello passus, <u>dum</u> conderet urbem
> Inferretque deos Latio, genus unde Latinum
> Albanique patres atque altae moenia Romae.
> <u>Musa</u>, mihi causas memora ...   (*Aeneid* 1.1-8)

> Of **man**'s <u>fir</u>st disobedience, <u>and</u> the **fr**uit
> Of that forbidden tree, <u>whose</u> **m**ortal **taste**
> Brought death into the world, <u>and</u> **all** our **woe**,
> With loss of Eden, <u>till</u> one greater man
> Restore us, and regain the blissful seat,
> <u>Sing</u> heavenly <u>Muse</u> ...   (*Paradise Lost* 1.1-6)

6.2   "Thee I Revisit"/*Sociosque Revisit*

Another type of opening may serve to exemplify ways in which a bilingual signifier can operate on an inter- and intratextual level. Milton opens book 3 with a salutation not dissimilar to that of his native language in *At A Vacation Exercise*.[40] But instead of proclaiming a vernacular that gave him the power of speech, he salutes "holy Light"[41] from which he, a now blind speaker, is perpetually excluded:

> Hail holy light, offspring of heaven first-born,
> Or of the eternal co-eternal beam
> May I express thee unblamed (*Paradise Lost* 3.1-3)

In what follows the speaker's self-fashioning is as an infernal soul caught in its own external darkness and longing to revisit (and this discussion, like Milton's lines, emphasizes this word) the upper world. He signals

---

[40] See pages 90-93.

[41] For debates concerning the nature of the light invoked by Milton, see, among others, W.B. Hunter, "The Meaning of 'Holy Light' in *Paradise Lost* III," *MLN* 74.7 (1959), 589-592; M.Y. Hughes, "Milton and the Symbol of Light," *SEL* 4.1 (1964), 1-33; A.R. Cirillo, "'Hail Holy Light' and Divine Time in *Paradise Lost*," *JEGP* 68 (1969), 45-56; L.L. Martz, "*Paradise Lost*: The Realms of Light," *ELR* 1.1 (1971), 71-88; Estelle Haan, "Heaven's Purest Light: Milton's *Paradise Lost* 3 and Vida," *CLS* 30.2 (1993), 115-136; Hee-Won Lee, "Light in *Paradise Lost*, Book III: A Metaphor for Incarnation and Mimesis," *Journal of Classical and English Renaissance Literature* 12.1 (2003), 159-178.

this through the verb "revisit"—a verb that is actually "both English and Latin." And it occurs three times in eleven lines:

> Thee I <u>revisit</u> now with bolder wing,
> Escaped the Stygian pool, though long detained
> In that obscure sojourn, while in my flight
> Through utter and through middle darkness borne
> With other notes than to the Orphean lyre
> I sung of Chaos and eternal Night,
> Taught by the heavenly Muse to venture down
> The dark descent, and up to reascend,
> Though hard and rare: thee I <u>revisit</u> safe,
> And feel thy sovereign vital lamp; but thou
> <u>Revisitst</u> not these eyes, that roll in vain
> To find thy piercing ray, and find no dawn;
> So thick a drop serene hath quenched their orbs,
> Or dim suffusion veiled. (*Paradise Lost* 3. 13-26)

The verb "revisit" (derived from the Latin *reviso-ere*) functions perhaps as a bilingual signifier of a classical intertext: that of the underworld of Virgil's *Aeneid*, an intertext also signaled by a series of thematic and structural parallels and contrasts. In book 6 of the *Aeneid* the Latin verb *revisere* occurs significantly three times, and in all instances of characters in the darkness of an underworld. Milton, however, seems to reverse the Virgilian sequence,[42] presenting events in backward motion as the speaker's quest for light is mirrored by a reverse infernal itinerary, beginning in the depths of the underworld but progressing backward to the pre-infernal conditions of the upper world. Upon the first occurrence of the verb the speaker proclaims:

> Thee I revisit now with bolder wing,
> Escaped the Stygian pool, though long detained

In *Aeneid* 6 Aeneas and his guide, the Sibyl, encounter Charon, the stern ferryman of the river Styx. About him throng souls of the unburied begging for transportation across the river. The Sibyl explains to an inquisitive Aeneas that only those whose bodies have been buried in the upper world may cross; all the unburied can do is wander about the Stygian pool for one hundred years; then when eventually buried and thus

---

[42] On Virgil's underworld, see among others, Frances Norwood, "The Tripartite Eschatology of *Aeneid* 6," *CP* 49 (1954), 15-26; R.D. Williams, "The Sixth Book of the *Aeneid*," *G&R* 11 (1964), 48-63; W.A. Camps, "The Role of the Sixth Book in the *Aeneid*," *Proceedings of the Vergil Society* 7 (1967-8), 22-30; Friedrich Solmsen, "The World of the Dead in Book 6 of the *Aeneid*," *CP* 67 (1971), 31-41; E.L. Harrison, "Metempsychosis in *Aeneid* Six," *CJ* 73 (1977-78), 193-197.

admitted into Charon's boat, they "revisit" that pool for which they have been longing:

> portitor ille Charon; hi, quos vehit unda, sepulti.
> nec ripas datur horrendas et rauca fluenta
> transportare prius quam sedibus ossa quierunt.
> centum errant annos volitantque haec litora circum;
> tum demum admissi stagna exoptata <u>revisunt</u>. (*Aen.* 6.326-330)

The verb *revisunt* reinforces the fact that these are souls who have had to wait for a long time. The Miltonic speaker has, like those unburied souls who have wandered for one hundred years, been hovering for some time about his metaphorical Styx ("though long detained" [14]). Virgil had compared those hovering souls to autumn leaves falling in the woods in a simile reworked by Milton in *Paradise Lost* 1 to describe Satan and his crew.[43] But now the speaker himself has been transported ("Escaped the Stygian pool" [14]). And the longed-for pool revisited by Virgil's souls (*stagna exoptata*) is replaced by light itself: "thee I revisit" (13). The speaker's "bolder wing" enables him to "overleap" the boundaries, the conditions of his underworld just as the poem itself has escaped the hell of books 1 and 2, elevated as it is now to the world of heaven. As the hymn to light continues the speaker elaborates on that long detainment:

> though long detained
> In that obscure sojourn, while in my flight
> Through utter and through middle darkness borne
>
> (*Paradise Lost* 3.14-16)

The language here, especially lines 15 and 16, conducts the reader back some fifty lines previous in *Aeneid* 6 as Aeneas and the Sibyl commence their infernal journey. And they do so in famous lines marked by their slow spondaic movement, vowel sounds and juxtaposition of nouns and adjectives:

> **Ibant obscuri so**la sub nocte ... (*Aen.* 6. 268)
> **In that obscure so**journ, while in my flight (*Paradise Lost* 3.15)

> ... **per** umbram
> **Perque** domos Ditis vacuas **et** inania regna (*Aen.* 6. 268-269)
> **Through** utter **and through** middle darkness borne (*Paradise Lost* 3.16)

Milton's English actually looks and sounds like the Latin lines: "In that obscure sojourn"/*ibant obscuri sola*. Indeed Austin's pertinent remark concerning Virgil's Latin ("the opening spondaic disyllable sets the grave

---

[43] *Paradise Lost* 1. 301-304.

tone")[44] is equally applicable to Milton's English, which recreates those multiple vowel-sounds ee, ah, aw, u, o. The syntactical repetition of "through" "and through" replicates the Latin *per* and *perque*, and "darkness" parallels the Virgilian *umbram*. But more than that. Phonological replication takes the reader on an infernal journey of sorts. Just as the Miltonic speaker sung of Chaos and Eternal Night

> With other notes than to the Orphean lyre
> I sung of Chaos and eternal Night   (*Paradise Lost* 3.17-18)

so the Virgilian speaker in lines immediately preceding the *ibant obscuri* passage had invoked Chaos and the powers of darkness:

> Di, quibus imperium est animarum, umbraeque silentes
> Et Chaos et Phlegethon, loca nocte tacentia late,
> Sit mihi fas audita loqui, sit numine vestro
> Pandere res alta terra et caligine mersas (*Aen*. 6. 264-267)

So from unburied souls flitting about the Styx, back to Aeneas and the Sibyl beginning their infernal journey, back to the poetic invocation of darkness, the reader is conducted via one further backward step to the font of Miltonic inspiration (19-21). Now in terms of the Virgilian intertext we are transported back a further one hundred and thirty lines prior to the speaker's invocation of Chaos. Before even entering the underworld Aeneas approaches the Sibyl, and is warned by her that the descent to the underworld is easy, but to retrace one's steps and get back to the upper world is the difficult task:

> Tros Anchisiade, facilis **de**scensus Averno:
> noctes atque **di**es patet atri ianua **Di**tis;
> sed revocare gradum superasque evadere ad auras,
> **hoc opus, hic labor est** (*Aen* 6. 126-129)[45]
>
> Taught by the heavenly Muse to venture **do**wn
> The **d**ark **d**escent, and up to reascend,
> **Though hard and rare**. (*Paradise Lost* 3. 19-21)

Although the Virgilian prophetess is replaced by the Miltonic Heavenly Muse, named in book 7 as Urania,[46] Milton recreates Virgil's

---

[44] Virgil, *Aeneid VI*, ed. R.G. Austin (Oxford, 1992), 116.

[45] Cf. *Paradise Lost* 2. 432-433: "long is the way/And hard, that out of hell leads up to light."

[46] *Paradise Lost* 7. 1-5.

linguistic patterning of threefold alliterative *d*s and their subsequent varying vowel-sounds: *descensus, dies, Ditis* in his own "down," "dark," "descent." He recreates also the pattern of descent/ascent: the difficulty of reascending conveyed in Virgil's four-word phrase *hoc opus, hic labor* becomes the Miltonic four-word phrase "though hard and rare." In what follows the Miltonic speaker laments:

> thee I revisit safe,
> And feel thy sovereign vital lamp; but thou
> Revisitst not these eyes, that roll in vain
> To find thy piercing ray, and find no dawn;
> So thick a drop serene hath quenched their orbs,
> Or dim suffusion veiled. (*Paradise Lost* 3. 21-26)

The lines transport the reader to yet another region of the Virgilian underworld. The verb *revisere* in its second occurrence describes another category of souls flitting this time around another river, Lethe, the river of forgetfulness. Virgil had compared them to bees in a simile echoed in *Paradise Lost* 1 to describe swarming demons.[47] Aeneas, once gain amazed, asks his father: *quae lucis miseris tam dira cupido?* (6. 721), a desire surely at the heart of the Miltonic hymn and a blind bard's quest for light. Aeneas is told that these are souls awaiting reincarnation. Thus the god of the underworld summons them to the river Lethe so that they may drink its waters of oblivion and then revisit (*revisant*) the upper air:

> has omnis, ubi mille rotam volvere per annos,
> Lethaeum ad fluvium deus evocat agmine magno,
> scilicet immemores supera ut convexa revisant
> rursus, et incipiant in corpora velle reverti. (*Aen.* 6. 748-751)

In his quest for light, Milton, like these souls, longs to quench his lips in the waters, but by a process of inversion, instead of drinking of Lethe, a "drop serene" has "quenched" the "orbs" of his eyes, or they have been "veiled" by "dim suffusion." Milton's English may actually translate two Latin terms for eye conditions: "drop serene"/*gutta serena*; "dim suffusion"/*suffusio nigra*. It is his eyes, not Lethean waters, that have been quenched. Where Virgil's souls have an active wish to return to their dwelling in the body, the Miltonic speaker is already trapped in a body marred by blindness. His eyes roll in vain to find the piercing ray and find no dawn.[48] One of the Latin words for eye (*lumen*) is also the word for

---

[47] *Paradise Lost* 1. 767-776.

[48] Cf. the dying Dido: *ter revoluta toro est oculisque errantibus alto/quaesivit caelo lucem ingemuitque reperta* (*Aeneid* 4. 691-692).

light. He revisits light but by contrast light does not revisit his eyes. His blindness is its own underworld. "Revisit" here operates on a bilingual level but also signals the Virgilian intertext with which the passage engages. When at the end of book 6 Aeneas himself leaves the underworld and makes his way to the world above, he is described as "revisiting" his comrades:

> his ibi tum natum Anchises unaque Sibyllam
> prosequitur dictis portaque emittit eburna,
> ille viam secat ad navis sociosque revisit. (*Aen.* 6. 897-899)

No such escape to society for the Miltonic speaker who in virtue of his blindness is "from the cheerful ways of men/Cut off" (3. 46-47), his severance emphasized by the development of that revisiting motif into a complaint about the lack of reciprocity.

Nonetheless this Miltonic hymnist, like the great classical blind bards and prophets, possesses an inner light that gives him the power of speech, of language itself. He announces this in an invocation that inverts and transcends that Virgilian invocation to night and darkness:

> So much the rather thou celestial light
> Shine inward, and the mind through all her powers
> Irradiate, there plant eyes, all mist from thence
> Purge and disperse, that I may see and tell
> Of things invisible to mortal sight. (*Paradise Lost* 3. 51-55)

Milton's reverse itinerary through a metaphorical underworld leads back to the priestess of Apollo, the Sibyl, but ultimately to the authorial voice—to speech itself.

6.3 *Serpens Bilinguis*: "Tongue of Brute"/*Brutus Orator*

Speech, and the power of speech, are in fact central to the epic and to its double-tongued tempter, a *serpens bilinguis*, whose success and failure frequently reside in the use and abuse of Latinate rhetoric. Satan in effect becomes a Roman orator in performance, to whom he is likened in the poem itself. At a key moment in book 9 as Satan girds himself for a series of climactic temptation speeches Milton proclaims:

> ... when now more bold
> The tempter, but with show of zeal and love
> To man, and indignation at his wrong,
> New part puts on, and as to passion moved,
> Fluctuates disturbed, yet comely, and in act

> Raised, as of some great <u>matter</u> to begin.
> As when of old some orator renowned
> In Athens or free Rome, where eloquence
> Flourished, since mute, to some great <u>cause</u> addressed,
> Stood in himself collected, while each <u>part</u>,
> <u>Motion</u>, each <u>act</u> won audience ere the tongue,
> Sometimes in height began, as no delay
> Of preface, brooking through his zeal of right.
> So standing, moving, or to height upgrown
> The tempter all impassioned thus began. (*Paradise Lost* 9. 664-678)

Even before the simile, aspects of the language seem to signal a classical oratorical intertext. The authorial voice articulates the prerequisites of the accomplished orator perhaps as delineated by Cicero in such works as *De Oratore* and *Brutus Orator*. Thus "act" (668 and 674) denotes *actio*, an orator's exterior form and being. For Cicero the orator's *actio* constitutes a form of physical eloquence.[49] "Matter" (669) denotes *materia* or *materies*, the rhetorical word for a theme for declamation. Cicero expounds eloquently on the importance of the orator's *materia*.[50] "Cause" (672) signals the *causa*, a legal case; "motion" (674), the *motus* by which the orator's physical gestures could win over an audience; "part" (673), *pars*, the standpoint or side taken in a rhetorical dispute.[51] In *De Oratore* 1.5 Cicero stresses the importance of physical deportment, gestures of the arms, facial expression, voice-production, and the avoidance of monotony, and he does so by striking an analogy with the actor on the stage,[52] a pertinent comparison that likewise seems to underlie Milton's account of the "new part" (667), "each part" (673) assumed by Satan. And as Satan proceeds in his series of temptation speeches the vocabulary and syntax in which he expresses that temptation become increasingly Latinate—nouns and verbs with Latin

---

[49] *est enim <u>actio</u> quasi corporis quaedam eloquentia, cum constet e voce atque <u>motu</u>* (*Brutus Orator* 17.55). Text is that of *Cicero: Orator*, ed. and trans. H.M. Hubbell (Cambridge Mass.: Loeb Classical Library, 1952).

[50] *De <u>materia</u> loquor orationis* (*Brutus Orator* 34.119).

[51] For Cicero every "part" of an oration should be worthy of praise: *omnis <u>pars</u> orationis esse debet laudabilis* (*Brutus Orator* 35.125).

[52] *Nam quid ego de <u>actione</u> ipsa plura dicam? quae <u>motu</u> corporis, quae gestu, quae vultu, quae vocis confirmatione ac varietate moderanda est; quae sola per se ipsa quanta sit, histrionum levis ars et scaena declarat* (*De Oratore*, 1.5.18). Text is that of *Cicero: De Oratore*, ed. E.W. Sutton (Cambridge Mass.: Loeb Classical Library, 1948).

roots, an abundance of quasi-Ciceronian subordinate clauses, highly convoluted syntax with inflected word order:

> Wonder not, sovereign mistress, if perhaps
> Thou canst, who art sole wonder, much less arm
> Thy looks, the heaven of mildness, with disdain,
> Displeased that I approach thee thus, and gaze
> Insatiate, I thus single, nor have feared
> Thy awful brow, more awful thus retired.
> Fairest resemblance of thy maker fair. (*Paradise Lost* 9.532-538)

Satanic rhetoric[53] commences with a *proemium* that functions as a *captatio benevolentiae*, addressing Eve in grandiloquently regal language ("sovereign mistress" [532], "sole wonder" [533], "fairest resemblance" [538]). In *De Oratore* Cicero emphasizes the importance of the *proemium* as a means of winning over the mind of the audience.[54] But this "proem" (549) is couched in verbal and syntactical ambiguities whereby language serves to flatter, to confound and ultimately to entrap. Thus the imperative "wonder" (532) becomes the noun "wonder" (533).[55] This

---

[53] On Satanic rhetoric in this speech, see Masahiko Agari, "Logical Equivocation in *Paradise Lost*," in *Language and Style in English Literature: Essays in Honour of Michio Masui*, ed. Michio Kawai (Tokyo, 1991), 542-556, who argues that Satan commences with courtly rhetoric followed by logical equivocation. Hideyuki Shitaka, "Satan's Language and Its Influence on the Linguistic Deterioration of Adam and Eve in *Paradise Lost*, Book 9: A Note Mainly From a Rhetorical Viewpoint," *ERA* 3 (1983), 1-18, provides an analysis of the compartmentalization of Satanic rhetoric into *ethos*, *comprobatio*, *parrhesia*, *procatalepsis* and *meiosis*. Neither discussion, however, situates the Satanic orator within a Ciceronian context.

[54] *initio conciliandos eorum esse animos, qui audirent* (*De Oratore* 1.31.143).

[55] Indeed it is as though a Satanic Ferdinand is being mesmerized by a second Miranda. Satan's language, like that of Shakespeare's Ferdinand, conveys a sense of awe in words that may likewise pun on the name Miranda "to be wondered at." Cf. the initial encounter between Ferdinand and Miranda: "*Ferdinand*: 'Most sure, the goddess/On whom these airs attend! Vouchsafe my prayer/May know if you remain upon this island;/And that you will some good instruction give/How I may bear me here: my prime request,/Which I do last pronounce, is, O you wonder!/If you be maid or no?' *Miranda*: 'No wonder, sir;/But certainly a maid'" (*The Tempest* 1.2.424-431). Later the noun "wonder" is transformed into the verb as Ferdinand describes himself as one "that wonders/To hear thee speak of Naples" (1.2.435-436). Cf. also "Admir'd Miranda" (3.1.37). With Satan's self-description as "I thus single" (9. 536), cf. Ferdinand's self-description as "A single thing, as I am now" (1.2.435). Like Ferdinand ("I am the best of them that speak this speech" [1.2. 432]), Satan is the orator par excellence, addressing a somewhat naïve female. But the ironies are apparent. Miranda will proclaim of Ferdinand: "There's nothing ill can dwell in such a temple" (1.2 460). In regard to Satan, the "author of all ill" (2. 381), nothing could

linguistic entrapment is enhanced through the repetition of "awful" (537) or "fairest" and "fair" (538) or through the assonance of "disdain" (534) and "displeased" (535).[56] And the labyrinthine and even serpentine syntax of these lines is achieved by an orator's quasi-Ciceronian manipulation of language. This is evident in the wealth of clauses: the subordinate "if" clause (532-534) containing within it the relative clause "who art sole wonder" (533); the shift in subject in 536-537 from Eve as addressee to the Satanic first person. This *captatio benevolentiae* is followed by Satan's hymn in praise of Eve:

> Thee all things living gaze on, all things thine
> By gift, and thy celestial beauty adore
> With ravishment beheld, there best beheld
> Where universally admired. (*Paradise Lost* 9. 539-542)

The hymnic nature of these lines is signaled by the varying forms of the second-person address, from "thee" (539) as object to "thine" (539) and "thy" (540) as possessive. The language suggests a divine lifeforce admired and revered by the whole of creation, as though this Edenic goddess mirrors the Lucretian Venus hymned in a series of *te*, *tuum* and *tibi* clauses in the *proemium* of the *De Rerum Natura*.[57] In what follows the language becomes explicitly pagan and indeed quasi-Lucretian in its references to "goddess" and "gods" ironically juxtaposed in this instance with "angels." Thus Eve "shouldst be seen/A goddess among gods, adored and served/By angels numberless, thy daily train" (9.546-548).

As beast becomes orator Eve is surprised by this instantaneous acquisition of language:[58]

> "What may this mean? Language of man pronounced
> By tongue of <u>brute</u>." (*Paradise Lost* 9. 553-554)

> "How cam'st thou speakable of mute, and how
> To me so friendly grown above the rest
> Of <u>brutal</u> kind." (*Paradise Lost* 9. 563-565)

---

be further from the truth. Indeed it is his rhetorical language that serves as a means of concealing such "ill."

[56] On *dis-* words in *Paradise Lost* see page 122.

[57] See Lucretius, *De Rerum Natura* 1.1-9.

[58] Cf. Fish, *Surprised By Sin*, 13: "Eve (innocently) surrenders her mind to wonderment ('much marvelling') at the technical problem of the seeming-serpent's voice."

In Satan's reply the beast of "abject thoughts and low" (572) is transformed into the orator who can employ language to maximum effect. According to Cicero, there is nothing more agreeable to the understanding and ear of the audience than a speech adorned with wise thoughts and fine language.[59] Key to the orator's success is his ability to magnify and adorn what is pleasant and attractive.[60] Satan appeals to the senses of his audience by describing in hissingly seductive language (9. 575-588) his feigned experience of eating the forbidden fruit.[61]

The rhetorical powers of this beast are encapsulated in a possible pun on "brute" and Brutus, perhaps Marcus Brutus, the famed orator of classical Rome, eponymously equated with oratory itself in Cicero's *Brutus Orator*, and more famous as the assassin of Julius Caesar.[62] The pun finds precedent in Shakespeare. Thus Mark Anthony after Brutus's assassination of Caesar:

> Mark Antony: O judgment! thou art fled to *brutish* beasts,
> And men have lost their reason (*Julius Caesar* 3.2.105-106)

Compare Hamlet to Polonius:

> Hamlet: My lord, you
>   Played once i' th' university, you say?
> Polonius: That did I, my lord, and was accounted a good actor.
> Hamlet: What did you enact?
> Polonius: I did enact Julius Caesar. I was killed i' th' Capitol.
>   Brutus killed me.
> Hamlet: It was a *brute* part of him to kill so capital a calf there.
>   (*Hamlet* 3.2.97-103)[63]

---

[59] *Aut tam iucundum cognitu atque auditu, quam sapientibus sententiis gravibusque verbis ornata oratio et polita?* (*De Oratore* 1.8.31).

[60] *ea, quae vulgo expetenda atque optabilia videntur, dicendo amplificat atque ornat.* (*De Oratore* 1.51.221).

[61] "savoury" (579), "sense" (580), "smell" (581), "sweetest" (581), "unsucked" (583), "satisfy" (584), "sharp" (584), "desire" (584), "tasting" (585), etc. For the anticipation of this methodology in Milton's *Apologus De Rustico et Hero*, see pages 45-46.

[62] On the Shakespearean Brutus as orator, see among others R.W. Zandvoort, "Brutus's Forum Speech in *Julius Caesar*," *RES* 16.61 (1940), 62-66; Nathan Norman, "Brutus' Oratory," *San Jose Studies* 8.1 (1982), 82-90. Compare Michael West's discussion of Coriolanus as orator in "The Controversial Eloquence of Shakespeare's Coriolanus: An Anti-Ciceronian Orator?" *MP* 102.3 (2005), 307-331.

[63] The lines may refer to the neo-Latin drama *Caesar Interfectus* performed in Christ Church Hall, Oxford (1581-1582) and perhaps even witnessed by Shakespeare.

The possibility of Satan's identification with Brutus is strengthened perhaps when it is remembered that the two are closely associated in Dante's *Inferno*. There Satan stands forth out of the ice. He has three faces, and in each of his mouths he champs a sinner with his teeth. Three sinners are named: Judas Iscariot, who has his head within; Brutus who hangs from Satan's black visage, writhing and not uttering a word, and Cassius:

> De li altri due ch'hanno il capo di sotto,
> quel che pende dal nero ceffo è Bruto:
> vedi come si storce, e non fa motto!
> e l'altro è Cassio, che par sì membruto. (*Inferno* 34.64-67)[64]

But if in Dante the silenced Brutus dangles from Satan's mouth, thereby enduring a form of eternal and infernal punishment, in Milton by a process of inversion it is the "brute" Satan who willingly enters a mouth—that of the serpent. Brutus, the Devil, and the serpent are conflated to function as one, the wily orator: "in at his mouth/The devil entered, and his *brutal* sense,/In heart or head, possessing soon inspired/With act intelligential" (9.187-190).[65] In *Hamlet* the Brutus/ "brute" pun is paired with one on the Capitol, the hill of Rome (where in Shakespeare's version Caesar met his end), and the adjective "capital." Interestingly, Milton's Satan is likewise associated with the Capitol. Thus his serpentine beauty surpasses a whole series of classical serpents, including Jupiter Capitolinus, who assumed the form of a snake to father Scipio Africanus:

> ... nor to which transformed
> Ammonian Jove or Capitoline was seen,
> He with Olympias, this with her who bore
> Scipio the height of Rome. With tract oblique
> At first, as one who sought access, but feared
> To interrupt, sidelong he works his way.
> As when a ship by skilful steersman wrought
> Nigh river's mouth or foreland ... (*Paradise Lost* 9. 507-514)[66]

---

[64] Text is that of *Dante Alighieri, La Divina Comedia: Inferno*, eds. Umberto Bosco and Govanni Reggio (Florence, 1979).

[65] Italics are mine.

[66] Emphasis is mine.

The serpentine Satan,[67] surpassing Jupiter of the Capitol, envelops the language and sentiment in the possible acrostic (SATAN 510-514). His sidelong movement is mirrored by the language itself as vernacular is literally side by side and framing the classical allusion. Earlier in book 1 a demonic conference was convened in Pandaemonium "the high capital/Of Satan and his peers" (1. 756-757) located on "a hill" (1. 670). Is Milton punning here on "capital"/"Capitol," the hill of Rome, upon which were held debates on peace and war? Does "high capital" recall perhaps the Virgilian "high Capitol" (*Capitolia ... alta* [*Aen*. 6.836])[68] with Satan's richly laid temple that is Pandaemonium equated with the Capitol "now all gold" (*Capitolia ...aurea nunc* [*Aen*. 8.347-348])?[69] Interestingly, the original manuscript reading was "Capitol" at this point, but was changed in a later hand to "capital."[70] Will brute Satan ultimately become a second Brutus, assassinating Eve, a second Caesar?

6.4 "Words" and the "Sword": Assassinating Eve?

Before discussing the "assassination scene" proper in Milton's epic, it might be pertinent to comment on several wider points of contact and contrast between Shakespeare's Brutus and Milton's Satan. The whole conspiratorial opening of Shakespeare's play is paralleled perhaps by the demonic plotting that occupies *Paradise Lost* 1 and 2. Both Brutus and Satan are tormented by what is essentially a very private, a very personal, inner turmoil, which they try to veil in different ways. Thus Brutus proclaims: "Vexed I am/Of late passions of some difference,/ Conceptions only proper to myself" (1.2.38-40); Satan, though putting a

---

[67] Cf. Fish, *Surprised by Sin*, 74: "Satan's fallacies are wrapped in serpentine trains of false beginnings, faulty pronoun references, missing verbs and verbal schemes which sacrifice sense to sound."

[68] *ille triumphata Capitolia ad alta Corintho/victor aget currum caesis insignis Achivis* (*Aen*. 6. 836-837).

[69] *hinc ad Tarpeiam sedem et Capitolia ducit/aurea nunc, olim silvestribus horrida dumis* (*Aen*. 8.347-348).

[70] Helen Darbishire, *The Manuscript of Milton's Paradise Lost, Book 1* (Oxford, 1931), favors the earlier reading. R.M. Adams, *Ikon: John Milton and the Modern Critics* (Ithaca, 1955), 88, supports the emendation, while acknowledging the possibility of a subtextual allusion. Cf. R.G. Moyles, *The Text of "Paradise Lost": A Study in Editorial Procedure* (Toronto, 1985), 143.

brave face on things, is "in pain" (1.125) and "racked with deep despair" (1.126). Both rebuke their peers for lethargy. Thus Brutus: "Awake, I say!" (2.1.5);[71] Satan: "Awake, arise, or be for ever fall'n." (1.330). Both resent the position of subservience in which they find themselves, yet simultaneously state that they had rather abide by their current circumstances than endure servitude under a tyrannical power. "Brutus had rather be a villager/Than to repute himself a son of Rome/Under these hard conditions as this time/Is like to lay upon us." (1.2.170-173).[72] Satan famously proclaims "Here we may reign secure, and in my choice/To reign is worth ambition though in hell:/Better to reign in hell, than serve in heaven." (1.261-263). For Brutus and Cassius, as indeed for Satan, that power is equated with tyranny and the chains of enslavement. Shakespeare's Brutus moreover is described in terms that associate him with both the devil and the serpent. Thus, according to Cassius, he could in former times have surpassed the devil himself: "There was a Brutus once that would have brook'd/Th'eternal devil to keep his state in Rome/As easily as a king" (1.2.157-159). Later Brutus employs the image of the serpent, proclaiming "It is the bright day that brings forth the adder" (2.1.14); "And therefore think him as a serpent's egg/Which, hatch'd, would as his kind, grow mischievous/And kill him in the shell" (2.1.32-34). Both present their "mission" as inspired not by personal motivation but by the good of the "general cause." Thus Brutus: "It must be by his death; and for my part,/I know no personal cause to spurn at him,/But for the general. He would be crowned" (2.1.10-12); Satan announces: "while I abroad/Through all the coasts of dark destruction seek/Deliverance for us all" (2.463-465), is venerated by his crew, and praised "that for the general safety he despised/His own" (2. 481-482). The key motivation of both missions is conspiratorial resentment at the advancement of (one) man: "Why, man, he doth bestride the narrow world/Like a Colossus, and we petty men/Walk under his huge legs" (1.2.133-135); "some new race called Man" (2.348).[73]

It is within this wider context that Milton's Eve, the ultimate victim of the "brute" Satan, might be regarded as a second Caesar, undergoing

---

[71] Cf. *Marullus*: And do you now cull out a holiday?" (1.1.49) and the exhortation in the letter received by Brutus: "Brutus, thou sleep'st; awake, and see thyself" (2.1.45). See also Milton's Latin verses on early rising discussed at pages 25-36.

[72] Cf. Cassius: "And the man/Is now become a god, and Cassius is/A wretched creature, and must bend his body/If Caesar carelessly but nod on him" (1.2.115-118).

[73] Cf. "What should be in that 'Caesar'?/Why should that name be sounded more than yours?/Write them together, yours is as fair a name" (1.2.141-143); "but one man" (1.2.154); "one only man" (1.2.156).

an "assassination" of sorts, or, more accurately, a series of assassinations. Even before the cumulative assassination scenes proper, Eve's behavior is in several respects similar to that of Caesar. Both leave their spouse's side against that spouse's advice. Thus Calphurnia: "What mean you, Caesar? Think you to walk forth?/You shall not stir out of your house today" (2.2.8-9), and later: "Do not go forth to-day" (2.2.50). In a subtly gendered inversion it is the male spouse who exhorts Eve: "leave not the faithful side/That gave thee being" (9.265-266), yet ultimately yields, stating: "Go; for thy stay, not free, absents thee more" (9. 372). Calphurnia's attempts to detain Caesar are instigated by a series of enigmatic dreams she has had the previous night, including one of a bleeding statue, prefiguring, as she believes, his untimely end (2.2.75ff.).[74] Such dreams are, however, described by Decius as nothing more than a fair "vision" (2.2.84ff).[75] As a consequence Caesar, governed by what is in effect a grave misinterpretation of the Macrobian *somnium* or enigmatic dream,[76] leaves her side.[77] The reality is, however, that Calphurnia's dream is a prophetic dream (*visio*),[78] prefiguring Caesar's end. Eve had initially assumed a role equivalent to that of Calphurnia, narrating to Adam her troublesome dream of the fall. Significantly, however, Eve's dream is not about her spouse, but about herself[79]—a

---

[74] "Calphurnia here, my wife, stays me at home./She dreamt to-night she saw my statue,/Which like a fountain with an hundred spouts/Did run pure blood" (2.2.75-78). See in general T.N. Tice, "Calphurnia's Dream and Communication with the Audience in Shakespeare's *Julius Caesar*," *The Shakespeare Yearbook* 1 (1990), 37-49.

[75] "This dream is all amiss interpreted;/It was a *vision* fair and fortunate" (2.2. 83-84). Italics are mine.

[76] Cf. Macrobius, Commentary on Cicero's *Somnium Scipionis*, 1.3.10: *somnium proprie vocatur quod tegit figuris et velat ambagibus non nisi interpretatione intellegendam significationem rei quae demonstratur.*

[77] Cf. "How foolish do your fears seem now, Calphurnia!/I am ashamed I did yield to them./Give me my robe, for I will go." (2.2.105-107).

[78] According to Macrobius, Commentary on Cicero's *Somnium Scipionis*, the *visio* or prophetic dream was useful in divination especially when a dream came true: *visio est autem cum id quis videt quod eodem modo quo apparuerat eveniet* (1.3.9). Cf. Caesar's ironic praise of Decius's misguided interpretation of the dream: "And this way have you well expounded it" (2.2.91).

[79] On Eve's dream, cf. E.J. Bellamy, "Milton's Freud: The Law of Psychoanalysis in Eve's Dream," *Literature and Psychology* 42.3 (1996), 36-47; Sung-Kyun Yim, "Eve's Dream and Myth Making in Milton's *Paradise Lost*," *The Journal of Milton Studies in Korea* 7 (1997), 237-256; D.T. Benet, "Milton's Toad, or Satan's Dream,"

point that she emphasizes. Thus she has "dreamed,/If dreamed, not as I oft am wont, of thee" (5.31-32). As she relates her dreams of her own fall, she seems to echo the emphasis upon "walking forth" in the Calphurnia/Caesar interchange, stating: "methought/Close at mine ear one called me forth to walk" (5.35-36). As in Shakespeare, these dreams are subsequently dismissed in pseudo-Macrobian language, in this instance as nothing more than an *insomnium*,[80] a dream originating, Adam suggests, from the previous evening's conversation: "Some such resemblances methinks I find/Of our last evening's talk, in this thy dream,/But with addition strange" (5.114-116).

And thus the scene is set for the assassination attempt or attempts. When in book 9 Eve yields to temptation, that yielding is depicted as the gradual and cumulative piercing of her heart, a heart penetrated on more than one occasion by the oratorical powers of Satan. It could be argued moreover that Eve as a second Caesar is repeatedly stabbed by Satan's "words" (in a Miltonic anagram perhaps of "sword"): "So glozed the tempter, and his proem tuned;/Into the *heart* of Eve his *words* made way" (9. 549-550).[81] Later "his *words* replete with guile/Into *her heart* too easy entrance won" (9. 733-734).[82] And as she commits the fatal act, that act is described as the double wounding of both Nature and Eve herself. Thus "Earth felt the wound, and nature from her seat/Sighing through all her works gave signs of woe,/That all was lost" (9. 782-784), while Eve "engorged without restraint,/And knew not eating death" (9. 791-792). Her deed has implications that move far beyond this Edenic immediacy, signaling a death that has universal implications. Comparable perhaps are the words of Mark Antony after Caesar's death: "A curse shall light upon the limbs of men;/Domestic fury and fierce civil strife/Shall cumber all the parts of Italy" (3.1.262).

And if Eve is a second Caesar, so Adam is perhaps a second Mark Antony: "For Antony is but a limb of Caesar" (2.1.165); Eve was begotten from the rib of Adam ("bone of my bone, flesh of my flesh" [8. 495]). Upon learning of the fall, Adam's initial reaction, not unlike that of Mark Antony ("*Brutus*: O Antony, beg not your death of us" [3.1.164]), is to profess the wish for death itself: "Certain my resolution is to die" (9. 907). Adam utters a lament on the loss of nobility and virtue (9. 1067-

---

MS 45 (2006), 38-42. See also K.P. McColgan, "'God is Also in Sleep': Dreams Satanic and Divine in *Paradise Lost*," *MS* 30 (1993), 135-148.

[80] On the Macrobian *insomnium*, see pages 72-75.

[81] Italics are mine.

[82] Italics are mine.

1090). Similar sentiments underlie Mark Antony's funeral oration on Caesar's fall and its universal consequences: "O mighty Caesar! dost thou lie so low?" (3.1.148); "great Caesar fell./O, what a fall was there, my countrymen!/Then, I and you, and all of us fell down" (3.2.191-193).

But what ultimately of Satan's "brute part"? After the assassination of Caesar, Brutus's followers turn against him, and many of them flee. He ascends a pulpit and defends his action as a deed undertaken for the common good; after the fall Satan returns to hell, ascends his throne, and defends his deed. But his expectations of applause are defeated when his audience responds with an "exploding hiss" (10. 546), the Latinate adjective hissing him off his stage,[83] as they and he are transformed into serpents. Brutus will finally meet his end by running against a sword; Satan, as the war in heaven proved, can be wounded, but cannot die. Instead the brute beast in Dantesque terms is silenced and reduced to eternal torment. His last word spoken in the poem, ironically "bliss,"[84] mirrors the hissing brute that he has now become. The orator is rendered incapable of speech (*infantia linguae*)[85] as his eloquently "bilingual" tongue becomes the forked tongue of a serpent: "He would have spoke,/But hiss for hiss returned with forked tongue/To forked tongue." (10. 517-519). Thus does the *serpens bilinguis* meet his epic end.

6.5 Epic Endings: *Facies*/Faces/Firebrands

Although there has been much debate concerning the closing lines of Milton's epic, the complexity of their engagement with a Latin intertext has failed to receive due attention.[86] For as Adam and Eve "in the saddest passage of the poem"[87] bid their final farewell to Eden, that paradise

---

[83] See *OLD* sv *explodere*: "To drive off the stage by clapping, etc." Cf. Cicero, *Pro Roscio* 30: *e scaena non modo sibilis sed etiam convicio explodebatur*. See also Casca (of Caesar): "If the tag-rag people did not clap him and hiss him, according as he pleased and displeased them, as they use to do the players in the theatre, I am no true man" (*Julius Caesar* 1.2.255).

[84] "Ye have th'account/Of my performance: what remains, ye gods,/But up and enter now into full bliss." (10. 501-503).

[85] See page 92.

[86] With one exception: M.C.J. Putnam, "The *Aeneid* and *Paradise Lost*: Ends and Conclusions," *Literary Imagination* 8.3 (2006), 387-410.

[87] Nuttall, *Openings*, 90.

comes to function as a second Troy, a Troy that has been lost. The equation is established by means of a series of intertextual and at times interlingual links with two scenes from *Aeneid* 2: 1) the departure of Aeneas and his family from the burning city; 2) Aeneas's return to the city in search of his wife Creusa, his surprise encounter with her ghost, and his subsequent departure in exile and in quest of a new order. It is with the second of these episodes that this discussion will begin. Milton, it will be argued, reverses the sequence of Virgilian events, before allowing the whole to come full circle.

A number of parallels can be cited at the outset. Both Aeneas and Adam rush back to look for their "spouse," find her in a condition different to that of which they were last aware, and receive from her a verbal *consolatio*, describing some sort of privileged alliance that she seems to enjoy with the divine. She emphasizes the guiding role of providence, conveying a sense of contentment, and offering the male some form of reassurance in regard to her own future circumstances.

Aeneas, having realized that he has lost his wife, returns to Troy in a frantic search that causes him to rush endlessly through buildings in the city (*quaerenti et tectis urbis sine fine ruenti* [2.771]). To his surprise, however, he encounters not Creusa herself, but her ghost, a shade, which seems even greater than the person he had known in actuality (*infelix simulacrum atque ipsius umbra Creusae/visa mihi ante oculos et nota maior imago* [2.772-773]). Adam, having received an epiphanic vision from Michael, runs back to the bower where Eve lay sleeping, but finds her not asleep as had expected (after all, Michael had proposed: "let Eve (for I have drenched her eyes)/Here sleep below while thou to foresight wak'st,/As once thou slepst, while she to life was formed" [11.367-369]), but in a waking state ("Adam to the bower where Eve/Lay sleeping ran before, but found her waked" [12.607-608]). That "but" conveys some element of surprise, conveying, as in Virgil, a contrast between two states.

In both instances the female takes the initiative and addresses the male: Creusa consoles Aeneas with her words (*et curas his demere dictis* [2.775]) as she explains that all that they both have suffered has happened in accordance with divine will (*non haec sine numine divum/eveniunt* [2.777-778]). Nonetheless part of that divine plan is the tragic reality that he is not permitted to take her out of Troy with him (*nec te hinc comitem asportare Creusam/fas, aut ille sinit superi regnator Olympi* [2.778-779]). As if to illustrate her affinity with divine providence, she utters a prophecy, predicting that Aeneas will eventually reach Italy (*et terram Hesperiam venies* [2.781]), enjoy success, and will acquire a new kingdom and a new wife (*illic res laetae regnumque et regia coniunx/parta tibi* [2.783-784]).

As Adam comes upon Eve, he is received by her with "words not sad" (12. 609). Like Creusa, Eve reveals a personal alliance with a wider providential plan that is seen as transcending the suffering underlying their current circumstances ("Whence thou returnst, and whither wentst, I know;/For God is also in sleep" [12.610-611]). But the Virgilian situation is inverted in two ways: first, unlike Creusa, Eve has not had to die to acquire this insight into the divine; instead, she has received this by means of a series of dreams sent to her by God himself ("and dreams advise,/Which he hath sent propitious, some great good/Presaging" [12. 611-613]). Second, in this instance the message that she delivers is the direct antithesis of Creusa's: for Eve proclaims unreservedly her willingness to *accompany* Adam in his departure from Eden. And as if to emphasize the contrast with Creusa, Milton highlights at this point that sense of conjugal unity ("but now lead on;/in me is no delay; with thee to go,/Is to stay here; without thee here to stay,/Is to go hence unwilling" [12.614-617]). Still, she resembles Creusa in her offer of "further consolation" [12.620]), a consolation that in both instances is closely linked to the future fate of the respective female. Creusa reassures Aeneas that she will not behold the Myrmidons or Dolopes nor will she suffer enslavement at the hands of Greek matrons (2.785-787). Rather in death she has found a resting place in Troy (2.788). Eve can likewise offer some comfort and hope as a means, albeit slight, of compensating for the loss of a homeland, so to speak; "though all by me is lost,/Such favour I unworthy am vouchsafed,/By me the promised seed shall all restore" [12.621-623]). The allusion is to the unnamed Christ, a second Adam, who will be born of Mary. The old order must give way to the new just as Creusa must make way for Lavinia, Aeneas's second unnamed wife (*regia coniunx*).

But the ultimate contrast between the eventual fates of Eve and Creusa has deeper Virgilian resonances. Eve's professed willingness to leave without delay "but now lead on;/<u>in me is no delay</u>" [12.614-615]) and the terms in which that willingness is expressed seem to look back to a previous episode in *Aeneid* 2. It is an episode that serves as a point of departure for the Miltonic passage. Having witnessed the brutal murder of King Priam, Aeneas thinks of his own father and rushes back home to rescue him and his family from the burning city. But Anchises refuses to go, a refusal conveyed in the forceful repetition of *abnegat* (2.637; 2.654). He believes that if the gods had wanted him to live, they would have saved Troy (*me si caelicolae voluissent ducere vitam/has mihi servassent sedes* [2.641-642]), and announces his intention to commit suicide (*ipse manu mortem inveniam* [2.645]), firm in his conviction that he is *invisus divis* (2.647). This speech evokes in Aeneas a crazed desire to rush into the fighting and seek certain death. Suddenly, however, a tongue of fire appears over the head of Iulus. Anchises asks Jupiter to confirm the omen (*da deinde augurium, pater, atque haec omina firma* [2.691]). In response to his prayer, a comet comes gliding through the air, illuminating the skies and marking the path of their departure. Addressing the gods of his fatherland, Anchises significantly proclaims that he will delay no longer: " *iam iam nulla mora est. sequor et quo ducitis, adsum/ di patrii*" (2.701-702), for now he recognizes this sign as an *augurium* (703) confirming divine will and indicating that the fate of Troy is in the hands of the gods. Then turning to Aeneas, he states "*cedo equidem nec, nate, tibi comes ire recuso*" [2.704]). He is at last willing to relinquish the old order for the new.

Eve, however, does not seem to require such an *augurium*. The divine insight afforded her in dreams functions as confirmation in itself. After all, she and Adam had already contemplated that Anchises-like option of suicide.[88] Her explicit eagerness to accompany Adam ("in me is no delay") counters Anchises's refusal (*abnegat*) to leave—a refusal itself reminiscent of a female voice, that of the Euripidean Hecuba.[89] It may contain a verbal echo of Anchises's statement in regard to *nulla mora*, but with a difference. Whereas he had invoked the gods for guidance (*qua ducitis adsum* [701]), her request for guidance is addressed to Adam alone: "now lead on" as if in testimony to that famous dictum "she for god in him" (4.299).

Ironically, however, the Miltonic passage is not without an *augurium* of its own. The lines neatly dovetail into a passage which engages with that familial and familiar scene in Virgil of Anchises/ Aeneas/Creusa/Iulus. The shooting star that glides down leading a comet in its train (*et de caelo lapsa per umbras/stella facem ducens multa cum luce cucurrit* [2.693-694]) is, as it were, transformed by Milton into the descending cherubim "gliding meteorous" (12.629). And to reinforce the parallel, the archangel Michael wields the sword of God which blazes like a comet–but a comet with a difference: "The brandished sword of God before them blazed/Fierce as a comet; which with torrid heat,/And vapour as the Libyan air adust,/Began to parch that temperate clime" (12. 633-636). Unlike the harmless *augurium* that served to provide illumination as

---

[88] Thus Eve: "Let us seek death, or he not found, supply/With our own hands his office on ourselves" (10. 1001-1002]). Cf. Adam "for with thee/Certain my resolution is to die;/How can I live without thee" (9.906-908); "Certain to undergo like doom, if death/Consort with thee, death is to me as life" (9.953-954); "Why do I overlive,/Why am I mocked with death, and lengthened out/To deathless pain" [10. 773-775]).

[89] Cf. De la Cerda, *P. Virgilii Maronis Aeneidos Libri Sex Priores*, I, 245 *Abnegat exscissa] ductum fortasse ex Eurip. imitatione, apud quem in Troad. Hecuba non vult vivere, exscisso Ilio.*

it marked the way (*signantemque vias* [2.697]), unlike the harmless tongue of fire that did not scorch Iulus's head (*tactuque innoxia mollis/lambere flamma comas et circum tempora pasci* [2.683-684]), this sword/comet is threatening, austere and potentially destructive, depicted as parching and scorching its environs. This particular comet moreover recalls that to which Satan was compared:[90] "Incensed with indignation Satan stood/Unterrified, and like a comet burned,/That fires the length of Ophiucus huge/In the Arctic sky, and from his horrid hair/Shakes pestilence and war" (2.707-711).[91] Both seem to draw upon an equivalent simile used of Aeneas in book 10:

> Ardet apex capiti cristisque a vertice flamma
> Funditur et vastos umbo vomit aureus ignis:
> Non secus ac liquida si quando nocte cometae
> Sanguinei lugubre rubent, aut Sirius ardor
> Ille sitim morbosque ferens mortalibus aegris
> Nascitur et laevo contristat lumine caelum   (*Aen.* 10. 270-275)

Here aspects of the Iulus scene are disturbingly transmuted into something very sinister: the *fundere lumen apex, tactuque innoxia mollis/ lambere flamma comas et circum tempora pasci* (2. 683-684) recalled in *ardet apex* (10. 270), *flamma/funditur* (10.270-271).

And as Adam and Eve prepare to leave Eden they enact a rather transmuted version of the Virgilian escape from Troy scene. Having assembled his family, Aeneas takes his father upon his back, holds the hand of his son Iulus (*dextrae se parvus Iulus/implicuit* [2.723-724]),[92] while Creusa follows behind (*pone subit coniunx* [2. 725]). But urged to hasten by his father, Aeneas fails to look back at his wife (*nec prius amissam respexi ...* [2.741]), who has either wandered off course or grown tired (*erravitne via seu lassa resedit* [2.739]). Thus does he lose her. In the first of two references Milton picks up the hand-in-hand (*dextra*) motif central to Virgil's depiction of Aeneas. In Virgil, the motif not only signifies the Trojan hero's concern for his son, but also signals elsewhere in the epic a very human desire for physical contact: reflected

---

[90] Cf. Neil Forsyth, *The Satanic Epic* (Princeton, 2003), 346: "God's sword, even at the very end of the poem, still echoes Satan."

[91] "hair," as Fowler, 146, notes, plays etymologically on "comet" "Gk ἀστὴρ κομήτης, 'long-haired star.'" For the juxtaposition of "horrid" and "hair," cf. Aeneas's reaction to Mercury's rebuke at 4.280: *arrectaeque horrore comae*. Unlike the "unterrified" Satan, however, Aeneas was significantly *attonitus tanto monitu imperioque deorum* (4. 282).

[92] Cf. Servius, ad loc: *implicuit puerilem expressit timorem, ne manu excidat patris*.

in his poignant request to his divine mother (*cur dextrae iungere dextram/non datur* [1.408-409]) and to the ghost of his father in the underworld (*da iungere dextram,/da, genitor* [6.697-698]). At other times it functions as a symbol of help,[93] trust[94] or formal treaty.[95] The motif likewise underlies the Adam/Eve relationship and operates on a variety of levels. At times it indicates a sense of idyllic and idealized unity between the pair in prelapsarian Eden ("So hand in hand they passed" [4.321]; "with that thy gentle hand/Seized mine" [4.488-489]; "hand in hand alone they passed" [4.689]). In postlapsarian Eden it functions by inversion as a symbol of separation "from her husband's hand her hand/Soft she withdrew" [9.385-386]), and lust ("Her hand he seized" [9.1037]).

Michael, however, seems to usurp and surpass Aeneas as "<u>In either hand</u> the hastening angel <u>caught</u>/Our <u>lingering</u> parents" [12.637-638]). Although he is "hastening" as indeed was Aeneas (*"fuge" nate* [2.733]) in his escape from Troy, he has "caught" both of his charges by the hand. That "lingering" on the part of Adam and Eve implies reluctance, but also perhaps conveys something of Anchises's initial wish to remain with the burning city, refusing to live on once Troy has fallen, and reluctant to endure the trials and tribulations of exile (*abnegat excisa vitam producere Troia/exsiliumque pati* [2.637-638]).

As Adam and Eve take their final steps through Eden they cast a quasi-Virgilian retrospective glance—a glance that was in fact central to *Aeneid* 2 and to intertextual links between Virgil's passage and the Orpheus/Eurydice story of *Georgics* 4. When Aeneas first witnesses the death of Priam he describes his behavior in the following terms: <u>respicio</u> *et quae me circum copia lustro* (2.564), conveying his realization (2. 565-566) that he has been abandoned and that his comrades have committed suicide either by hurling their bodies to the ground or by running into the flames (*aut ignibus aegra dedere* [*corpora*] [2.566]). Later, just before urging his father to leave, he hears the fires burning and feels them approaching (*et iam per moenia clarior ignis/auditur, propiusque aestus incendia volvunt* [2.705-706]). In the course of his departure from the city he is urged to speed up by his father, who can see the enemy's blazing shields and gleaming bronze (*ardentis clipeos atque aera micantia cerno* [2.734]). But in an inversion of the *respicio* motif, an inversion that is

---

[93] Cf. *ipse pater dextram Anchises .../dat iuveni* (3.610-611); *da dextram misero et tecum me tolle per undas* (6.370).

[94] Cf. Dido to Aeneas: *per ego has lacrimas dextramque tuam* (4.314); *en dextra fidesque* (4.597).

[95] Cf. *dextrae coniungere dextram* (8.164); *iungunt dextras* (8.467); *nec foedera nec quas/iunximus hospitio dextras* (11.164-165).

also an inversion of the Orpheus/Eurydice story, Aeneas loses Creusa because he *fails* to look back (<u>nec</u> ... <u>respexi</u> [2.741]). Loss of spouse is the microcosmic mirror-image of Aeneas's loss of his homeland. And as the book closes the Greeks have thronged the city gates (*Danaique obsessa tenebant/limina portarum* [802-803]).

The motifs of looking back, blazing weaponry, and thronged gates seem to be conflated in the closing lines of Milton's epic. Adam and Eve "<u>looking back</u>" (641) see their fallen Troy, as it were, that "happy seat" now "waved over by that <u>flaming brand</u>, the gate/With <u>dreadful faces</u> thronged and <u>fiery</u> arms" (644). In regard to the latter phrase Martindale compares the *dirae facies* of the gods threatening Troy[96] as observed by a horrified Aeneas (*apparent <u>dirae facies</u> inimicaque Troiae/numina magna deum* [Aen. 2. 622-623]).[97] This stark realization on his part is the culmination of an encounter with his mother, Venus, who had removed the cloud obscuring his vision, only to show him Neptune, Juno, Pallas all actively engaged in Troy's destruction. She promises him protection and urges him to flee; then she disappears into night's shadows: "*eripe, nate, fugam finemque impone labori;/nusquam abero et tutum patrio te limine sistam."/dixerat et spissis noctis se condidit umbris.* (2.619-621). Linguistically "dreadful faces" replicates the sinister and horrific *dirae facies*, all the more terrifying precisely because they are divine. De la Cerda glosses it well: *induerant ipsa numina torvitatem diritatemque et quandam veluti saevitiam, quo formidabiliora appareant*.[98] The Miltonic lines seemingly fail to offer that final Virgilian *consolatio* in that Michael "then disappeared" (640). Instead, the final image of Eden is of a paradise engulfed by the imagery of fire ("flaming brand" [643], "fiery arms" [644]), a second Troy (*tum vero omne mihi visum considere in ignis/Ilium* [2.624-625]). It is as though those "dreadful <u>faces</u>" are, by means of a macaronic pun, synonymous with firebrands (*faces*: plural of *fax*). In Virgil, the *dirae facies* passage is immediately followed by a simile in which the battered city of the falling Troy is compared to a tree being hacked down, gradually tottering and eventually collapsing. Its fate symbolizes a loss of pastoral not far removed from postlapsarian Eden now lost as the consequence of the "fruit" of another tree: "that forbidden tree," its inhabitants themselves transplanted from their soil.[99]

---

[96] Cf. Charles Martindale, *John Milton and the Transformation of Ancient Epic* (Bristol, 2002), 134: "This is perhaps the supreme moment of terror in the *Aeneid*."

[97] Cf. Forsyth, *The Satanic Epic*, 346-347.

[98] De la Cerda, *P. Virgilii Maronis Aeneidos Libri Sex Priores*, I, 243.

[99] On the metaphor of transplanting in *Paradise Lost*, see pages 49-50.

> iamque iugis summae surgebat Lucifer Idae
> ducebatque diem, Danaique obsessa tenebant
> limina portarum, nec spes opis ulla dabatur.
> cessi et sublato montes genitore petivi. (*Aen.* 2.801-804)

There has been much debate about the mood of the closing lines of *Aeneid* 2. Nuttall sees "a hope" in "the imagery of the star, the lifted father, and the movement out towards higher ground at the very end."[100] The passage is marked by continuous motion conveyed via the imperfect tense (*surgebat* [801], *ducebatque* [802], *tenebant* [802], *dabatur* [803]), the urgent *iamque* (801) signaling the rising of the Morning Star, and the use of conjunctions such as the enclitic *que* and *nec*. Creusa had, after all, urged Aeneas to dispel his tears: <u>lacrimas</u> *dilectae* <u>pelle</u> *Creusae* (2.784). But one can hardly ignore the starkly grim statement: *nec spes opis ulla dabatur* (803). As Milton's epic nears its conclusion Adam and Eve seem collectively to become a second Aeneas ("some natural <u>tears</u> they dropped, but <u>wiped them soon</u>" [645]), drying their tears as if in obedience to a Creusa-like injunction. Like Aeneas, they are exiles, facing a future that is unknown. That sense of uncertainty in exile is emphasized in the opening lines of *Aeneid* 3: *diversa exsilia et desertas quaerere terras/auguriis agimur divum* (3.4-5); *incerti quo fata ferant, ubi sistere datur* (3.7). As Putnam notes, Milton's epic ends where Virgil's began:[101] loss of kingdom and subsequent exile. It is an ending couched in ambiguity as the hand-in-hand motif recurs for one last time:

> The world was all before them, where to choose
> Their place of rest, and Providence their guide:
> They hand in hand with wandering steps and slow,
> Through Eden took their solitary way. (*Paradise Lost* 12.646-649)

Now the husband securely holds his wife's hand, but as they wander, they pace their departure slowly. This ambiguity is reflected in the rallentando effect achieved both metrically and, as Ainsworth notes, by the vowel sounds in each of the lines' final words—sounds that "slow the pace of the poem," thereby "creating a sense of serenity."[102] However, Aeneas's *cessi* (804) was in fact quite telling. Despite that sense of serenity and unity, Adam and Eve have had to yield to divine will. And although they

---

[100] Nuttall, *Openings*, 90.

[101] Putnam, "Ends and Conclusions," 387.

[102] Ainsworth, *Milton and the Spiritual Reader*, 140.

are together, they are alone.[103] The poem's final ambiguity is mirrored intertextually as our first parents both assume and also vacillate between the roles of Aeneas and Creusa. That "wandering" motif, widely debated by scholars,[104] is reminiscent of Creusa's loss of direction as conjectured by Aeneas (<u>erravitne</u> via seu lassa resedit [2.739]).[105] As Fowler notes, "it implies erring."[106]

> Before the fall, the Tongue of man was like the pen of a swift writer ... and uttered those thinges which his heart indited: but since the fall, it is a world of iniquity, and defileth the whole bodie ... Before the fall, he spake with one Tongue; but since the fall, he is *bilinguis*, he speakes with a double tongue.[107]

Ultimately the Miltonic *lingua bilinguis* is symbolized by a *Latinitas* that has proceeded hand in hand with its vernacular into a new world, which now lies "all before" future scholarship.

---

[103] Cf. the proleptic "hand in hand alone they passed" (4. 689).

[104] See Fish, *Surprised by Sin*, 130-141

[105] Cf. (of the lost 1645 volume) *Rous.* 39: *semel erraveris agmine fratrum*, and page 145.

[106] *Paradise Lost*, ed. Fowler, 678.

[107] John Weemse, *The Portraiture of the Image of God in Man* (London, 1632), 19.

BIBLIOGRAPHY

1. MANUSCRIPTS

AUSTIN
University of Texas: Humanities Research Center
Pre-1700 MS127.

FLORENCE
Biblioteca Nazionale Centrale
MSS Magliabecchiana, MSS.Cl. IV, cod. 61.
MSS Magliabecchiana, MSS. Cl. IX, cod. 60.
MSS Magliabecchiana, MSS. Cl. VI, cod. 163.

Biblioteca Marucelliana
MS A.36.

Biblioteca Riccardiana Fiorentina
Cod. Riccardiano 1949.

LONDON
British Library
BL MS Harley 1706.
BL MS Harley 7038.
BL Add.MS 5016.

Lambeth Palace Library
MS 770.

OXFORD
Bodleian MS Lat. Misc. d.ff (kept at Arch.F.D.38).
8^0M.168.Art. (kept at Arch.G.f.17).

2. MILTON: EDITIONS/COMMENTARIES

Poems of Mr John Milton Both English and Latin, Compos'd at Several Times (London, 1645).
Poems &c Upon Several Occasions by Mr John Milton: Both English and Latin &c Composed at Several Times (London, 1673).
Poems upon Several Occasions ... by John Milton, ed. Thomas Warton (London, 1791).
The Poetical Works of John Milton, ed. David Masson (London, 1874), 3 vols.
The Latin Poems of John Milton, ed. Walter MacKellar (New Haven, 1930).
The Works of John Milton, eds. F.A. Patterson, *et al.* (New York: Columbia University Press, 1931-1940), 18 vols.

John Milton: Paradise Regained, The Minor Poems and Samson Agonistes, ed M.Y. Hughes (New York, 1937).
Milton: The Minor Poems, ed. M.Y. Hughes (New York, 1947).
John Milton: Complete Shorter Poems, ed. John Carey (London and New York, 1997).
The Riverside Milton, ed. Roy Flannagan (Boston, 1998).
John Milton, Latin Writings: A Selection, ed. J.K. Hale (Arizona, 1998).
Paradise Lost, ed. Alastair Fowler (London and New York, 2006).
John Milton: Complete Shorter Poems, ed. S.P. Revard (Wiley-Blackwell, 2009).
A Variorum Commentary on the Poems of John Milton: Volume I: The Latin and Greek Poems, ed. Douglas Bush (New York, 1970).
A Variorum Commentary on the Poems of John Milton, ed. M.Y. Hughes (New York, 1972).

3. OTHER PRIMARY TEXTS AND ANTHOLOGIES

ALBERTI, Leon Battista, *Opere Volgari* (Florence, 1843-9).
ANDREWES, Lancelot, *XCVI Sermons*, eds. William Laud and John Buckeridge (London, 1629).
APHTHONIUS, *Progymnasmata, Partim a Rodolpho Agricola, Partim a Ioanne Maria Catanaeo Latinitate Donata cum Scholiis R. Lorichii* (London, 1596).
ARIOSTO, Ludovico, *Orlando Furioso* (London, 1591).
ARISTOPHANES, *Frogs*, ed. Kenneth Dover (Oxford, 1993).
ARNOLD, Matthew, *On Translating Homer* (London, 1861).
ASCHAM, Roger, *The Scholemaster* (1570), ed. Edward Arber (London, 1870).
AUBREY, John, *Minutes of the Life of Mr John Milton*, in *The Early Lives of Milton*, ed. Helen Darbishire (London, 1932).
BATTISTA, Giuseppe, *Le Giornate Accademiche* (Venice, 1673).
BRINSLEY, John, *Ludus Literarius or The Grammar School*, ed. E.T. Campagnac (Liverpool, 1917).
BUCHANAN, George, *Poemata Quae Extant* (Amsterdam, 1687).
BULLOKAR, William, *Aesop's Fables in True Orthography* (London, 1585).
BUONMATTEI, Benedetto, *Della Lingua Toscana Libri Due* (Florence, 1643).
Carmina Illustrium Poetarum Italorum, ed. G.G. Bottari (Florence, 1719-1726).
CHAUCER, Geoffrey, *Works*, ed. F.N. Robinson, reproduced in *The Riverside Chaucer* (Oxford, 1991).
CICERO, Marcus Tullius, *De Oratore*, ed. E.W. Sutton (Cambridge Mass.: Loeb Classical Library, 1948).
—————, *Orator*, ed. and trans. H.M. Hubbell (Cambridge Mass.: Loeb Classical Library, 1952).
COMENIUS, Johan Amos, *Orbis Sensualium Pictus*, trans. Charles Hoole (London, 1659).
DANTE Alighieri, *La Divina Comedia: Inferno*, eds. Umberto Bosco and Govanni Reggio (Florence, 1979).
DATI, Carlo Roberto, *Lettere* (Florence, 1825).
DE LA CERDA, Juan Luis, *P. Virgilii Maronis Aeneidos Libri Sex* (Cologne, 1628).
DRYDEN, John, *Works*, eds. E.N. Hooker and H.T. Swedenberg Jr (University of California Press, 1956).

DU BARTAS, Guillaume de Salluste, *Divine Weekes and Workes*, trans. Joshua Sylvester (London, 1605).
ELYOT, Sir Thomas, *The Book Named the Governor* (1531), ed. S.E. Lehmburg (London, 1962).
ERASMUS, Desiderius, *De Civilitate Morum Puerilium Libellus* (Frankfurt, 1547).
— — — — — —, *Prudentii Opera* (London, 1824).
GOODMAN, Godfrey, *The Fall of Man or the Corruption of Nature, Proved by the Light of Our Naturall Reason* (London, 1616).
GIL, Alexander (Sr), *Logonomia Anglica* (London, 1619; rev. 1621).
The Greek Anthology (London: Loeb Classical Library, 1916-18).
HAKEWILL, George, *An Apologie of the Power and Providence of God in the Government of the World* (Oxford, 1627).
HARVEY, Gabriel, *Works*, ed. A.B. Grosart (London, 1884).
HESSUS, Helius Eobanus, *Poetic Works*, ed., trans., and annotated by Harry Vredeveld (Binghamton, 2004).
HILL, Thomas, *The Most Pleasant Art of the Interpretation of Dreams* (London, 1576).
HOMER, *Iliad*, trans. A.T. Murray, rev. W.F. Wyatt (Loeb Classical Library: Harvard, 1999).
HOOLE, Charles, *A New Discovery of the Old Art of Teaching Schoole*, ed. E.T. Campagnac (Liverpool, 1913).
Iusta Edovardo King (Cambridge, 1638).
JOHNSON, Samuel, *Lives of the Poets*, ed. G.B. Hill (Oxford, 1905).
LANE, John, *Triton's Trumpet* (London, 1621).
LANGHAM, Robert, *A Letter*, ed. R.J.P. Kuin (Leiden, 1983).
Le Glorie degli Incogniti O vero Gli Huomini Illustri dell' Accademia de' Signori Incogniti di Venetia (Venice, 1647).
LELAND, John, *Principum ac Illustrium Aliquot et Eruditorum in Anglia Virorum, Encomia, Trophaea, Genethliaca et Epithalamia* (London, 1589).
— — — — — —, *Cygnea Cantio* (London, 1658).
Le Tre Sirocchie di Benduccio Riboboli da Mattelica (Pisa, 1635).
LILY, William, *A Shorte Introduction of Grammar*, intro. J. Flynn (New York: Scholars' Facsimiles and Reprints, 1945).
LIVY, *Ab Urbe Condita*, ed. R.M. Ogilvie (Oxford, 1974).
LOREDANO, Francesco, *Vita del Cavalier Marino* (Venice, 1633).
LUCRETIUS, *De Rerum Natura*, ed. Cyril Bailey (Oxford, 1977).
— — — — — —, *De Rerum Natura* V, ed. C.D.N. Costa (Oxford, 1984).
LYDGATE, John, *The Dance of Death*, ed. Florence Warren (Oxford: Early English Text Society, 1931).
MACROBIUS, Ambrosius Theodosius, *Commentarii In Somnium Scipionis*, ed. Iacobus Willis (Leipzig, 1970).
MANSO, Giovanni Battista, *Poesie Nomiche* (Venice, 1635).
— — — — — —, *Vita di Torquato Tasso* (Venice, 1621).
MANTUAN, Baptista, *Primus (Secundus, tertius) Operum ... tomus in quo sunt Commentariis Murrhonis, Brantii et Ascensii haec illustrata* (Paris, 1513).
— — — — — —, *The Eclogues*, ed. W.P. Mustard (Baltimore, 1911).
MARTIAL, *Epigrammaton Libri*, ed. Jacobus Borovskij (Leipzig, 1976).
MARVELL, Andrew, ed. Gordon Campbell (Everyman: London, 1997).
MINTURNO, *De Poeta* (1559; rpt. Munich, 1970).
MULCASTER, Richard, *Positions* (1581), ed. R.H. Quick (London, 1888).

NASHE, Thomas, *The Terror of the Night* (London, 1594).
NIETZSCHE, Friedrich, *Twilight of the Idols and The Anti-Christ*, trans. R.J. Hollingdale (Penguin, 1990).
OGILBY, John, *The Fables of Aesop Paraphras'd in Verse* (London, 1651).
OWEN, John, *Epigrammatum*, ed. J.R.C. Martyn (Leiden, 1978).
PLAUTUS, *Persa*, ed. Erich Woytek (Wien, 1982).
Poesie de' Signori Accademici Fantastici di Roma (Rome, 1637).
QUINTILIAN, *Institutionis Oratoriae Libri Duodecim*, ed. Michael Winterbottom (Oxford, 1970).
RUGGLE, George, *Ignoramus* (London, 1630).
SALMASIUS, Claudius, *Ad Ioannem Miltonum Responsio* (London, 1660).
SCALIGER, Joseph, *Poetices Libri Septem* (Geneva, 1561).
SHAKESPEARE, William, *Love's Labour's Lost*, ed Richard David (Methuen: Arden, 1951).
——————, *Twelfth Night*, eds. J.M. Lothian and T.W. Craik (London: Arden Shakespeare, 2003).
SHELLEY, Percy Bysshe, *Selected Poetry and Prose*, ed. A.D.F. Macrae (London, 1991).
STIGLIANI, Tomaso, *Lettere* (Rome, 1664).
STOW, John, *Survey of London* (London, 1598).
TASSO, Torquato, *Gerusalemme Conquistata* (Rome, 1593).
——————, *Il Manso, overe Dell' Amicitia Dialogo del Sig. Torquato Tasso al Molte Illustre Sig. Giovanni Battista Manso* (Naples, 1596).
VERGERIUS, Petrus Paulus, *De Ingenuis Moribus*, in *Humanist Educational Treatises*, ed. and trans. C.W. Kallendorf (I Tatti Renaissance Library, 2002).
VIRGIL, *Opera*, ed. F.A. Hirtzel (Oxford, 1942).
———, *Aeneid VI*, ed R.G. Austin (Oxford, 1992).
WEEMSE, John, *The Portraiture of the Image of God in Man* (London, 1632).
WESLEY, John, *The Duty and Advantage of Early Rising* (London, 1786).
WITHAL, John, *A Short Dictionarie for Young Begynners* (London, 1553).
WORDSWORTH, Dorothy, *Journals*, ed. Ernest De Selincourt (London, 1941).

4. **WORKS OF REFERENCE**

Dizionario Biografico degli Italiani (Rome: Istituto della Enciclopedia Italiana, 1977).
FRENCH, J.M., *The Life Records of John Milton* (New York, 1966).
JOHNSON, A.F., and Scholderer, Victor, *A Short-Title Catalogue of Books 1470-1600* (New York, 1964).
King James Bible (Peabody, MA, 2006).
LE COMTE, E.S., *A Dictionary of Puns in Milton's English Poetry* (New York, 1981).
LOCKWOOD, L.E., *Lexicon to the English Poetical Works of John Milton* (New York, 1907; rpt 1968).
Oxford Latin Dictionary (Oxford, 1968).

5. SECONDARY LITERATURE

ADAMS, R.M., *Ikon: John Milton and the Modern Critics* (Ithaca, 1955).
AGARI, Masahiko, "Logical Equivocation in *Paradise Lost*," in *Language and Style in English Literature: Essays in Honour of Michio Masui*, ed. Michio Kawai (Tokyo, 1991), 542-556.
AINSWORTH, David, *Milton and the Spiritual Reader: Reading and Religion in Seventeenth-Century England* (Routledge, 2008).
APPLEFORD, Amy, "John Carpenter, John Lydgate, and the Daunce of Poulys," *Journal of Medieval and Early Modern Studies* 38.2 (2008): 285-314.
ARNBERG, Lenore, *Raising Children Bilingually: The Pre-School Years* (Clevedon, 1987).
BAKER, Colin, *A Parents' and Teachers' Guide to Bilingualism* (Clevedon, 1995).
─────, *Foundations of Bilingual Education and Bilingualism* (Clevedon, 1996).
─────, *The Care and Education of Young Bilinguals* (Clevedon, 2005).
BALDI, Sergio, "The Date of Composition of *Epitaphium Damonis*," *Notes and Queries* 25 (1978): 508-509.
BALDWIN, T.W., *Shakspere's Small Latine and Lesse Greeke* (Urbana: University of Illinois Press, 1944).
BAUGH, A.C., *A History of the English Language* (London, 1951).
BELLAMY, E.J., "Milton's Freud: The Law of Psychoanalysis in Eve's Dream," *Literature and Psychology* 42.3 (1996): 36-47.
BENET, D.T., "Milton's Toad, or Satan's Dream," *Milton Studies* 45 (2006): 38-42.
BENJAMIN, Walter, "The Task of the Translator," in *Illuminations*, trans. Harry Zohn, ed. Hannah Arendt (London, 1970), 69-82.
BENVENUTI, Edoardo, *Agostino Coltellini e L'Accademia degli Apatisti a Firenze nel Secolo XVII* (Pistoia, 1910).
BERRY, Herbert, "The Miltons and the Blackfriars Playhouse," *Modern Philology* 89 (1992): 510-514.
BINNS, J.W., *Intellectual Culture in Elizabethan and Jacobean England: The Latin Writings of the Age* (Leeds, 1990).
BLANC, M.H.A. and HAMERS, J.F., *Bilinguality and Bilingualism* (Cambridge, 1989).
BLOOMFIELD, Josephine, "The Doctrine of These Olde Wyse': Commentary on the Commentary Tradition in Chaucer's Dream Visions," *Essays in Medieval Studies* 20 (2003): 125-133.
BOONE, L.P., "The Language of Book VI, *Paradise Lost*," *SAMLA Studies in Milton*, ed. J. Max Patrick (Gainesville, 1953), 114-127.
BRADNER, Leicester, "Milton's *Epitaphium Damonis*," *Times Literary Supplement* 18 August 1932, 581.
BROWN, J.C., "The Verbal Art of Horace's *Ode to Pyrrha*," *Transactions of the American Philological Association* 111 (1981): 17-22.
BURBERY, T.J., "John Milton, Blackfriars Spectator?: 'Elegia Prima' and Ben Jonson's *The Staple of News*," *Ben Jonson Journal* 10 (2003): 57-76.
─────, *Milton The Dramatist* (Pennsylvania, 2007).
BURNETT, Archie, "The Fifth Ode of Horace, *Lib.* I, and Milton's Style," *Milton Quarterly* 16 (1982): 68-72.
CAMPBELL, Gordon, "Francini's Permesso," *Milton Quarterly* 15 (1981): 122-133.
─────, "Imitation in *Epitaphium Damonis*," *Milton Studies* 19 (1984): 165-177.
─────, *A Milton Chronology* (New York, 1997).

———————, "Shakespeare and the Youth of Milton," *Milton Quarterly* 33 (December 1999): 95-105.
——————— and CORNS, T.N., *John Milton, Life, Work, and Thought* (Oxford, 2008).
CAMPS, W.A., "The Role of the Sixth Book in the *Aeneid*," *Proceedings of the Vergil Society* 7 (1967-8): 22-30.
CANDY, H.C.H., *Some Newly Discovered Stanzas Written by John Milton on Engraved Scenes Illustrating Ovid's Metamorphoses* (London, 1924).
CANEVARI, Henrico, *Lo Stile del Marino nell'Adone* (Pavia, 1901).
CARRITHERS, G.H., Jr, "*Poems* (1645): On Growing Up," *Milton Studies* 15 (1981): 161-179.
CASALI, Sergio, "Nisus and Euryalus: Exploiting the Contradictions in Virgil's 'Doloneia,'" *Harvard Studies in Classical Philology* 102 (2004): 319-354.
CASOTTI, Giovanni Battista, *Vita di Benedetto Buommattei* prefixed to *Della Lingua Toscana di Benedetto Buommattei Libri Due* (Milan, 1807).
CHANEY, Edward, *The Grand Tour and the Great Rebellion* (Geneva, 1985).
CINQUEMANI, A.M., *Glad to Go For a Feast: Milton, Buonmattei, and the Florentine Accademici* (New York, 1998).
CIRILLO, A.R., "'Hail Holy Light' and Divine Time in *Paradise Lost*," *Journal of English and Germanic Philology* 68 (1969): 45-56.
CLARK, D.L., *John Milton at St Paul's School* (New York, 1948; rpt Hamden, 1964).
CLAVERING, Rose and SHAWCROSS, J.T., "Milton's European Itinerary and His Return Home," *Studies in English Literature* 5 (1965): 49-59.
COFFTA, David, "Programme and Persona in Horace, *Odes* 1.5," *Eranos* 96 (1998): 26-31.
COLEBROOK, Claire, *Milton, Evil and Literary History* (London, 2008).
COLOMBO, Michele, "Benedetto Buonmattei e La Questione della Lingua nel Primo Seicento," *Aevum*, 77 (2003): 615-634.
CONDEE, R.W., "Ovid's Exile and Milton's Rustication," *Philological Quarterly* 37 (1958): 498-502.
——————, "The Structure of Milton's *Epitaphium Damonis*," *Studies in Philology* 62 (1965): 577-594.
——————, *Structure in Milton's Poetry: From the Foundation to the Pinnacles* (Pennsylvania, 1974).
CORNS, T.N., "Ideology in the *Poemata* (1645)," *Milton Studies* 19 (1984): 195-203.
—————, *Milton's Language* (Oxford, 1990).
—————— and CAMPBELL, Gordon, *John Milton, Life, Work, and Thought* (Oxford, 2008).
CROCE, Francesco, "Nuovi Compiti della Critica del Marino e del Marinismo," *Rassegna della Letteratura Italiana* 61 (1957): 459-473.
CUMMINS, James, "Bilingualism, Language Proficiency and Metalinguistic Development," in *Childhood Bilingualism: Aspects of Linguistic, Cognitive and Social Development*, eds. Peter Homel, Michael Palij and Doris Aaronson (New Jersey, 1967), 57-73.
CURR, Matthew, *The Consolation of Otherness: The Male Love Elegy in Milton, Gray and Tennyson* (London, 2002).
DAMIANI, Guglielmo, *Sopra la poesia del Cavalier Marino* (Turin, 1899).
DARBISHIRE, Helen, *The Manuscript of Milton's Paradise Lost, Book 1* (Oxford, 1931).
—————, ed. *The Early Lives of Milton* (London, 1932).

DE FILIPPIS, Michele, "Milton and Manso: Cups or Books?" *Publications of the Modern Language Association of America* 51 (1936): 745-756.
DE-KEYSER, Robert and LARSON-HALL, Jenifer, "What does the Critical Period Really Mean?" in J.F. Kroll and A.M.B. De Groot, eds. *Handbook of Bilingualism: Psycholinguistic Approaches* (Oxford, 2005), 88-108.
DEVOTO, Giacomo, *The Languages of Italy* (Chicago, 1978).
DIJKSTRA, Ton, "Bilingual Visual Word Recognition and Lexical Access," in *Handbook of Bilingualism: Psycholinguistic Approaches*, eds. J.F. Kroll and A.M.B. De Groot (Oxford, 2005), 179-201.
DORIAN, D.C., "Milton's *Epitaphium Damonis*, lines 181-197," *Publications of the Modern Language Association of America* 54 (1939): 612-613.
—————, *The English Diodatis: A History of Charles Diodati's Family and His Friendship with Milton* (New Brunswick, 1950).
DRAPER, J.W., *The Twelfth Night of Shakespeare's Audience* (New York, 1975).
DUST, Philip, "Milton's *Epitaphium Damonis* and *Lycidas*," *Humanistica Lovaniensia* 32 (1983): 342-346.
EDWARDS, K.L., *Milton and the Natural World: Science and Poetry in Paradise Lost* (Cambridge, 2005).
EDWARDS, Viv, *Reading in Multicultural Classrooms* (Reading, 1995).
—————, *The Other Languages: A Guide to Multilingual Classrooms* (Reading, 1996).
ELIOT, T.S., "Milton," *Proceedings of the British Academy* 33 (1947): 61-79.
————, *On Poetry and Poets* (London, 1957).
EMMA, R.D., *Milton's Grammar* (London, 1964).
FINK, Z.S., "Wine, Poetry, and Milton's *Elegia Sexta*," *English Studies* 21 (1939): 164-165.
————, "Milton and the Theory of Climatic Influence," *Modern Language Quarterly* 2 (1941): 67-80.
FIORELLO, Piero, "Il *Trattato della Pronunzia* di Benedetto Buommatei," *Studi Linguistici Italiani* 1 (1960): 117-161.
FISCHER, S.R., "Dreambooks and the Interpretation of Medieval Literary Dreams," *Archiv für Kutturgeschichte* 65 (1983): 1-20.
FISH, Stanley, *Surprised by Sin: The Reader in Paradise Lost* (Macmillan, 2nd ed., 1997).
FITZGERALD, G.J., "Nisus and Euryalus: A Paradigm of Futile Behavior and the Tragedy of Youth," in *Cicero and Virgil: Studies in Honour of Harold Hunt*, ed. J.R.C. Martyn (Amsterdam, 1972), 114-137.
FLANNAGAN, Roy, "Reflections on Milton and Ariosto," *Early Modern Literary Studies* 2.3 (1996): 4, 1-6.
FLETCHER, H.F., "Milton and Thomas Young," *Times Literary Supplement* 21 Jan. (1926), 44.
—————, *The Intellectual Development of John Milton* (Illinois, 1956).
—————, "Milton's *Apologus* and its Mantuan Model," *Journal of English and Germanic Philology* 55 (1956): 230-233.
—————, "The Seventeenth-Century Separate Printing of *Milton's Epitaphium Damonis*," *Journal of English and Germanic Philology* 61 (1962): 788-796.
FORSYTH, Neil, "Of Man's First Dis," in *Milton in Italy: Contexts, Images, Contradictions*, ed. M.A. Di Cesare (Binghamton, 1991): 345-369.
—————, *The Satanic Epic* (Princeton, 2003).

FREDRICKSMEYER, E.A., "Horace's Ode to Pyrrha *(Carm.* 1.5)," *Classical Philology* 60 (1965): 180-185.
FREEMAN, J.A., "Milton's Roman Connection: Giovanni Salzilli," *Milton Studies* 19 (1984): 87-104.
GARCÍA, Eugene, *Early Childhood Bilingualism* (Albuquerque, 1983).
GARCÍA, Ofelia and BAKER, Colin, *Bilingual Education: An Introductory Reader* (Toronto, 2007).
GLECKNER, R.F., *Gray Agonistes* (London, 1997).
GODOLPHIN, F.R.B., "Notes on the Technique of Milton's Latin Elegies," *Modern Philology* 37 (1939-40): 351-356.
GRAYSON, Cecil, *A Renaissance Controversy: Latin or Italian?* (Oxford, 1960).
GREENBLATT, Stephen, *Renaissance Self-Fashioning: From More to Shakespeare* (Chicago, 1980).
HAAN, Estelle, *John Milton's Latin Poetry: Some Neo-Latin and Vernacular Contexts* (PhD thesis, The Queen's University of Belfast, 1987).
—————, "Heaven's Purest Light: Milton's *Paradise Lost* 3 and Vida," *Comparative Literature Studies* 30.2 (1993): 115-136.
—————, "Milton's Latin Poetry and Vida," *Humanistica Lovaniensia* 44 (1995): 282-304.
—————, "Milton and Buchanan," *Humanistica Lovaniensia* 46 (1997): 266-278.
—————, "Milton and Two Italian Humanists: Some Hitherto Unnoticed Neo-Latin Echoes in *In Obitum Procancellarii Medici* and *In Obitum Praesulis Eliensis*," *Notes and Queries* 44 (June 1997): 176-181.
—————, "John Milton Among The Neo-Latinists: Three Notes on *Mansus*," *Notes and Queries* 22.2 (June, 1997): 172-176.
—————, "Milton's *Naturam Non Pati Senium* and Hakewill," *Medievalia et Humanistica* 24 (1997): 147-167.
—————, "Milton's *Ad Patrem* and Grotius's *In Natalem Patris*," *Notes and Queries* 45.4 (1998): 442-447.
—————, *From Academia to Amicitia: Milton's Latin Writings and the Italian Academies* (Philadelphia: Transactions of the American Philosophical Society, 88.6, 1998).
—————, *Andrew Marvell's Latin Poetry: From Text to Context* (Collection Latomus 275: Brussels, 2003).
—————, "Milton's *Ad Ioannem Rousium* and the 1645 Volume," *Notes and Queries* 51 (2004): 356-360.
—————, "'Both English and Latin': Milton's Bilingual Muse," *Renaissance Studies* 21.5 (2007): 679-700.
—————, "From Neo-Latin to Vernacular: Marvell's Bilingualism and Renaissance Pedagogy," in *New Perspectives on Andrew Marvell*, ed. Gilles Sambras (Reims, 2008), 43-64.
—————, "'The Adorning of my Native Tongue': Latin Poetry and Linguistic Metamorphosis," in *The Oxford Handbook of Milton*, eds. Nicholas McDowell and Nigel Smith (Oxford, 2009), 51-65.
—————, "*Defensio Prima* and the Latin Poets," in *The Oxford Handbook of Milton*, eds. Nicholas McDowell and Nigel Smith (Oxford, 2009), 291-304.
HALE, J.K., "Milton Playing with Ovid," *Milton Studies* 25 (1982): 115-130.
————, "Milton's Self-Presentation in Poems ... 1645," *Milton Quarterly* 25.2 (1991): 37-48.

————, "Notes on Milton's Latin Word-Formation in the *Poemata* of 1645," *Humanistica Lovaniensia* 43 (1994): 405-410.
————, *Milton's Languages: The Impact of Multilingualism on Style* (Cambridge, 1998).
————, *Milton's Cambridge Latin: Performing in the Genres 1625-1632* (Cambridge, 2005).
HALL, R.A., *The Italian Questione della Lingua, An Interpretative Essay* (Chapel Hill, 1942; *Univ. of No. Carolina Stud. in Romance Lang. and Lit.*, No. 4).
HALLIDAY, M.A.K., *Learning How to Mean: Explorations in the Development of Language* (London, 1975).
HAMERS, J.F. and BLANC, M.H.A., *Bilinguality and Bilingualism* (Cambridge, 1989).
HANFORD, J.H., *The Youth of Milton* (Michigan, 1925).
HARDING, D.P, *Milton and the Renaissance Ovid* (University of Illinois Studies in Language and Literature, 30.4: Urbana, 1946).
————, *The Club of Hercules: Studies in the Classical Background of Paradise Lost* (Illinois, 1962).
HARDING, Edith and RILEY, Philip, *The Bilingual Family: A Handbook for Parents* (Cambridge, 1986).
HARRIS, Brian and SHERWOOD, Bianca, "Translating as an Innate Skill," in *Language, Interpretation and Communication*, eds. David Gerver and H.W. Sinaiko (New York, 1978), 155-170.
HARRIS, Neil, "Galileo as Symbol: The 'Tuscan Artist' in *Paradise Lost*," *Annali dell' Istituto e Museo di Storio della Scienza di Firenze* 10 (1985): 3-29.
HARRIS, Victor, *All Coherence Gone* (Chicago, 1949).
HARRISON, E.L., "Metempsychosis in *Aeneid* Six," *Classical Journal* 73 (1977-78): 193-197.
HARTWELL, Kathleen, *Lactantius and Milton* (Cambridge: Harvard University Press, 1929).
HIND, A.M., *Engraving in England in the Sixteenth and Seventeenth Centuries* (Cambridge, 1964).
HORWOOD, A.J., *A Commonplace Book of John Milton* (London, 1876; rev. 1877).
HUGHES, M.Y., "Milton and the Symbol of Light," *Studies in English Literature* 4.1 (1964): 1-33.
HUNT, Leigh, *Literary Examiner*, 6 Sept 1823.
HUNTER, W.B., "The Meaning of 'Holy Light' in *Paradise Lost* III," *Modern Language Notes* 74.7 (1959): 589-592.
JOHNSON, F.R., "Two Renaissance Textbooks of Rhetoric: Aphthonius' *Progymnasmata* and Rainolde's *A Booke Called the Foundation of Rhetorike*," *Huntington Library Quarterly* 6 (1943): 427-444.
JOHNSON, R.M., "The Politics of Publication: Misrepresentation in Milton's 1645 'Poems,'" *Criticism* 36.1 (1994): 45-71.
JOHNSON, Samuel, *Lives of the Poets*, ed. G.B. Hill (Oxford, 1905).
JONES, Edward, "'Ere Half my Days': Milton's Life, 1608-1640," in *The Oxford Handbook of Milton*, eds. Nicholas McDowell and Nigel Smith (Oxford, 2009), 3-25.
KELLY, Maurice, "Grammar School Latin and John Milton," *Classical World* 52.5 (1959): 133-136.
KENNEDY, G.A., *Greek Rhetoric* (Princeton, 1963).
KNIGHT, Sarah, "Milton's Student Verses of 1629," *Notes and Queries* 255.1 (2010): 37-39.

KOEHLER, Stanley, *Milton and the Roman Elegists: A Study of Milton's Latin Poems in their Relation to the Latin Love Elegy* (Unpublished dissertation: Princeton, 1941).
LABENDE-JEANROY, Thérèse, *La Question de la Langue en Italie* (Strassburg, 1925).
LAZZERI, Allessandro, *Intellettuali e Consenso nella Toscana del Seicento: L'Accademia degli Apatisti* (Milan, 1983).
LEACH, A.F., "Two Notes on Milton," *Modern Language Review* 2 (1906-7): 121-128.
————, "Milton as Schoolboy and Schoolmaster," *Proceedings of the British Academy* 3 (1908): 295-318.
LEAVIS, F.R., *Revaluation* (Harmondsworth, 1967).
LE COMTE, E.S., *Milton's Unchanging Mind* (New York, 1973).
————, "Sly Milton: The Meaning Lurking in the Contexts of His Quotations," *English Studies Collection* 1 (1976): 1-15.
LEE, Hee-Won, "Light in *Paradise Lost*, Book III: A Metaphor for Incarnation and Mimesis," *Journal of Classical and English Renaissance Literature* 12.1 (2003): 159-178.
LEEDHAM-GREEN, E.S., *Books in Cambridge Inventories: Book-Lists From Vice-Chancellors' Court Probate Inventories in the Tudor and Stuart Periods* (Cambridge, 1986).
————, *Private Libraries in Renaissance England* (New York, Binghamton, 1994).
LEOPOLD, W.F., *Speech Development of a Bilingual Child: A Linguist's Record* (New York, 1939-49).
LEWALSKI, B.K., *The Life of John Milton* (Blackwell, 2000).
LEWIS, E.G., *Bilingualism and Bilingual Education* (Perganon Press, 1981).
LIEB, Michael and SHAWCROSS, J.T. eds., *Achievements of the Left Hand: Essays on the Prose of John Milton* (Massachusetts, 1974).
LOEWENSTEIN, David and TURNER, J.G., eds., *Politics, Poetics, and Hermeneutics of Milton's Prose* (Cambridge, 1990).
LOW, Anthony, "The Unity of Milton's *Elegia Sexta*," *English Literary Renaissance* 11 (1981): 213-223.
LUPTON, J.H., *Life of Dean Colet* (London, 1887).
LYON, Jean, *Becoming Bilingual: Language Acquisition in a Bilingual Community* (Philadelphia, 1996).
MACNEICE, Louis, *Carpe Diem* Third Programme, Monday 8th October 1956, 7.30-8.15 p.m.
MACWHINNEY, Brian, "A Unified Model of Language Acquisition," in *Handbook of Bilingualism: Psycholinguistic Approaches*, eds. J.F. Kroll and A.M.B. De Groot (Oxford, 2005), 49-67.
MANFREDI, Michele, *Giovanni Battista Manso nella Vita e nelle Opere* (Naples, 1919).
MARTINDALE, Charles, "Unlocking the Word-Hoard: In Praise of Metaphrase," *Comparative Criticism*, 6 (1984): 47-72.
————, *Redeeming The Text: Latin Poetry and the Hermeneutics of Reception* (Cambridge, 1993).
————, *John Milton and the Transformation of Ancient Epic* (Bristol, 2002).
MARTZ, L.L., "The Rising Poet, 1645," in *The Lyric and Dramatic Milton*, ed. J.H. Summers (New York, 1965), 3-33.

――――, "*Paradise Lost*: The Realms of Light," *English Literary Renaissance* 1.1 (1971): 71-88.
――――, *Poet of Exile: A Study of Milton's Poetry* (New Haven, 1980).
MASSON, David, *The Life of John Milton: Narrated in Connexion with the Political, Ecclesiastical, and Literary History of his Time* (Cambridge, 1859-94).
MAYLENDER, Michele, *Storia dell'Accademie d'Italia* (Bologna, 1926-1930).
MCCOLGAN, K.P., "'God is Also in Sleep': Dreams Satanic and Divine in *Paradise Lost*," *Milton Studies* 30 (1993): 135-148.
MCGANN, M.J., *Studies in Horace's First Book of Epistles* (Latomus: Brussels, 1969).
MEUTER, R.F.I., "Language Selection in Bilinguals: Mechanisms and Processes," in *Handbook of Bilingualism: Psycholinguistic Approaches*, eds. J.F. Kroll and A.M.B. De Groot (Oxford, 2005), 349-370.
MICHAEL, E.B. and GOLLAN, T.H., "Being and Becoming Bilingual: Individual Differences and Consequences for Language Production," in *Handbook of Bilingualism: Psycholinguistic Approaches*, eds. J.F. Kroll and A.M.B. De Groot (Oxford, 2005), 389-407.
MILLER, Leo, "Milton's Portraits: An Impartial Inquiry into their Authentication," *Milton Quarterly* (Special Issue, 1976): 1-43.
MIROLLO, J.V., *The Poet of the Marvelous: Giambattista Marino* (New York, 1963).
MOSELEY, C.W.R.D., *The Poetic Birth: Milton's Poems of 1645* (Aldershot: Scolar Press, 1991).
MOSS, Ann, *Printed Commonplace-Books and the Structuring of Renaissance Thought* (Oxford, 1996).
MOYLES, R.G., *The Text of "Paradise Lost": A Study in Editorial Procedure* (Toronto, 1985).
MYERS, W.T., *The Relations of Latin and English as Living Languages in England During the Age of Milton* (Dayton, 1913).
NAGLE, B.R., *The Poetics of Exile: Program and Polemic in the Tristia and Epistulae ex Ponto of Ovid* (Collection Latomus 170: Brussels, 1980).
NISBET, R.G.M. and HUBBARD, Margaret, *A Commentary on Horace Odes Book I* (Oxford, 1970).
NORMAN, Nathan, "Brutus' Oratory," *San Jose Studies* 8.1 (1982): 82-90.
NORWOOD, Frances, "The Tripartite Eschatology of *Aeneid* 6," *Classical Philology* 49 (1954): 15-26.
NUTTALL, A.D., *Openings: Narrative Beginnings From the Epic to the Novel* (Oxford, 1992).
OBERHELMAN, S.M. and MULRYAN, John, "Milton's Use of Classical Meters in the *Sylvarum Liber*," *Modern Philology* 81 (1983): 131-145.
PARKER, W.R.,"Milton and Thomas Young, 1620-1628," *Modern Language Notes* 53 (1938): 399-407.
――――, "Milton and the News of Charles Diodati's Death," *Modern Language Notes* 72 (1957): 486-488.
――――, *Milton: A Biography*, ed. Gordon Campbell (Oxford, 1996).
PATTERSON, Annabel, *Pastoral and Ideology: Virgil to Valery* (Berkeley, 1987).
――――, *Milton's Words* (Oxford, 2009).
PAVLOVITCH, Millivoïe, *Le Lange Enfantin: Acquisition du Serbe et du Français* (Paris, 1920).
PEACOCK, A.J., "Louis MacNeice: Transmitting Horace," *Revista Alicantina de Estudios Ingleses* 5 (1992): 119-130.

PECHEUX, Mother M. Christopher, "Another Note on 'This Fell Sergeant,'" *Shakespeare Quarterly* 26.1 (1975): 74-75.

―――――, "The Nativity Tradition in Milton's *Elegia Sexta*," *Milton Studies* 23 (1987): 3-19.

PEDEN, Alison, "Macrobius and Medieval Dream Literature," *Medium Aevum* 54 (1985): 59-73.

PHILIP, Ian, *The Bodleian Library in the Seventeenth and Eighteenth Centuries* (Oxford, 1983).

PIEPHO, Lee, "Versions by Thomas, Lord Fairfax of Some Poems by Mantuan and Other Neo-Latin Writers," *Renaissance and Reformation* 8 (1984): 114-120.

―――――, "Mantuan's Religious Poetry in Early Tudor England: Humanism and Christian Latin Verse," *Medievalia et Humanistica* 20 (1993): 65-83.

PITTS, R.E., "'This Fell Sergeant, Death,'" *Shakespeare Quarterly* 20.4 (1969): 486-491.

PIZZOLATO, L.F., "'Fortunati ambo': per Niso ed Eurialo," in *Studia Classica Iohanni Tarditi Oblata* (Milan, 1995): 1.265-283.

PLESSOW, Max, *Geschichte der Fabeldichtung in Englan bis zu John Gay (1726); nebst Neudruck von Bullokars "Fables of Aesop" 1585*, Palaestra 52 (1906).

PÖSCHL, Viktor, "Die Pyrrhaode des Horaz (c. 1.5)," *Hommages à J. Bayet*, eds. Marcel Renard and Robert Schilling (*Collection Latomus* 70: Brussels, 1964), 579-586.

POUND, Ezra, *ABC of Reading* (New York, 1934).

PUTNAM, M.C.J., "Horace, *Carm.* 1.5: Love and Death," *Classical Philology* 65 (1970): 251-254.

―――――, "The *Aeneid* and *Paradise Lost*: Ends and Conclusions," *Literary Imagination* 8.3 (2006): 387-410.

QUINN, Kenneth, "Horace as a Love Poet: A Reading of *Odes* 1.5," *Arion* 2 (1963): 59-77.

RADZINOWICZ, M.A., "To Play in the Socratic Manner: Oxymoron in Milton's *At a Vacation Exercise in the College*," *University of Hartford Studies in Literature* 17 (1985): 1-11.

REVARD, S.P., "*Ad Ioannem Rousium*: Elegiac Wit and Pindaric Mode," *Milton Studies* 19 (1984): 205-226.

―――――, *Milton and The Tangles of Neaera's Hair: The Making of the 1645 Poems* (Columbia, 1997).

RICHEK, Roslyn, "Thomas Randolph's Salting (1627): Its Text, and John Milton's Sixth *Prolusion* as Another Salting," *English Literary Renaissance* 12 (1982): 102-131.

RICKS, Christopher, *Milton's Grand Style* (Oxford, 1963).

RONJAT, Jules, *Le Développement du Lange Observé chez un Enfant Bilingue* (Paris, 1913).

SAID, E.W., *Beginnings: Intention and Method* (New York, 1975).

SANDERS, Julie, "'Powdered with Golden Rain': The Myth of Danae in Early Modern Drama," *Early Modern Literary Studies* 9.2 (2002): 1.1-23.

SAUNDERS, George, *Bilingual Children: From Birth to Teens* (Clevedon, 1988).

SCHIPPERS, Arie, "Hebrew Andulasian and Arabic Poetry: Descriptions of Fruit in the Tradition of the 'Elegants' or Zurafa," *Journal of Semitic Studies* 33.2 (1988): 219-232.

SCHULTZ, Howard, "Satan's Serenade," *Philological Quarterly* 27 (1948): 17-26.

SCHWARTZ, Louis, *Milton and Maternal Mortality* (Cambridge, 2009).

SEBASTIÁN-GALLÉS, Núria and BOSCH, Laura, "Phonology and Bilingualism," in *Handbook of Bilingualism: Psycholinguistic Approaches*, eds. J.F. Kroll and A.M.B. De Groot (Oxford, 2005), 68-87.
SESSIONS, W.A., "Milton's *Naturam*," *Milton Studies* 19 (1984): 53-72.
SHAWCROSS, J.T., "*Epitaphium Damonis*: lines 9-13 and the Date of Composition," *Modern Language Notes* 71 (1956): 322-324.
——————, "Of Chronology and the Dates of Milton's Translation from Horace and the New Forcers of Conscience," *Studies in English Literature* 3 (1963): 77-84.
——————, "Milton and Diodati: An Essay in Psychodynamic Meaning," *Milton Studies* 7 (1975): 127-163.
SHEPHERD, William, *The Life of Poggio Bracciolini* (Liverpool, 1802).
SHITAKA, Hideyuki, "Satan's Language and Its Influence on the Linguistic Deterioration of Adam and Eve in *Paradise Lost*, Book 9: A Note Mainly From a Rhetorical Viewpoint," *ERA* 3 (1983): 1-18.
SOLMSEN, Friedrich, "The World of the Dead in Book 6 of the *Aeneid*," *Classical Philology* 67 (1971): 31-41.
STAROBINSKI, Jean, *Les Mots Sous Les Mots: Les Anagrammes de Ferdinand de Saussure* (Paris, 1971).
STEADMAN, J.M., "Chaste Muse and *Casta Iuventus*: Milton, Minturno and Scaliger on Inspiration and the Poet's Character," *Italica* 40 (1963): 28-34.
STORRS, Ronald, *Ad Pyrrham: A Polyglot Collection of Translations of Horace's Ode to Pyrrha (Book 1, Ode 5)* (London, 1959).
STROUP, T.B., *Religious Rite and Ceremony in Milton's Poetry* (Lexington, 1968).
STUBBS, Michael, "Language and the Mediation of Experience: Linguistic Representation and Cognitive Orientation," in *The Handbook of Sociolinguistics*, ed. Florian Coulmas (Oxford, 1997), 358-373.
SULLIVAN, J.P., *Martial: The Unexpected Classic: A Literary and Historical Study* (Cambridge, 1991).
SUMMERS, J.H., "The Masks of *Twelfth Night*," in *Shakespeare: Twelfth Night: A Casebook*, ed. D.J. Palmer (Macmillan, 1980), 86-97.
TAESCHNER, Traule, *The Sun is Feminine: A Study on Language Acquisition in Bilingual Children* (Berlin, 1983).
THOMSON VESSEY, D.W., "Pyrrha's Grotto and the Farewell to Love: A Study of Horace, *Odes* 1.5," in *Why Horace? A Collection of Interpretive Essays*, ed. W.S. Anderson (Bolchazy-Cardicci, 1999), 20-30.
TICE, T.N., "Calphurnia's Dream and Communication with the Audience in Shakespeare's *Julius Caesar*," *The Shakespeare Yearbook* 1 (1990): 37-49.
TILLYARD, E.M.W., *Milton* (New York, 1966).
VITALE, Maurizio, *La Questione della Lingua* (Palermo, 1978).
VIVALDI, Vincenzo, *Storia della Controversie Linguistiche in Italia de Dante ai Nostri Giorni* (Catanzaro, 1925).
VYGOTSKY, L.S., *Thought and Language* (Cambridge Mass., 1962).
WELLS, G.G., *Learning through Interaction: The Study of Language Development* (Cambridge, 1981).
WEST, Michael, "The Controversial Eloquence of Shakespeare's Coriolanus: An Anti-Ciceronian Orator?" *Modern Philology* 102.3 (2005): 307-331.
WHEELER, A.L.,"Topics from the Life of Ovid," *American Journal of Philology* 46 (1925): 26-28.

WHITE, Peter, "The Presentation and Dedication of the *Silvae* and the *Epigrams*," *Journal of Roman Studies* 64 (1974): 40-61.
WILLIAMS, G.D.,"Representations of the Book-Roll in Latin Poetry: Ovid, *Tr*.1,1, 3-14 and Related Texts," *Mnemosyne* 45.2 (1992): 178-189.
WILLIAMS, R.D., "The Sixth Book of the *Aeneid*," *Greece and Rome* 11 (1964): 48-63.
WILSON, F.P., *The Plague in Shakespeare's London* (Oxford, 1927).
WOODHOUSE, A.S.P., "Milton's Pastoral Monodies," in *Studies in Honour of Gilbert Norwood*, ed. M.E. White (Toronto, 1952), 266-277.
————————, *The Heavenly Muse: A Preface to Milton* (Toronto, 1972).
YIM, Sung-Kyun, "Eve's Dream and Myth Making in Milton's *Paradise Lost*," *The Journal of Milton Studies in Korea* 7 (1997): 237-256.
ZANDVOORT, R.W., "Brutus's Forum Speech in *Julius Caesar*," *Review of English Studies* 16.61 (1940): 62-66.

INDEX NOMINUM

Abra, 135
Accademia Fiorentina, 113
Adam, 25, 34, 46, 47, 48, 50, 51, 52, 53, 169, 173, 176-180, 182, 188-190, 190-198
Adimari, Allessandro, 97, 100, 101
Adonis, 81, 82, 126
Aeneas, 173, 176, 178, 179, 191-198
Aeschylus, 117
Aesop, 41, 43
Africanus, Scipio, 185
Agamemnon, 33
Agricola, Iulius, 128
Agricola, Rodolpho, 28
Aguecheek, Sir Andrew, 26
Alaunus, 135
Alberti, Leon Battista, 138, 149
Alcinous, 74
Alcyone, 73
Alexandria, 81, 155
Alps, 96, 109
Ambrogi, G.M., 111
Ambrose, 88
Amphitryo, 47
Anchises, 128, 180, 192-195
Andalusia, 48
Andrewes, Lancelot, 69, 70-75
Antenor, 173
Anthony, Mark, 184, 189-190
Antinori, 100
Antioch, 28
Aonia, 64, 86, 171
Apatisti, Accademia degli, 101-102, 107, 114, 139
Aphthonius, 28, 29, 32, 44-45
Apollo, 67, 85, 129, 130, 146, 162, 180
Apuleius, 77
Aquilo, 79
Arcadia, 151, 157
Ariosto, Ludovico, 105, 131, 136-137
Aristophanes, 61-62
Aristotle, 64
Arno, 104, 134
Arnobius, 77-79
Arnold, Matthew, 171-172
Arthur, King, 130-131, 133
Ascanius, 173
Ascensius, J. Baldius, 41
Ascham, Roger, 9, 10, 12, 16, 19, 29, 30, 39-40, 41

Asserino, 101
Athens, 104, 136, 181
Atreus, 33
Aubrey, John, 1, 56, 61
Aurora, 71
Ausonia, 127, 156
Avernus, 178
Avon, 123

Baalim, 87, 162
Bacchus, 84, 85
Baiae, 145
Baroni, Leonora, 102, 158
Bartolommei, Giovanni, 98, 100, 101
Barzizza, Gasparino, 138
Bassus, Saleius, 117
Battista, Giuseppe, 125
Beckett, Samuel, 40
Belch, Sir Toby, 26
Belisarius, 132
Bembo, Pietro, 136, 137, 138
Blackfriars Theatre, 59
Boccaccio, Giovanni, 105
Bodleian Library, 141, 146, 149
Bonin, P., 100
Bouillon, Godfrey of, 130, 132
Bracciolini, Poggio, 118, 138
Brignole, Anton Giulio, 122
Brinsley, John, 5-6, 9, 10, 12, 13, 16-17, 20, 22, 23, 28, 31, 40, 41, 43, 44, 91
Brutus, Marcus, 184-190
Buchanan, George, 58, 61
Buckeridge, John, 70, 74
Bullokar, William, 41, 43, 46, 47, 51, 52
Buonmattei, Benedetto, 93, 97, 98, 101, 102, 104-118, 139

Cacace, Gio. Camillo, 125
Caesar, Augustus, 148
Caesar, Julius, 31, 184-190
Callimachus, 117, 118
Calphurnia, 188-189
Cam, 61
Cambridge University, 6, 7, 55-93, 95, 99, 103, 122, 123, 142-143, 161, 162
Camden, William, 82
Camerarius, Ioachim, 27

Camoena, 83, 120
Campania, 129
Capitol, 184-186
Cardoini, Camillo, 95
Caroli, Gioffredo, 44
Carpenter, John, 68
Casca, 190
Casotti, Giovanni Battista, 107, 115
Cassius, 185, 187
Castalia, 64
Castiglione, Baldassare, 47
Catanaeus, Ioannes Maria, 28
Catullus, 143, 144, 149
Cavalcanti, Andrea, 97, 101
Cephalus, 71
Ceres, 84, 85
Ceyx, 73
Chappell, William, 58, 61
Charlemagne, 132
Charon, 176, 177
Chateauneufare, 75
Chaucer, Geoffrey, 71-75, 84, 125
Chimentelli, Valerio, 161
Chiron, 64, 130
Christ, 85-88, 162, 173, 192
Cicero, 12-13, 34, 39, 72, 138, 181-182, 183, 184, 188, 190
Citolini, Alessandro, 138
Claudian, 91, 92, 135
Clio, 64
Codner, David, (= Selvaggi, Matteo) 150
Codrus, 151
Colet, Dean, 2-3, 38
Colossus, 187
Coltellini, Agostino, 102
Comenius, Johan Amos, 10-11
Corinna, 71
Corinth, 186
Coriolanus, 184
Cortesi, Paolo, 138
Corus, 79
Creusa, 191-198
Criseyde, 72, 125
Cromwell, Oliver, 19
Crusca, Accademia della, 108, 114, 139
Cumbria, 28
Cupid, 44, 72
Cypris, 79

Damon, 103, 134, 135, 164-165 (see also *Epitaphium Damonis*)
Danae, 24
Daniello, Bernardino, 105
Dante, 104, 105, 107, 113-114, 185, 190
Dati, Carlo, 97, 98, 99, 101, 103, 105, 133, 134, 135, 142, 157
Daunus, 33
Decius, 188
Dee, 123
Deipoea, 120
De La Cerda, Ludovico, 172, 173-174, 193, 196
De L'Aubespine, Charles, 75
Delia, 78
Delphi, 162
Demosthenes, 117, 118
Dido, 179, 195
Diodati, Charles, 77, 80-83, 103, 105, 122, 124, 132-136, 161, 162
Diodati, Theodore, 77, 87-88
Diodorus, 137, 155
Dis, 122, 178, 179
Dolopes, 192
Doni, Niccolo, 98, 101
Dryden, John, 14, 16
Du Bartas, Guillaume de Salluste, 67
Dun, 123

Eden, 24, 35, 50, 170, 172, 175, 190, 192, 195, 196, 197
Eliot, T.S., 167, 172
Elizabeth I, Queen, 124
Ely, 18, 69
Elyot, Sir Thomas, 2
England, 99, 121, 123, 125, 150, 151, 156, 157
Ennius, 117
Epicurus, 76
Erasmus, Desiderius, 27, 28, 30, 86
Erato, 84
Erythraeus, Janus Nicius, 127
Euripides, 117, 118, 193
Euryalus, 33-34
Eurydice, 195-196
Eusebius, Dr, 100, 107
Eve, 24, 25, 34-36, 46, 47, 48, 50, 51, 52, 53, 169, 170, 182, 183, 186-190, 190-198

Fabricius, 86
Fairfax, Mary, 40
Fairfax, Thomas, 37
Fantastici, Accademia dei, 99, 120, 123
Farrini, Abat., 100
Faustinus, Julius, 144, 146
Favonius, 74
Felton, Nicholas, 69
Ferdinand, Prince, 182-183
Ferdinand II, King, 102
Fiesole, 104
Flaccus, Valerius, 117
Florence, 7, 93, 96, 99, 100-104, 133, 134, 139, 142, 157, 164
Foglietta, Uberto, 138
Forster, John, 75
Fortunatus, 86
France, 70, 99, 100
Francini, Antonio, 98, 99, 103, 109, 134
Franciscans, Order of, 31

Gaddi, Jacopo, 100, 107
Galilei, Galileo, 107
Galilei, Vincenzo, 98
Gallus, 118
Geloni, 79
Geneva, 95
Gherardini, Bartolommeo, 100
Gil, Alexander Sr, 30, 41
Girolami, V., 100
Goodman, Godfrey, 77
Gorgo, 81-82
Gori, Anton Francesco, 101
Gostlin, John, 69
Goths, 132
Graham, Sir Frederick, 28
Gray, Thomas, 82
Greece, 99, 150, 152
Gregory, Edmund, 153
Grossi, Gennaro, 126-127
Grotius, Hugo, 4

Hakewill, George, 77-79
Hamburg, 62, 64
Hamlet, Prince, 60, 67-68, 184, 185
Harington, John Sir, 136-137
Harpies, 156
Harvey, Gabriel, 37-38

Hebe, 84
Hecuba, 193
Hercules, 15
Hermaphroditus, 60
Hermione, 66
Herodotus, 117, 118, 128
Hesiod, 117
Hesperia, 191
Hesperus, 151
Hessus, Helius Eobanus, 81-82
Hill, Thomas, 73-74
Hobson, Thomas, 66
Holland, 75
Holofernes, 37
Holstenius, Lucas, 102
Homer, 19, 33, 117, 118, 131, 150, 171, 172, 174
Hoole, Charles, 6, 10-11, 13, 28, 38, 41
Horace, 1, 15-25, 45, 83, 93, 95, 99, 101, 121, 124, 125, 129, 144, 147, 150
Horeb, 170
Horwood, A.J., 2, 28
Humber, 123

Icarus, 124
Ida, 197
Ilissus, 104
Incogniti, Accademia degli, 122
India, 78
Iscariot, Judas, 185
Iulus, 193-194 (*see also* Ascanius)

James I, King, 60, 124
Jerusalem, 129, 130
Job, 118, 132
Johnson, Samuel, 167
Jonson, Ben, 59-60, 124
Judith, Book of, 37
Juliet, 60
Juno, 120, 171, 175, 196
Jupiter (deity), 24, 66, 84, 127, 185, 186, 193
Jupiter (planet), 79
Juvenal, 46
Juvencus, 38

Kenilworth, 41
King, Edward, 142-143

Lactantius, 38
Landino, Cristoforo, 149
Lane, John, 71-72
Langham, Robert, 41
Latium, 171, 173, 175
Lavinia, 192
Lavinium, 171, 175
Leda, 66
Lee, 123
Leland, John, 124
Leo, Pope, 149
Leonidas, 155
Lesbos, 122, 124
Lethe, 179
Libitina, 70
Libya, 193
Lily, William, 26-27, 31
Livy, 66, 89-90, 118, 137
Lombards, 105, 132
London, 1, 2, 58, 59, 60, 61, 62, 68, 70, 119, 132, 134, 162
Longtown, 28
Loredano, Francesco, 128
Lorich, Reinhard, 28, 29, 32, 44-45
Lucan, 117
Lucca, 133
Lucifer, 197
Lucilius, 155
Lucretius, 49, 76, 91-93, 117, 169, 183
Lydgate, John, 68-70
Lydia, 98

Macbeth, 25, 60
Macer, 117
MacNeice, Louis, 21
Macrobius, Ambrosius Theodosius, 72-75, 188-189
Maecenas, 127
Makin, Bathsua, 153
Manso, Giovanni Battista, 124-132, 133
Mantuanus, Giovanni Baptista, 36-53
Marino, Giambattista, 126-129, 130
Mars (deity), 131
Mars (planet), 78, 79
Marshall, William, 18, 152-155
Martial, 144-146, 148, 152
Marullus, 187
Marvell, Andrew, 10, 19-20, 40, 174
Mary, Virgin, 192

Medway, 123
Mercury (deity), 194
Mercury (planet), 79
Michael, Archangel, 50, 191, 193, 195, 196
Milton, Christopher, 61
Milton, John
— *Ad Ioannem Rousium*, 141-157, 198
— *Ad Leonoram*, 102, 158, 160
— *Ad Patrem*, 4, 98, 102, 160
— *Ad Salsillum*, 102, 119-123, 160, 161
— *Animadversions*, 156
— *Apologus de Rustico et Hero*, 1, 16, 36-53, 184
— *Apology Against a Pamphlet*, 77
— *Apology for Smectymnuus*, 15, 156
— *Arcades*, 160
— *Areopagitica*, 146
— *At a Solemn Music*, 160, 169
— *At a Vacation Exercise*, 5, 36, 88-93, 122, 123, 175
— *Carmina Elegiaca*, 1-2, 28-36
— *Commonplace Book*, 28, 29, 72, 105
— *Comus*, 18, 95, 160, 161, 162, 163-165
— *Defensio Prima*, 24, 26, 66
— *Defensio Secunda*, 4, 11, 108
— *De Idea Platonica*, 75, 160
— *Doctrine and Discipline of Divorce*, 156
— *Elegia Prima*, 58-62, 82, 103, 129, 134, 160, 161-162
— *Elegia Secunda*, 18, 65-70, 160
— *Elegia Tertia*, 18, 69, 70-75, 160
— *Elegia Quarta*, 3, 18, 62-65, 160
— *Elegia Quinta*, 18, 36, 160
— *Elegia Sexta*, 60-61, 80-88, 103, 120, 160
— *Elegia Septima*, 18, 72, 160
— Epigrams on the Gunpowder Plot, 158, 160
— *Epistolae Familiares*, 104-118, 122, 124, 142, 157
— *Epitaphium Damonis*, 6, 80, 81, 98-99, 102-103, 132-139, 150-151, 160, 161, 162-165, 167
— *Epitaph on the Marchioness of Winchester*, 160

Index Nominum

— *History of Britain*, 137
— *Il Penseroso*, 72, 76, 83, 84, 160, 161
— *In Effigiei Eius Sculptorem*, 155
— *In Obitum Praesulis Eliensis*, 18, 69, 160
— *In Obitum Procancellarii Medici*, 18, 66, 69, 160
— *In Quintum Novembris*, 18, 31, 35, 98, 160, 169
— *L'Allegro*, 76, 83, 84, 153, 160, 161
— *Latin Grammar*, 26
— *Lycidas*, 6, 18, 41, 61, 142, 143, 160, 162, 163
— *Mansus*, 61, 99, 102, 124-132, 160, 161, 165
— *Naturam Non Pati Senium*, 75-79, 98, 102, 160
— *Of Education*, 1, 5, 156
— *Of Prelatical Episcopacy*, 156
— *Of Reformation*, 137, 156
— *On Shakespeare*, 18, 160
— *On the Death of a Fair Infant*, 36
— *On the Morning of Christ's Nativity*, 18, 41, 61, 81, 83, 84-88, 160, 162
— *On the University Carrier*, 66, 160
— *On Time*, 160
— *Paradise Lost*, 7, 15, 21, 22, 24-25, 26, 34-36, 41, 45-47, 48, 49-50, 55, 63, 92, 107, 122, 139, 167-198
— *Philosophus ad Regem*, 160
— *Prolusions*, 56, 61-65, 88-90, 103, 122, 123
— *Pro Se Defensio*, 152-153
— *Psalm 114* (English), 18, 160
— *Psalm 114* (Greek), 160
— *Psalm 136*, 160
— *Reason of Church Government*, 3, 74, 96, 115, 118, 131-132, 136, 151-152, 154, 156
— *Song On a May Morning*, 160
— *Sonnets*, 103, 160, 161
— *The Passion*, 160
— Translation of Horace, *Odes* 1.5, 1, 17-25, 101
— *Upon the Circumcision*, 160
Milton, John Sr, 3-4, 71-72
Mincius, 121
Minerva, 127 (*see also* Pallas)
Minturno, 83

Miranda, 182-183
Moloch, 87, 162
Mole, 123
Mulcaster, Richard, 4
Mycale, 127
Myrmidons, 192

Naples, 96, 102, 125, 126, 129, 133, 182
Narcissus, 79
Nashe, Thomas, 37, 74-75
Neaera, 141, 143, 144, 158, 159
Neptune, 196
Netherby Hall, 28
Nietzsche, Friedrich, 23
Nisus, 33-34
Nun Appleton House, 40
Nuwas, Abu, 48

Ogilby, John, 41
Olympias, 185
Olympus, 27, 78, 125, 191
Ophiucus, 194
Orkney Islands, 135
Orpheus, 1, 84, 127, 176, 195-196
Ouse, 123, 135
Ovid, 1, 2, 12, 14, 46, 58-62, 62-65, 71, 76, 117, 137, 144, 147-149, 157, 161-162
Owen, John, 87-88
Oxford, 141, 145, 146, 149, 184
Oziosi, Accademia degli, 124, 125-128

Pallas, 66, 196
Pan, 127
Pandaemonium, 186
Paphos, 128, 129
Paris, 68
Parnassus, 64, 128, 156
Pegasus, 63, 124
Peor, 87, 162
Perilla, 62-65
Periz, Gonsalvo, 19
Permessus, 102
Persephone, 81, 82
Persia, 122
Petrarch, Francesco, 104
Phlegethon, 178
Phoebus, 27, 67, 78, 79, 130 (*see also* Apollo)

Phoenix, 64
Pieria, 3, 64
Pindar, 100, 117, 118, 141
Pitti, Giulio, 101
Plato, 117
Plautus, 47, 169-170
Pliny the Younger, 39
Poitiers, Hilary of, 88
Poliziano, Angelo, 69
Polonius, 184
Porphyrion, 93
Porta Capena, 83
Portumnus, 122
Pound, Ezra, 167-168
Praxinoa, 81-82
Priam, King, 192, 195
Proba, 38
Probus, 145
Propertius, 59, 117
Prudentius, 38, 86
Ptolemy, King, 81
Pyrrha, 17

Quintilian, 13, 19, 30, 115-118

Rainolde, 28
Ramus, 76
Randolph, Thomas, 89
Remus, 89
Rich, Henry, 75
Richard III, King, 60
Ridding, Richard, 65-70
Rome, 57, 58, 59, 61, 62, 65, 66, 83,
    89, 96, 99, 102, 104, 115, 119, 121,
    122, 123, 129, 133, 134, 136, 138,
    144, 146, 147, 148, 150, 152, 162,
    171, 172, 175, 181, 184, 185, 186
Romeo, 60
Romulus, 89, 93
Roscius, Quintus, 190
Rotherhithe, 4
Rouse, John, 141-157, 198
Rovai, Francesco, 97, 101
Rovitto, Ferrante, 125
Rubicon, 173
Ruggle, George, 60
Rutulians, 33
Sabine women, 66
Sallust, 118
Salmasius, 66, 87

Salzilli, Giovanni, 119-123, 150
Sarrocchi, Margherita, 127
Satan, 31, 34-36, 45, 47, 49, 169, 177,
    180-190
Saturn, 78, 79
Saturnalia, 83
Saxons, 131
Scaliger, Joseph, 83
Scaramuzza, Angelita, 130
Scythia, 123
Sebetus, 121
Sedulius, 38
Selvaggi, Matteo (*see* Codner, David)
Seneca, 49, 150
Servius, 173-174, 194
Severn, 123
Severus, Cornelius, 117
Shakespeare, William, 2, 7, 18, 25, 26,
    37, 60, 67, 68, 70, 124, 182-183,
    184, 185, 186-190
Shelley, Percy Bysshe, 9, 24
Sibyl, 176-180
Sicily, 134
Siena, 164
Siloa, 171
Sinai, 170
Sion, 171
Sirius, 194
Socrates, 26, 64, 91
Solomon, 35
Sophocles, 117, 118
Spain, 99, 126
Speght, Thomas, 72
Spenser, Edmund, 84, 124, 125
Speroni, Sperone, 138
St Paul's Cathedral, 68
St Paul's School 1, 2, 3, 6, 7, 9-53, 55,
    57, 95
Statius, 46
Stigliani, Tomaso, 120
Stockwood, M., 44
Stow, John, 68
Strozzi, Ercole, 138
Styx, 60, 61, 176-178
Suetonius, 145
Sulpicius, 30
Surrey, Earl of, 19
Svogliati, Accademia degli, 97-101,
    106, 138
Sylvester, Joshua, 67

Index Nominum

Tacitus, 128
Tamara, 135
Tarpeia, 186
Tasso, Torquato, 118, 121, 126, 128, 129-132
Tennyson, Alfred Lord, 82
Terence, 38, 41
Terracina, 145
Thames, 61, 102, 121, 123, 124, 134, 135, 156
Theocritus, 6, 33, 81, 82, 117
Thrace, 87
Thucydides, 117, 118
Thyrsis, 150, 151, 161, 163-165
Tiber, 104, 121
Tibullus, 117, 144
Titan, 31, 32
Tityrus, 125
Tivoli, 145
Tomis, 61, 148
Tovey, Nathaniel, 61
Trebula, 145
Trent, 123, 135
Triton, 72
Troilus, 72, 125
Troy, 171, 172, 175, 191-198
Turnus, 33
Tuscany, 164
Tweed, 123
Tyne, 123

Ulysses, 99
Urania, 178

Valeriano, G.P., 138
Valla, Lorenzo, 138
Varro, 61
Vatican Library, 149
Venice, 37, 109, 122, 125
Venus (deity), 84, 126, 129, 183, 196
Venus (planet), 79
Vergerius, Petrus Paulus, 4
Vida, Marco Girolamo, 4, 47, 84
Virgil, 6, 34, 46, 66, 86, 117, 118, 120, 132, 137, 150, 152, 158, 162, 168
— *Aeneid*, 33, 66, 86, 120, 129, 168, 171-180, 186, 190-198
— *Eclogues*, 41, 129, 150-151
— *Georgics*, 19, 62, 195-196
Volscians, 33
Vulcan, 120

Weemes, John, 198
Wesley, John, 25, 29, 32, 33
Winchester, 70
Withal, John, 170
Wooton, Sir Henry, 163
Wordsworth, Dorothy, 81

Young, Rebecca, 63
Young, Thomas, 3, 62-65

Zephyritis, 31

www.ingramcontent.com/pod-product-compliance
Lightning Source LLC
Chambersburg PA
CBHW080923100426
42812CB00007B/2358